One man's journey of re
addiction and cancer t(

LIVE A LIFE
TO DIE FOR

Roger Davies

Roger Davies © Copyright 2022

This 2nd edition published by Goldcrest Books International Ltd
www.goldcrestbooks.com
publish@goldcrestbooks.com

ISBN: 978-1-913719-60-9

A CIP catalogue record of this book is available from the
British Library.

1st edition published by New Generation Publishing

*For Lesley, Georgina and those I trudged
the road of Happy Destiny with …*

CONTENTS

INTRODUCTION

On New Year's Day 2020, I found myself standing in our hallway before two Guinness World Records with 'Roger Davies' inscribed on them. Every story has a beginning: mine started at the age of ten, when a surgeon told me I was disabled, never to enjoy physical activities again. Over time there have been many challenges and demons to fight in my 'interesting' roller coaster ride of a life.

Through necessity and chance, from a violent criminal and alcoholic, I evolved into an entrepreneur, honorary eccentric, charity worker in Africa and an adventurer. More than half a century later, at the tender age of 71, on Mt Everest, I played in the two highest games of rugby in history, and entered the record books.

I relish unusual experiences, from hard core expeditions, pulling my sled over some of the most desolate terrain on the planet, trekking 650 km from Resolute Bay in Canada to the North Pole, to the altitude problems of the world's highest trek, in the Himalayas, and the fearsome heat of the Sahara.

And then there are the extreme rowing challenges, including the brutal and, sadly, ultimately tragic world-record attempt to row across the violent, uncompromising North Atlantic in the world's toughest rowing race. I like to think I have done all this with commitment, humour and unbridled enthusiasm. And I only achieved all this by remaining clean and sober, one day at a time, since 2nd February 1981. As I have grown older, travelled more and become somewhat better informed, I have come to truly appreciate that time is my most precious resource. I accept that I am trekking, a day at a time, through life – just this once! I choose not to waste the adventure!

Then, at 9.30 a.m. on 29th October 2020, I was given the diagnosis: I had the big C ...

Obstacles do not block the path. They are the path.

Zen Proverb

And now begins possibly the most challenging and important journey of my life and one which, and I say this with humility, I intend to tackle using the life skills I have acquired in my career as an adventurer. Blessed am I to have the help and support of my wife, close friends, colleagues and an incredible medical team.

As a cancer survivor, I was encouraged to paddle a single kayak across the English Channel from Dungeness, UK to Boulogne, France on 3rd August 2021, celebrating six months, to the day, since my last chemotherapy cycle, and on 8th October kayaked the return journey. I smashed it both ways!

While this is my story of transformation, I hope that others (maybe you) will read it and understand that there is no limitation to what human beings can achieve. If there is a message to this book it's that I'm just an ordinary guy who went out and did extraordinary things.

Believe in yourself, your mountain is waiting ...

CHAPTER 1

Me, Disabled?

As a small boy I enjoyed all forms of physical activity, and I especially loved playing sports. However, I developed a serious problem with my feet. Initially the doctors tried to blame poor footwear, suggesting my shoes were too small. My parents persisted and took me to an orthopaedic consultant who diagnosed hammer toes. At the age of ten I was admitted to Mount Vernon Hospital, Middlesex, to have toes on both feet operated on. The top joints (DIP joint) on three middle toes on each foot were fused together. This operation was carried out in the 1950s with the very best of intentions and with the best knowledge available at that time. Medical and surgical procedures have advanced since then. I woke from the operation to find I was bedbound, with a cage over my feet. Nobody ever explained anything to me; being left in this position was strange and worrying. Happily it only lasted for about a week before I got promoted into a wheelchair, which enabled me to escape the boredom of the ward and any restrictions set by the nurses. During my bedbound week Mum, Dad and my little brother, Brian, visited me. Brian was intrigued by the cage, which was open to all who passed by, with only a modesty blanket over my bits and down to my knees; apart from dressings on my toes, both bare feet were poking out. Today I can understand the irresistible temptation to tickle my feet but not at the time.

My wheelchair was adapted with elevating leg rests so my legs were permanently set straight out in front of me, with the foot plates upright protecting my feet, obviously cunningly designed to function as a battering-ram. With practise I acquired the necessary skills to reach the optimum speed needed to crash through hospital swing doors before they swung back and got me!

Exploring, I went wheeling my chariot around the maze of hospital corridors. At the beginning nurses and porters found it refreshing – a disabled boy could have fun – but the novelty soon wore off. I decided to branch out, exploring the hospital grounds. On one occasion I ventured out of the campus to enjoy a speedy descending slalom, eventually stranding myself near the bottom of a steep road called White Hill. I was found struggling to wheel back up the hill; a kindly hospital visitor assisted me by pushing me back up to the hospital.

I treated the painful experience more as a temporary extended game until a meeting involving the consultant, my parents and me. The consultant's opening words hit me almost as hard as the first of many beatings I received from Brother Eugene (of whom more anon). 'Roger may never be able to enjoy physical activities again.' My mind closed down to the rest of the discussion.

Me, disabled? Nah.

It's not always my feet

Some years later, I was briefly worried about my feet for entirely different reasons. Did I have something in my boot or was one of my socks bunching up? I didn't have time to investigate. Most days I would take my dogs to the park or woods first thing in the morning. One drizzly, damp, winter Saturday was no different, just a little later than usual. As soon as I put my coat on, Jodie, our Rhodesian Ridgeback, followed by her cheeky little friend Julie, the Welsh terrier, were both ready for mischief. I padded out, still waking up, with a mug of hot coffee in one hand, to where my wellies were waiting for me, sheltering under the veranda. One boot at a time, left then right; was there something in the right boot? A little shuffling, wriggling and stomping and it became sort of OK. Off we went to the Land Rover, dogs in the back and me driving.

As I recall the walk was lovely, apart from the discomfort in my right foot. Arriving home, after a good hour's walk with two dogs and a slight limp, I was greeted by the wife and daughter waving smugly from the kitchen window. The dogs ran off through the dog flap in search of their breakfast, leaving me to take off my muddy boots. My right sock was covered in blood; my wife saw this and asked what I had done.

Both were watching, eager to see the damage! I pulled off my sock to reveal the wound; but there was no wound, much to their disappointment. However, when I tipped up my welly, out fell the body of a squished mouse. The little chap had been sheltering from the weather in the safety of my boot.

CHAPTER 2

School: Bullies are Made Not Born

For much of my life I felt different – out on the edge, not part of things. School was the start.

In the 1950s, as a lower middle-class boy, I went to a private school in Hampstead, where all the boys talked posh. At the end of junior school I left under a cloud and was sent to St Marylebone CE School, where I was different alright – I dressed different, I talked different and I lived many miles away. To survive I had to learn how to fight and stand up for myself. During my three years there I won some, and lost some, but most importantly I earned respect; not the respect trumpeted by today's hoodie culture but the kind you work for, and that opens the door to friendships – friendships that are not based on fear.

When my dad's circumstances changed for the better, we moved out to Hertfordshire. My kid brother, Brian, and I were to start at a private Catholic school, St Columba's College, St Albans, run by the Brothers of the Sacred Heart. We arrived as self-conscious new boys, proudly decked out from head to foot in our brand-new school uniforms, shiny shoes and matching leather satchels. On the first day of the new term all the boys stood quietly in the playground until the headmaster called for attention. He called out each and every student by name and assigned us to our classes. On hearing your name you would immediately take your place in a line in front of your new class teacher. When complete, each class was led away by their teacher to their new classrooms.

The playground was empty. All the students had gone, except one – me. I stood alone in the empty school playground. Eventually Brother Eugene, the headmaster, summoned me and I was told to stand outside his office. Later this turned out to be a regular meeting place between me and him, always with painful results for me. After what felt like a whole morning I was eventually taken to a classroom and introduced to my new class. It turns out my younger brother had been accepted but I had not.

It was not a good start and it never got any better. On one occasion Brother Eugene came to our classroom and took out a classmate called Oliver Garvin, whom he beat with 12 strokes of the cane for a day's truancy. During this excessive beating Oliver cried out many times, and he obviously collapsed. We all knew this as we could hear him being shouted at by Brother Eugene to get up and then the thrashing continued. He was brought back into our classroom, in terrible pain and crying. Brother Eugene then left, slamming the door behind him.

I turned to the boy next to me in shock, but before I could say anything the door flew open again. Brother Eugene came in and ordered me to the front of the class where he beat me with six lashes of the cane. Yes it hurt, as it always did, but no matter what he said or did, he could never reach me. It is widely believed by researchers that regular exposure to painful beatings or stimuli can increase one's pain tolerance. Some individuals learn to handle pain by becoming more conditioned to it. Thanks to these twisted circumstances I acquired a high tolerance for physical pain. A little steel in your backbone is advantageous in an extreme adventure. A blacksmith will temper steel, so as to harden, strengthen and toughen it, then shape it by beating. I was born with steel but it was tempered by the beatings I received.

So physically I became as hard as nails but as it turned out, mentally I was damaged, so much so that in 1996 I was diagnosed with PTSD. I condemn all physical abuse.

To me, Brother Eugene was an evil monster in a frock who was only masquerading as a Christian. There are some who go around in frocks, and have this ordained authority, so people trust them implicitly, assuming they couldn't possibly harm anyone or anything.

There is more and more evidence being uncovered that chronic sexual frustration can and does contribute to violence and sexual perversion. Seclusion from secular life can lead some members of the clergy to significantly favour the latent traits of the Spanish Inquisition. If this is true, in my humble opinion and based on experience, I can certainly name at least one practitioner: Brother Eugene. I have never even bothered to hate him, to me he was just a cowardly bully hiding behind a frock. More so in recent years, I applaud the knowledge that he missed out on the mental, physical and all-embracing love of a wife or partner. He never enjoyed the supreme pleasure of the intimacy of a wife, a soulmate and family life. He was never blessed with the total trust needed to have a loved one, a child or grandchild fall asleep in your arms; it's one of the most loving and peaceful feelings in the world.

What loving father or mother would ever allow themselves to be represented here on earth or in heaven by anyone so sick, perverted and sadistic? I lost all belief, trust and faith in organised religion. I prefer a more open alternative, spirituality, which typically involves a search for the meaning of life. Sitting on top of a mountain, being at sea with no sight of land, or in a remote forest, certainly right sizes me; it gives my life a deeper purpose. I enjoy the feeling of serenity, wellbeing and emotional balance which I try to carry back to the modern urban world.

Over time, I also totally lost trust in bureaucracy, after being subject to unfair treatment meted out by teachers, police and people in authority that went unpunished (but that's a story for a later chapter). There are many good and decent people, and the majority of people in positions of authority and power are good and decent, unfortunately there are a few who are criminals and perverts. History repeatedly shows that the good ones did not constrain the bad ones.

For example, I received a hard slap to my head from Mr Coughlan, a lay teacher at St Columba's. For days afterwards, if I pinched my nose and blew, my school friends and I could hear the air coming out of my ear! The consequence was, my general hearing has never been great, and tinnitus doesn't help. Pressure changes when flying are a pain and scuba diving is out for me. Coughlan's excuse was, 'You were talking when you should've been listening.' Years later that's also how I got my nose broken.

My parents took me to the doctors and we got the diagnosis – confirmation that I had a ruptured eardrum. Dad went to the school but no action was ever taken. In the early 1960s, men in black frocks were above reproach. Today the teacher would be charged with assault and the school sued. Maybe I was lucky that I was never sexually abused but I was often severely beaten. The Brothers of the Sacred Heart (an order of monks), showed their real selves to be perverted sadists who ran the school through a regime of terror; I know I was not alone in living in constant fear. Much to the dismay of Brother Eugene and many others, a ban on corporal punishment came into force in 1986 in British state schools. Private schools took a lot longer: 1998 in England and Wales, 2000 in Scotland and 2003 in Northern Ireland.

The sudden, painful experience of ritual beatings inflicted on me as a young boy changed my mindset for life. Something happened inside my head. Never was anyone going to get to the inner me again. I never spoke to anyone about what had happened or how I felt inside.

But it changed me. Trust and faith in others were gone, from a tender age I was now on my own in the world. How profound and deep the damage was only came to the surface when my now ex-wife Gloria told me about a conversation she had had with my mum, who knew she was nearing the end of her life. My mum quietly confessed to Gloria that as a young boy, I had changed dramatically overnight from being her happy, fun-loving little boy. She didn't understand what she had done. Tragically, my mum blamed herself for how I had turned out. Mum died a week later.

I learnt of my mum's burden too late to set her mind at rest. For over forty years she had been unjustly condemning herself and she took that to her grave. Over all that time, no matter what anybody did to me or threatened me with, they could never reach me.

Bullies are made, not born; fighters are born and made better – I became a fighter. As a fighter, I attempted to achieve things in spite of great difficulties or the size of the opposition. After some time in the early recovery years my attitude changed; to the extent that in recent years I have come to seriously loathe any form of bullying. Did those beatings give me a physiological edge when dealing with pain?

As you can tell, school for me was neither a safe nor a happy place. I was extremely pleased to leave school, as a matter of fact, they let me go before taking O level exams. My academic education was blighted, I was labelled as lazy and dumb, rather than dyslexic. It wasn't until many years later that I learnt about this condition called dyslexia and realised that I had it (the first consensus definition of dyslexia finally appeared in 1968).

The only positive was that I did more than just OK in sport, and I represented my school in rugby and cricket. It was a privilege to have played for the London County Schools Association junior cricket team, both at county level and inter-school competitions within the London area.

Dad got me a job at the Brocks Firework Company in Hemel Hempstead. Dressed in a suit and tie, I worked in the costing/accounts department. Spelling and writing I found very hard, but I could juggle numbers well.

As a quiet and troubled seventeen-year-old, with money in my pocket, I began to visit a local village pub, the White Horse, and overnight I got the taste for booze. I started going to parties, the rowdier and noisier the better, like many of my generation. It wasn't long before I discovered sex, drugs and rock n' roll. Elvis Presley, the Who, the Rolling Stones, the Animals, Etta James, the Beatles, the Kinks, Tina Turner and the Beach Boys were some of my favourites.

I guess I gained a reputation for being a bit of a tearaway; often at local parties I was used as an unpaid bouncer. Dancing wasn't my thing so I gravitated to the kitchen with the booze. As a result of bottling up my aggression for years, all bets were off once I had a beer or three, and I could change into a loud and hostile pain in the arse. It wasn't long before the newly opened Hemel Hempstead Pavilion hired me as a doorman. Off came the suit, the tie and any veneer of respectability!

Little Rog, 1957

CHAPTER 3

Merchant Navy, 1965

As a mixed up, angry nineteen-year-old who was always in trouble, my parent's naive solution was to remove me from the root cause – they thought I was being led astray. As I was usually the ringleader, the opposite was true. Nonetheless, and with good intentions, they enlisted me in the Merchant Navy. Certainly peer pressure had played a role, but they failed to see the real triggers of alcohol and hormones! I was the guilty one. My mum and dad had my best interests at heart and always did the very best they could for me.

What could feasibly be achieved by putting the same person into different circumstances and situations? I don't really know what was in their minds when they shipped me off to sea. I expect that their hope, born of frustration and desperation, was that I would change, a sea change, perhaps. That the problems would disappear and the trouble would stop.

In reality, it was an open secret: wherever I went, I took me with me. I just created the same kind of havoc and chaos somewhere different. Every time the ship docked and I went ashore, you could be certain I found ways of creating some kind of mayhem – but never intentionally. I lasted all of nine months before the British Merchant Navy had had enough of me and I was thrown out. During that time I collected a couple of serious convictions.

The first conviction was for grievous bodily harm (GBH). The offence was committed during a nasty fight in the Port of Tyne at Tyne Dock, South Shields. The guy I fought with came to court with a big turban of a bandage wrapped around his head, off which I had bounced a full bottle of Newcastle Brown Ale. He was some fifteen or so years older than my nineteen and a good deal heavier than me. From the moment he came into court, he started shouting abuse both at me and the court officials. His behaviour added credibility to my testimony: 'He attacked me and I was only defending myself'.

However, I was found guilty of GBH and, in sentencing me, the Magistrate said, since I had used a bottle as a weapon, a standard custodial jail sentence was only suspended because I was a first offender. On reflection, fifty years later, I got off lightly.

My second conviction was committed barely a month later in Glasgow, Scotland. I was up on two charges: assaulting a police officer and 'Reset' (Reset, in Scottish criminal law, is feloniously receiving or retaining goods, obtained by theft, robbery etc., knowing that they have been dishonestly appropriated). In the Queen's English, that means I was in possession of property that had been taken by theft or robbery. I'd been shore-side for about four hours, drinking in a pub, when I was approached by someone with electrical gear that was dirt cheap, obviously it had fallen off the back of a lorry but stupidly I bought it. I got into a bit of a ruck in the bar, which was probably why, as I left the bar, I was stopped by some local coppers (referred to as 'Polis' in Glasgow) who were just arriving on the scene.

They pinned me up against the wall. I loudly declared my innocence regarding the problem in the bar. They began to frisk me and asked me what I was carrying. I didn't bother to reply so one of them grabbed me and I automatically slung a punch that connected, and that's when all hell broke loose. More Polis steamed in and I was carted off to the local nick. I remember standing in front of the desk sergeant. He asked me for my name and address to which I replied cockily, 'Off a boat.'

'Where's the boat?' he asked.

'I don't know,' I said, probably with my standard cocky smirk.

Next moment I was knocked back across the room – I never even saw the blow coming. They stood me up, charged me and said I'd be up in front of the sheriff. I thought they were taking the piss. I laughed and said, 'What's his name? Wyatt Earp?' The consequence was another blow around the head.

The sheriff is a legally qualified judge; the sheriff courts hear civil cases as a bench trial, without a jury. Next morning I was handcuffed and led from the police cells to a waiting prison van. I was placed in a large holding cell with roughly twenty other prisoners. One lad was pretty torn up. He said the Polis had set their dog on him. All the prisoners had their own stories and all seemed to say they were innocent victims. I kept quiet.

My experience of the inside of the infamous HM Prison Barlinnie was that it was definitely not an easy place for any Englishman, especially a teenager with a distorted view of life and a chip on his shoulder. However, once it was known that I had been nicked for assaulting the Polis, I became one of them and they accepted me without reservation. Also, I made it very obvious I would stand my ground, so they left me alone. This would have unquestionably changed, given time, so it was very lucky for me that my stay was relatively short.

PC Alan Tuffs was a friend of my dad and they played cricket together on the local village green, Leverstock Green, near Hemel Hempstead. He had driven up to Glasgow and he spoke up for me in court. However, I was found guilty by the sheriff, but as a first offender I received a suspended sentence. I was released into PC Alan Tuffs's care and he escorted me from Glasgow back to a quiet backwater in Hertfordshire.

The way I was at this time of my life, tough, angry and so cocksure of myself, I could have taken a polygraph test to prove beyond doubt that whatever the trouble, it was never my fault, it was always the other guy's.

In the 1960s there were no computer systems; the Police National Computer (PNC) was not set up until 1974. From that time, details of all my recordable offences will now remain on the PNC until I reach the age of 100.

As a dyslexic, filling in official forms was a headache for me. On occasions I may have made silly mistakes. Like misspelling my surname as Davis instead of Davies, or entering my DOB as 12.11.47 instead of the true date of 11.12.47. Dyslexics can be a bureaucratic nightmare; confusion may have reigned! Perhaps it was lucky for me that dyslexia hadn't yet been invented.

Could this, by any chance, be why I was deemed a first offender two or three times?

CHAPTER 4

Bouncer/Doorman, Debt Collector, 1966–1980

In more trouble – it followed me!

For much of this fifteen-year period of my life, I earned a living from the destructiveness that is better known as violence. From the not so tender age of nineteen I worked on and off as a bouncer or doorman. It was relatively easy money and a way of life that required no CV and no responsibility. Ultimately, I gave back nothing to society, and I got paid cash with no questions asked. Some of the venues I worked at included Hemel Hempstead Pavilion, the Trade Hall, a few local pubs and the Top Rank in Watford. There were psycho fruitcakes carrying knives and other weapons, so we needed to be tooled up. We kept our tools of the trade in an old leather cricket bag; it contained nothing sharp and no firearms, just a couple of wooden baseball bats, an assortment of batons and a fancy, lead-filled blackjack (a kind of cosh). Our war bag was usually kept near the street entrance, in the ticket booth or tucked away in the cloakroom. You would never get away with that today because of CCTV coverage, plus everyone has a smartphone.

By the time I was in my mid-twenties a team of us worked numerous venues, clubs and pubs in Bedfordshire, Hertfordshire, Middlesex and North London. Rogues attract more rogues; accordingly, some club owners and publicans hired some of those labelled as rogues, on the principle of poachers turned gamekeepers. In my late twenties to my early thirties, I worked similar venues, mainly in Central and West London, where most of the doors were run by known families. I was never the biggest or the best, but I was capable. It became a way of life when money became tight, or I just became too lazy to find real work. Bouncers in the 1960s and 70s were on the whole a dangerous breed, unlicensed and uncontrolled. Thugs with more than a scattering of total nutters, and yes, I include myself. Nevertheless, it was controlled by a core of genuinely hard men.

When I was working the doors of pubs, dance halls or clubs, the company I kept was a motley bunch, mostly bordering on and usually linked with career villains. You got to know all the local faces, and if you stayed around long enough you became one. There were perks to the job, on occasion these may have included, for some, debt collection, protection and drug dealing. We knew and did business with the local leading players, so when a small-time drug dealer was spotted working in the club he became our target. We kept a close eye on him and waited until a suitable moment to turn him over without things getting too messy. The best time was when the dealer visited the toilet, usually to do business.

That's when we would steam in and, depending on his attitude, he could hand over his stash quietly, or we would take his gear with what we thought was the appropriate degree of extreme force, then throw him out of the club. This was how we subsidised our income, we filled our pockets by selling the drugs we had confiscated. At one time we had old-fashioned, glass sweet jars full of purple hearts/speed/blues/black bombers (amphetamines) in all the pubs and clubs I worked. LSD (acid) made an occasional appearance in the clubs, but it made the punters go crazy, so it was unpopular with doormen. Marijuana, I noticed, was far trendier in the pubs than the clubs. Heroin belonged to the much darker side of the drug scene; I didn't see it in the pubs and clubs I worked. Ecstasy (MDMA) appeared in the 1970s, but I never worked the venues – raves – where it was most popular.

I did test our products with very limited success or enjoyment. Everybody knew when I took speed – I couldn't stop talking, mostly a lot of bollocks.

In the mid-seventies, while lying flat on my bed enjoying a joint, my head said I needed the toilet but my body didn't want to co-operate at first, and suddenly the thought of my vulnerability hit me. Marijuana made me paranoid, amplifying concerns into fears. That was the last time I touched marijuana. Talking bollocks and paranoia were not especially good attributes for a bouncer and debt collector. Drugs didn't suit me, so lucky for me that I drank!

Apart from gratuitous and occasionally warranted violence, there were some odd situations. For example, one night we got a call that there was a problem in the men's toilets and three of us steamed down. At first we thought it was a false alarm, until one of the others spotted two pairs of feet in one cubicle. I stood in front of the door flanked by another bouncer, while a third went into an adjacent, unoccupied cubicle, stood on the toilet seat, leant over the top and we heard a loud thump. The bouncer who leant over had given the poor lad an awful crack, right on the top of his head.

The door opened and a lad of about eighteen came tottering out towards me, his eyes totally crossed. The vision robbed me of any lucid thoughts and I got the giggles, leaving me unable to take the sorry event seriously. Adding to his distress, his trouser flies were open with his old chap peeking limply out. His friend sat frozen on the pan, wide-eyed and open-mouthed. With hindsight, I am a little ashamed to admit the incident set me off, howls of laughter exploding from me.

The job entailed what might now be called unsocial working hours, and we usually finished between three and four in the morning, which limited any normal socialising, but the strange subculture made our lives seem normal. Joe Public goes to work from nine to five, and then comes out in the evening to celebrate, have fun and get drunk. We looked down on Joe and all his mates and generally derided them.

I believe if I was smaller, less capable and did not have the insane ability to act with some kind of controlled violence, I might still be working on the darker fringes of the entertainment industry, possibly as a barman, but probably as a small-time drug dealer. We lived with the likelihood of the unexpected happening at any moment and when it did the adrenaline would fuel the system. The excitement and buzz, related usually to violence, did it for me. In hindsight I can see there was always a darker side that I connected with. It's just like a drug, you feed on it.

When I was working the doors, my job was to stop trouble or at least limit it. The vast majority of the clashes were usually drink and/ or drug related. Booze limits inhibitions, but exaggerates feelings and emotions. My observation, from working the doors and, later, confirmed in my sobriety, is that drink and drugs definitely take away inhibitions, limit self-control and lessen the effect of possible consequences.

Common kick-off triggers include disputes over a boyfriend or girlfriend, somebody feeling disrespected and gossip – 'someone said something about someone'. So often it's a trivial hassle, which if everyone were sober would be ignored or at worst result in a loud and foul-mouthed verbal. Sometimes the root of the trouble was simply a testosterone overdose. It's not unusual to see people under the influence acting stupidly and/or violently, actions far removed from their sober selves. I used to put myself at the top of that list.

I got into so much aggro with 'faces' and had so many brushes with the law that I decided I needed a change of scenery, so in May 1968 I went off backpacking around Europe. I left the family home in Leverstock Green, stopping at various towns I thought I might find interesting – and often did.

My timing could not have been worse. As soon as I arrived in France, I met with total disruption – the infamous workers and student riots were in full flow.

While hitching through France I was ignored by the locals, but not by the gendarmes, who stopped me many times. I guess I stood out as different, not a hippie or an average student off to join the riots. I showed them my British passport and they mocked me, telling me I was 'Anglais stupide'. I've been called a lot worse.

Opportunities – and surprises – so often arrive not from the direction you expect but from the side door – nothing could have prepared me for what lay ahead. The riots in Paris were eclipsed by one of the most nerve-wracking rides ever. It happened while I was thumbing a lift south through rural France.

An old Citroën 2CV (known as the 'tin snail') stopped. The driver was a priest, dressed in a black, full-length cassock, and sporting a square hat with three horns, a three-peaked biretta. The door opened but the wrong way – 'suicide doors' that hinged at the rear rather than the front. This should have been a hint of what was to come. The priest and I sat side by side on twin canvas picnic seats suspended on springs, trampoline style. Every bump, twist and turn in the road sent us ricocheting off the doors, dashboard and each other; safety belts hadn't yet been invented. The gear stick stuck out of the dashboard between us; one time when he braked unexpectedly hard, I shot forward and in self-defence put my hand out and crashed the gears. I am sure the loud string of angry French words that ensued were naughty ones despite his priestly attire.

I am not sure if he was short-sighted or just a lousy driver but he constantly wrenched the steering wheel with a heavy hand whenever we turned into a corner or to avoid obstacles, including other vehicles, sending the little car careering all over the country roads. Each time this happened, he recited loudly in French. I recognised the rhythm of the words, it was sometimes the Hail Mary or, on particularly close calls, the Our Father.

And then it started to rain. The windscreen wipers only worked when the car was in motion, and the faster he drove the quicker the wipers wiped – when we stopped, so did the wipers. Of the Citroën 2CV, the adverts famously promised 'On the level, you can get to 47 mph without difficulty'. He certainly squeezed out that promise!

Occasionally, whenever I see particularly bad driving, I wonder if the crazy priest made it into old age. I hope so.

I discovered Torremolinos, on Spain's Costa del Sol. I arrived during a particularly hot summer spell, when there were lots of like-minded backpackers who were there to party, tan, swim and generally goof around. Whether you're enjoying a siesta in sunny Spain, running a marathon, busy working or chasing around after your rugrats, without realising it you can easily get dehydrated. It's important to restore your body's water balance. It is medically proven we need a couple of litres of water throughout the day. This can be achieved with a few regular sips of water, vital for topping up your body fluids. If we don't there can be nasty side effects. Mild dehydration can be just uncomfortable and ruin your day. If it's severe you can experience seizures, and blood clots leading to potentially fatal complications.

That's why regular water stations are an absolute must during road races, not only on a warm summer's day but also throughout the seasons. In the Arctic, dehydration can also be a problem; we stopped every hour for a five-minute break to take on liquid fuel. Each of us carried two thermos flasks that we filled every morning with hot water made from melting ice.

In Torremolinos I got a job working at a beach bar. Oh boy, it was seriously thirsty work! I had to walk out, into the scorching sun, where the tables were scattered, and take customers' orders. Then I would trudge back to the air-conditioned bar, fill a tray with cool beers and margaritas, and then return to the open furnace. Each journey required me to partake of a liquid intake. I was looking after my health by regularly rehydrating! It took the Spanish owner a week to realise I had drunk his entire profits for the month! This very excitable Spaniard did a lot of shouting, waving of arms and hand gestures, none of which I understood. The gist was he was firing me. I blame him, it was his own fault – he told me to help myself to a beer!

Debt Collecting (1970s)

I was never any good at collecting monies owed to me – I could do it and did it for others, and was paid well for my services, but for myself, my emotions would come charging in, and the red mist descends. The next thing I knew ... bloody knuckles!

Everyone hates paying bills and nobody likes a confrontation. Straight people often act as if being asked to pay a bill is insulting and they can become very arrogant and mouthy. When I was a professional debt collector, I always got background info before a visit. Check out who you are collecting from. A straight punter is probably ashamed, flustered and will likely become defensive when you ask him or her to pay. I learnt to bite my tongue. I'd heard all the excuses before, but by letting the debtor explain why they hadn't paid or couldn't pay, I always gained the upper hand.

Silence from me could appear very intimidating, especially if I was just eyeballing, giving them a hard stare. Yet a little nod now and again gave them the feeling they were being heard, letting me feel I was more approachable than other debt collectors or bailiffs.

If they looked and sounded halfway genuine, offered solutions that could be considered, that could solve the problem. Straight punters will not want you to visit them at work or the golf club. So I'd drop a gentle hint regarding where a future visit could be, if an agreed arrangement was broken.

Doing these things lets customers know you care enough to listen to them and that you are giving them a couple of options to solve their problem. When customers get to choose a way that works best for them, the chances of them sticking with it are much higher than if you call and demand payment in full right now, without taking their situation into consideration. Offering a solution, offering a couple of options and remaining calm will give you the best chance of collecting from a past-due or late payer who might be yelling and swearing at you.

There are those who work in the grey market who feel they are immune from the law and from us; they are not illegal, but borderline, and are not authorised or controlled in the official way. So they think they are untouchable, and occasionally choose to feel that you're disrespecting them and quickly turn defensive. Hence, they may require a more physical approach; visiting them in their local drinking haunt was a favourite ploy.

We usually worked in pairs. One fellow debt collector, a serious big boy, with whom I often was teamed, had a strange way of opening negotiations by greeting them with a firm but friendly smack round the head, followed up by growling menacingly, 'I hope I have your full attention now'.

Many punters or clients may have been going through bad times and had every intention of paying their debt in full and on time, but shit happens. Then there are those ego-driven punters, who are deep in debt because they spend what they have, giving the inflated impression to their friends of what they believe they are making or earning.

Repossessing a car was easier than collecting cash. Then there's the punters who never have money to pay their debts because they have too much of something else! For example, the most common mistake was that the halfwit borrowed to buy goods, usually drugs, with the intention of selling them on for a profit and forgot not all the money is his, or else the idiot ended up sampling the product!

TV programmes today seem to suggest that everybody pays the official debt collectors, so you only see the positive results but in the real world there is a huge, unplugged black hole. Legit debt collectors can only collect what the punters are seen to own, and/ or what the court will allow. That's one reason why you have large interest rates on credit cards and overdrafts, and in the world of payday loans the APR could be up to 1,500%.

Films, books and TV have added drama and colour to thugs collecting debts. Of the many debts I and my associates collected over many years, I only recall serious violence when dealing with underworld characters who had taken the piss, who had stepped over the line and were in need of reminding of their place!

When an unlicensed debt collector arrives at your home, your favourite pub, golf club or place of work, you know they are there to collect. Embarrassment and intimidation are tools and there are no legal barriers, it's not exciting or glamorous!

To give you an idea of the sliding scale we often employed, when a minor drug dealer fails to pay his supplier he may get a few slaps as a gentle lesson. A face or serious player wants the deposit for a new set of wheels or opens a bar and needs stock or funding for a lorry load of booze and fags, and then defaults. The reminder becomes more serious, scaled to the amount of money outstanding.

My job was to collect debts from punters who owed money, not to destroy lives. Living, working and fighting in this subculture environment distorted our thinking, our humour and our values.

CHAPTER 5

My Attempt at Legit Businesses!

For a period during the late 1960s and in the 1970s, I lived in Hertfordshire, and earned a lucrative income in the grey (cash only) market. I quickly learnt to focus on my strengths and outsource the rest. For a few nights a week I was a bouncer on the doors of local nightclubs and pubs, depending on where I was living at the time. I started in the Pavilion in Hemel Hempstead at the age of nineteen. Other venues over the next decade included the Top Rank, Trade Union Hall and New Penny in Watford, and the Unicorn Club in Leighton Buzzard. This type of work had extra hidden cash benefits, in the form of occasional debt collecting and drug dealing.

In the daytime I ran a small building business, mainly to show the authorities I had the means to live. My way of making money and running a business in those days did not always coincide with legality. One time, I had my guys working on the refurbishment of an Indian Restaurant, including building a commercial brick tandoori oven to their specification. When I went to get the final payment, the owner started to renegotiate. He was attempting to screw me over, he didn't want to pay our agreed price – a very bad move on his part.

I walked out to my car and, marching back, in my own mind I was a cross between John Wayne, Charles Bronson and Rambo, carrying a sledge hammer instead of a shotgun.

I proceeded to totally demolish the tandoori oven right in front of him and his staff. His shouting and screaming did nothing but urge me on, just to show him. I kept on swinging the big hammer until the once-pristine oven was a pile of rubble.

The story went down well in the local pubs; from then on clients agreed a price, and didn't attempt to renegotiate. I got paid, in full, on time. However, the real cost to me financially was way out of proportion. Close examination of the contract revealed that the contract value was £1000; he wanted to pay £900, the total I had received was a £300 deposit, the cost to me in materials and labour was £500 – I was therefore out of pocket £200. His costs amounted to £300 for a pile of rubble! Lesson learnt – two losers and no winner.

The only positive for me was that word got out about how I would react to anyone who attempted to renege on the deal. I was a good builder but crazy. And although nobody ever knocked me again, it was a rubbish business model!

Black market, insurance and shady dealings

There are a couple of areas of insurance that I loosely brushed with during this period.

The market in stolen art is one of the most lucrative international black markets, third only to the trade in arms and drugs. Art-related crimes in countries like the United Kingdom total an average of over £300 million annually, with an average of six billion US dollars' worth of art stolen or forged worldwide each year. It's estimated that only 5% to 10% of stolen artworks (painting, sculpture, drawings, watercolours, graphics, pottery and jewellery are ever recovered. It's a very lucrative business, and regarded by some in authority as victimless.

A popular perception behind many major crimes, notably the theft of fine art, is that there is always a Mr Big in the background; a prime example was the Great Train Robbery.

Mr Big sounds dark, exciting and conspiratorial, but it's a myth. It has been strongly suggested that this particular myth is a convenient vehicle for some authorities to hide behind when awkward questions are being asked. Why? Here are some possible reasons:

- Legitimising stolen fine art is exceedingly difficult.
- Often it has been ruined, after being poorly stored for years in bank vaults, garages and under beds.
- Metal sculptures tend to be melted down for their scrap value.
- Dumped works of art that can't be sold are often destroyed.
- Some high-value fine art items are traded or fenced by a few international crime gangs as an easily transported currency.
- As with most stolen goods, there is a black market where items are traded at a fraction of their market value.

There is no single Mr Big but there are a number of organised criminal gangs around the world who specialise in high-value works of art. The gangs are usually linked to money laundering, firearms and often to drugs.

In the 1970s certain 'wide boys' appeared on the scene with antiques and fine art of questionable provenance. These were regularly sold at the 'midnight auctions' held at Bermondsey market, South London. Those of us in the know would spend Thursday night through to Friday morning picking up a bargain or three. The sale was subject to marché ouvert rules. You could buy valuable paintings, sculpture and architectural items, also genuine trinkets for the missus or girlfriend for a song. Profit on one late-night shift and one prudent bid bought me a nice car!

It's whispered that persons unknown (an iffy private syndicate nicknamed the Ring) occasionally employed a legit middleman to attend the Bermondsey auction with a pocketful of their money, thus enabling them to conceal their assets. A stooge would be instructed to bid for particular items that had been spotted and valued by a tame respected art dealer. Nobody dared bid against them.

They made a financial killing after reselling items with a legal title, at or near the true market value. By ancient royal decree, anyone who bought an article in Bermondsey market between the hours of sunset and sunrise immediately obtained legal title to the item, whatever its provenance. This law was finally repealed in 1995. A small percentage of businessmen and criminals who found this lucrative edge used dirty money – and effectively laundered it. In the 21st century, the scale of money laundering impacting the UK annually is in the hundreds of millions of pounds.

Today, it may seem that once stolen, art disappears and is lost forever. To make it even more difficult, art recovery is a legal minefield. Of course, the art insurance industry, led by fine art and specie underwriters in the City of London would like to find missing tainted works of art, as would the art world.

You may believe this actually happens – if so, how does it happen? Do the thieves just simply hand the items back? Do the thieves or their friends get rewards for information regarding the location? According to crime statistics only 1.5% of art theft results in the art being recovered and the thieves prosecuted. Could there be some form of secret (and highly lucrative) exchange?

You might think so, but I couldn't possibly comment, Your Honour …

CHAPTER 6

On the Run in France

I choose not to put in print all the colourful details of what I did to have half the French police force chasing me in the mid-seventies, it's sufficient to note it was the result of my stupid, alcohol-fuelled, violent behaviour. I was on the run due to my own actions, again!

To get away, I was hitchhiking from Antibes, in the south of France, heading for Paris. I got a few lifts and was drinking a beer, topping up my alcohol level in a little cafe bar just outside Lyon, when I saw a gendarme paying far too much attention to me. Quickly necking down the rest of the bottle, I grabbed my rucksack and made for the side door. Sprinting off in the opposite direction to the main road, I needed to get to the cover of undergrowth and scrub nearby. Minutes later I heard the distinctive siren sound of the French police – he had called for backup.

I ran and jogged away until I reached the side of a small, man-made canal which joined the main river. Moving quickly, I made my way along the bank until I reached a bridge, which carried the main road above it. I scrambled up the embankment and looked back towards the cafe. I could see that the gendarmes had created a road block just a few hundred metres back from where I was hidden, tucked behind a bush.

Clearly, I needed to put some distance between me and the police. My only option was to swim across the canal. I took a bottle of wine and my passport out of my rucksack, and stored the rucksack high up on a ledge, where the bridge's rocker bearing sits in the space high up between the bridge's pillar (abutment) and the underside of the horizontal deck of the bridge. Squeezing all my clothes and valuables into a plastic bag, I stripped down to my pants and tentatively waded out into the water.

As it got deeper, I turned onto my back, holding my gear above the water. I swam across the river like an upside-down frog. Reaching the other side, I climbed up the scrub-covered bank. As I ventured further, I realised I was on a sort of spit or island and, looking across, I saw for the first time that the main river was now acting as a serious obstacle. My memory is not perfect, but I do recall that the far bank seemed a bloody long way off. The Rhône is a big, wide and powerfully flowing river.

Lying down, I crawled to a position where I could see my route but be hidden from policemen's eyes. Oh hell. I heard a gunshot, then another. There was a lot of barking, growing ever closer. The booze I had consumed earlier mellowed any fear and stress that normally would have been eating into me. Two French coppers came out of the shrubs, in tow, behind a large and vocal Alsatian. It immediately started jumping up to where I had stashed my rucksack. Obviously, the dog was not making the right sound for finding a fugitive because the handler was impatiently yanking it away.

More gun shots: maybe they were trying to flush me out. I lay watching them with the sun beating down, drying me off. I remember opening the bottle of wine and thinking 'this is just like watching a movie or being the cameraman filming a movie.' As the afternoon wore on and the bottle became empty, I began to smell myself; at first, I had been distracted by fear, excitement and adrenaline, now the reality of my situation was sinking in. But the smell – it was me – I stank. In the evening when I bravely ventured back to the canal, I could see it was not an ordinary waterway but more akin to a large, slow-flowing, open sewer! Now I know why the gendarmes and their dog never followed me.

After that narrow escape, I managed to get to Paris, where I still had to lay low. Hotels were out, as was renting a flat, or even a room. I attempted sleeping on the Paris Metro but was quickly thrown off. My only option was to become a street person and look for a dosshouse (or an asile de nuit as the French call it). I found a Salvation Army Hostel.

In the 1970s, and possibly still today, there were two levels of society inside a Salvation Army Hostel in Paris, France. Those that worked and those that didn't. It was never clearer than at mealtimes, when there were two queues for your evening meal. At the head of the queue stood two great big cauldrons full of hot food. In the cauldrons was stew, one with meat for the workers and the other without meat for the dossers.

You could get a wash and a shave, even occasionally a tepid shower. The mattresses were tired, lumpy and hard, the woollen blankets were scratchy and worn. Every possession you wanted to keep you slept with or kept firmly tied down! It was warmer than the street, dry and, apart from petty theft, it was a relatively safe environment to sleep in. Breakfast was a large mug of hot chocolate with a hunk of bread. After eating and washing up you were shown the door, pushed back out on the street with a wrinkly old apple for the day in your hand.

I remember the Frenchman who ran the place; he was strict but fair. I never got to speak much with him, but I did feel he was a kind man under the regimental no-nonsense 'front' he put on. I will never say a bad word regarding 'Sally Ann'. They have helped thousands of men and women all over the world. Many of them are going through very difficult times, most are trying to deal with their own personal demons.

Due to problems of my own making in the UK, I was a marked man; adding to my problems I had become a wanted man in France, on the run, needing to keep a very low profile from the local authorities.

I believed I had limited options:

- Try and stay hidden in a foreign country
- Do time in a French prison

- Make a run for the border
- Join the French Foreign Legion

I recall having made my mind up, deciding upon the heroic and glamorous choice, I was going to join up and become a legionnaire. However, just before actually enlisting, I made a phone call. Unlike today, with mobiles, making a call then took effort and commitment, especially when making an international call. Both the caller and the recipient would be very aware of the importance of an international phone call!

I phoned a heavy contact, Wally L, in London, who knew I was overseas. I briefly told him I had made a decision to join the French Foreign Legion. He understood me and where I was coming from. I can clearly remember the impact his aggressive words had on me then. On paper they appear so tame, they were not threatening nor demanding. Someone from Nike's PR company must have heard him and copied him: Just Do It!

'Duck n' dive, duck n' dive, get the f*** back over the water fast.'

If I was standing in front of him, I knew the animated expression he would have been wearing, the saying 'bulldog chewing a wasp' was based on him. For a while back there, I was beginning to lose my appetite for the constant need and willingness to fight. In fact, I was going bloody soft when Wally L's positive, no-nonsense attitude gave me the kick up the bum I needed. His aggressive positivity triggered me to up my game, to fight and I did. I packed my kit, walked out of the hostel, headed for the outskirts of Paris and hitch-hiked to Calais.

I used almost the last of my cash on the ticket to get a ride home on Seaspeed's hovercraft, the largest in the world. I was sweating as I queued to collect my ticket, and again at passport control, but once on board I enjoyed a relaxing 35-minute ride. It wasn't until I stepped off at the port of Dover and cleared customs, a very long hour and half later, that I stopped anticipating the dreaded tap on my shoulder.

A key change in me, as I've hinted above, is that I now have respect and gratitude for the Salvation Army. They do a remarkable job offering practical help to people without discrimination. I admire and applaud the people who serve in the Salvation Army and I always give when I see them rattling their collection pots. I am ashamed to admit the times I sucked half a lemon while standing right in the eye line of the Salvation Army Brass Band, watching them struggle to keep playing. I was about twelve years old at the time.

CHAPTER 7

Who are the Real Villains? (1970s)

On occasions I have worked for and been involved with infamous crime families and leading members of the UK underworld. On reflection, some of them were highly intelligent. If they had applied their brains to running totally legitimate companies, they would have run large lucrative businesses, possibly even international corporations. Old hands, security services and senior officers know this frightening statement to be true. Sure, they employed heavies to do certain work, however, I quickly learnt never to underestimate their personal ability for extreme violence – it's a necessary tool of their trade.

There are others who never get past middle management and personal violence, still more who don't achieve the equivalent to management – you could refer to them as troops, soldiers, thugs and the occasional cretin. Years later I can confirm with absolute conviction that some of the real tough guys I have rubbed shoulders with hold down honest jobs and face life on life's terms; they stand firm and support their families and friends through all manner of crises.

Villains use intimidation as a weapon and a way of getting attention. It's proven behaviour that they know causes most ordinary people to fear real physical harm, mental damage or both. A conversation can begin with the hapless punter getting a firm slap. More extreme circumstances can involve violent threats, property damage, or someone getting seriously hurt. Bullying is a way of establishing social dominance, thugs and bullies crave recognition and respect. Real nasty action is normally reserved for gang warfare – it's just business.

In the 1970s I worked for a very enlightened hard man, later becoming his right-hand man. This face had to leave the Smoke after crossing swords with an infamous South London firm. He had escaped from the crime family's premises by jumping out of a closed first floor window because a man, associated with him, was being tortured – a Black and Decker drill was being applied to his kneecap. They were meting out punishment that didn't require the ultimate sanction. My boss, Wally, was a friendly and convivial character; he owned pubs, had interests in construction and fingers in other legitimate businesses.

On one occasion, I was having a quiet beer with him at his own bar in Leighton Buzzard town centre when he took a call. He put the phone down and he said we were off to a pub belonging to a friend of his right away, as in 'now'. I believe he may have had a financial hand in the pub we were visiting. We walked into the bar to be met by a group of travellers who were confronting our publican friend. He looked very nervous and had sensibly positioned himself with the bar counter between himself and the travellers.

As we walked towards the group of six men, Wally called out a friendly greeting to his friend the landlord, who was looking more than a little shaken. The group turned to face us – this didn't look good. These were men, not boys, with a three-to-one advantage, but you'd never have known by my facial expression – a mask I put out to the world. Wally stood inches from the gang, smiling and relaxed. I stood at his shoulder. His appearance alone made him look like a seriously bad man to cross. He had been a very capable heavyweight boxer in his day. On the other hand, he was an astute businessman who always chose to negotiate first. Things were a little tetchy to start with, but words were exchanged and the misunderstanding was sorted. They had expected the landlord to be an easy mark who would roll over, they had not expected him to have serious friends. I recall they bought us drinks and left on reasonable terms.

Two friends of Wally's acquired Beadlow Manor in the 1970s. It was an ambitious venture, with plans to further expand the golf club, refurbish the hotel and restaurant. At that time, on approximately 300 acres of their land, wild brown hares outnumbered golfers by 25 to 1!

Wally took over the refurbishment and building works, including a two-storey driving range. I was site agent/foreman, acting as the day-to-day manager on his behalf. Aside from the building work, for fun we created a skeet shoot. We bought a couple of mechanical skeets, which flung clay targets at about 40 mph into the air from different directions, the flight paths of the clay targets intersected in front of the guns. Allegedly, the skeet shoot was a distraction for locals and anyone else who might hear the sound of shotguns.

Colourful shady characters came up from the Smoke and took over the entire hotel. Reputedly, this gave them the opportunity to meet 'friends', discuss discreet business and arrange deals. Relax over a drink and enjoy some off-road racing around the golf course in street cars. Their appetite was for the freedom to bounce over rough ground, zooming around the fairways with their shotguns pointed out of the windows in pursuit of the hares. Hearsay, of course!

Far, far more damage was done to the grass fairways and local plant life than to any hares.

Real Hard Men or Hard Real Men?

I have read about some hard men – gangsters, rogues and doormen, many of whom I drank, rubbed shoulders and worked with – the stories sound so much more glamorous than I recall them to have been! Many of these men were seriously dangerous, especially when tooled up.

I have also met some genuine hard men, not only villains but forgotten, unsung hard real men. One was my grandad, Bryn Davies of Tredegar, Wales. Bryn was a contractor, collieries paid him for all the dangerous, back-breaking work involved in extracting coal on piecework. He was a sub-contractor who worked at the coalface himself, with his A team of hewers, and together they dug coal from a seam with a pick.

Then the B team of drawers, who are also called waggoners, would transport the tons of coal that he and his lads had hewn by hand from the bowels of the mountain, along tunnels to the 'pit-eye' at the foot of the 2,000-foot-deep shaft. At each fortnightly 'reckoning', the colliery paid Bryn for the recovered coal; he in turn paid his men. He supported not just his own family, but many in the village.

My dad, Elwyn R Davies of Tredegar didn't go down the pits or into the local steel mills. It was the beginning of the Second World War, and he joined the RAF and became a Brylcreem Boy. He was there at the beginning of the war, first crewing flying boats and later bombers. Despite witnessing lots of life-threatening action and losing many friends, he rarely spoke of it.

Dad was a first-rate rugby player; he started his playing career at Tredegar and went on to represent the Royal Air Force Rugby Union (RAFRU) 1st XV between his flying duties. After the war he played at a high standard for London Welsh, Harrow and Southern Counties of England. He hinted, with a wink, that he often received 'boot money'. As a boy I remember him going off to work every day with a bowler hat and an umbrella. Dad was upright and straight, he didn't appear to know how to bend the rules. Maybe there was a Cymry wildcatter gene that skipped a generation and jumped from Grandad Bryn to me!

My dad often reminded me of the time when I drove his car, a 'sit up and beg' Ford Popular 103e, across Harrow Rugby Club's pitch while he and 29 other players were in action! It was 1955 and I was eight years old. The game stopped as his car trundled forward across the pitch. A posse of muddy rugby players chased after me, the door was flung open and the car brought to a halt. I was promptly ejected and the car returned. It was some years later when all of my dad's embarrassment and anger was lost in the mists of time; he chuckled, recalling the sight of his car advancing while all that could be seen of the driver was a small pair of hands.

Early in 2016, I visited Harrow RFC Clubhouse – Elywn R Davies, my dad, was displayed on the wall, in a picture of the 1st team, of which he was captain, dated 1947 – the very year I was born! I am so proud of him. That picture is going with me up Mt Everest. My dad was my hero on the rugby field until I was twelve years old, when he was replaced by the 1970s Pontypool Front Row, their motto, 'We may go down; we may go up; but we never go back.' Today, it's my dad … again.

In tight situations some people freeze, some run and some stand! Experience has shown me that if my back is against the wall, top of my list would include many of my fellow adventurers. Some of them trekking to the North Pole, and others came with me up mountains, across the Sahara, the wild South Atlantic, and played extreme rugby with me. You will meet them soon, these are the hard real men and women of this world, unbeatable, untouchable and totally reliable.

CHAPTER 8

Working on Oil Rigs, 1978

Which is crazier and/or more dangerous?

- Being caught in high winds while working in a suspended cradle 200 ft above the North Sea?
- Getting involved in blood-splattered battles at the construction camp bar?

My circuitous journey from London's underworld to Loch Kishorn began when things were getting a little hot and I had to hurriedly exit London for health reasons. It was in my best interests if I lived out of the way, merely a temporary move until things quietened down. That's how I ended up under the radar, in Exeter, Devon.

On arriving in Exeter, I promptly found a cheap, clean and quiet B&B. Within a month I moved into unregistered digs in a house on an estate. Getting my money sent down from London was a struggle, leaving me a little light on cash, which was something I was not used to. In London I always knew how to get a few quid. Now I urgently needed beer and fag money.

To make money in my usual ways and not get my collar felt, I required local knowledge and contacts. I might as well have been on the moon as living in the backwaters of Britain. During this period I recall the mental torment of sitting in a pub, nursing a pint, watching the door, in the hope someone I knew would walk in. As a stranger in town, I was becoming desperate. The saying 'like gravitates to like' can't be just coincidence. It wasn't long before I discovered a local pub called the Dolphin that I found comfortable to drink in. Surprise, surprise it had a very bad reputation for trouble. After a few brushes with the locals and a couple of fights I became accepted. Money was still tight and my booze habit was costly. At that period in my life there was no way I would accept that drink was costing me more than money and increasingly difficult to control.

I hitch-hiked for three days, from Exeter to Aberdeen, because I'd heard it was overloaded with agencies desperate to hire bodies for well-paid rig work. On my arrival I swaggered into a few employment agencies, full of bulls**t, asking what vacancies were available. They urgently needed riggers. A rigger is a person who specialises in the lifting and moving of extremely large or heavy objects. My automatic response was, 'I can do that.' I was immediately hired as a rigger, my job would entail hanging and operating suspended cradles – something I had never done in my life!

Before I had time to think and change my mind I was given a contact name, handed a brief set of instructions and a train ticket. I walked out of the office, cocked and loaded, to start work on the Ninian Central Platform, the biggest floating structure ever built and the largest man-made moveable object in the world.

In May 1978, a total of eight tugs towed the completed platform out of Lock Kishorn, 480 miles to the Ninian oilfield, east of Shetland. It took over eleven days. There, the platform was sunk and fixed to the sea bed. The monolithic concrete gravity structure is reliant on its own incredible weight to remain stable. It went on to produce its billionth barrel of oil in 1996. It was designed and built for Chevron UK by Howard Doris Ltd in the 1970s, and it is now owned by Canadian Natural Resources (CNR). It dwarfs Trump Tower!

I took the train to my new job; arriving far from civilisation, it stopped at a bare and barren platform somewhere in the Scottish Highlands to disgorge scores of fellow tradesmen and manual

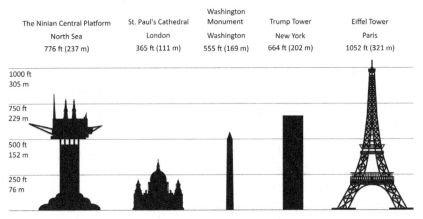

The Ninian Central Platform	St. Paul's Cathedral	Washington Monument	Trump Tower	Eiffel Tower
North Sea	London	Washington	New York	Paris
776 ft (237 m)	365 ft (111 m)	555 ft (169 m)	664 ft (202 m)	1052 ft (321 m)

Heights comparison chart

workers. We stood around waiting for transport to ferry us to the camp where, at its height in 1977, the total workforce of 3,000+ were employed in the construction and somehow accommodated. I wish I had £1 for everyone who said they had worked there – I'd certainly have a healthy pension pot! It was a Scottish winter evening, dark and cold, and as the train slowed and stopped there was nothing in sight, not a house, barn or shop. The unnamed and unmanned stop had no station buildings, no ticket office, just one empty track and a single platform – bizarre!

The train emptied of maybe 100 men carrying an assortment of luggage. In the middle of nowhere was a very brightly lit, square cinder block building. I followed the crowd into the building, which was already packed out. We stood four deep at the bar. As was standard practice we jostled, a polite expression for shoving, nudging and elbowing in our effort to get served. Sometimes, misjudging and crossing over the very thin line between bulldozers with a smile, to proper, full in-your-face, aggression.

The bar was heaving with drinkers, as were all the apparently unrestricted open-all-hours bars on the camp that I came to experience. Handy, since drinking was a major part of life between shifts for me and most other construction workers. I very quickly realised that bar fights regularly became full-on pitched battles.

The riggers and scaffolders wore heavy leather belts with tool frogs loaded with steel podgers (scaffolders' spanners). These were tools that soon became dangerous weapons; at any given moment they would deftly appear in their hands. They were not shy about using them! When the action kicked off, Security disappeared, after closing all the exits, locking us in the bar. They would appear again when all went quiet to pick up the fallen and the walking wounded. These battles kept the medics busy. In the morning, when we were boarding the catamaran, our transport to work, the security guards checked faces for the previous night's damage. You could be pulled aside, and the severity of the questioning depended on the damage caused both to property and persons. No one ever witnessed anything!

There was a line of parked camper vans just outside of the main gates. Rumour had it there were women in the vans, working girls. It was a large workforce, and for most of us it was two weeks on, two weeks off. During my two-week shift all my off time was spent in the bar; I decided I could wait rather than chance catching the clap. There were others, semi-resident in the camp for weeks/months at a time, who benefited from the company.

During my one and only interview, I casually remarked that the cradles were a little different to the ones down south, hence after ten minutes of rigorous training I became an instant expert and was promptly sent off to work. The catamaran ferried us from camp to the oil platform. To gain access we climbed the Haki stair tower up to the cellar deck.

The cradles were suspended from the cellar deck on wire cables, about 120 m above the sea. It wasn't just crazy, but wholly insane work! Health and safety officers were blindfolded. I am sure they did their best, but they had no chance. In any event, I don't ever remember bumping into any while dangling over a sea loch in the north-west Highlands of Scotland!

I am OK with heights, although in recent times I have issues with the consequences of gravity; as I have grown older I realise I do not bounce nor am I immortal. We would look down and see the seagulls circling way below us and beneath them, the safety boat that constantly circled the rig. Their job was to pull 'fallers' out of the sea. The only faller I witnessed was a scaffolder, who for some reason known only to himself was still gripping tightly to a scaffold tube all the way down. I never saw him after he hit the water. Nobody told us what happened to him.

Life in the camp was a parallel universe, akin to the days of the 1890s Klondike gold rush, but far more wild and brutish at times. For semi-skilled and skilled construction workers, prepared to work long hours in harsh conditions, it was a financial gold mine and it was also a lucrative opportunity for chancers such as me.

Insane times lead to insane moments

Swinging in an access cradle 60 metres in the air is hair-raising at the best of times. The trick is to look far out into the distance, at the horizon, or up at the clouds, but do not look down. In an attempt to grasp the height we operated from, I recall seeing far below us masses of little white dots circling and circling, it was only when we gradually lowered the cradle and got much closer that they materialised into seagulls. Operating the cradle is so simple anyone could do it after ten minutes of intense training. (This is certainly not what is encouraged by today's health and safety regime, and rightly so.) A suspended access cradle only moves up or down, or remains stationary: lever up, squeeze and up goes the cradle; lever down, squeeze and down goes the cradle. To stop you just let go of the dead man's handle.

The dead man's handle is a fail-safe device mounted in the control handle of the cradle. It is designed to be activated or deactivated if the human operator becomes incapacitated and loses his grip, when it will automatically engage the brake. In today's PC language, the dead man's handle is called a 'safety lock'. However, the difficult technical bit is that there are two operators, one at each end of the 12-foot-long cradle, who needed to work as a team. We would shout these very complicated instructions to each other: Up, Down or Stop. The 'passenger' in the middle did the

49

necessary work – maintenance, welding, acetylene burning or a general inspection.

Health and safety would have had a heart attack if they saw two of us riggers operating the large cradle, roping on two large gas cylinders, plus our passenger, Jack, a Glaswegian, who operated the acetylene torch. Our job was to remove all extruding debris off the monolithic Ninian's 45-metre circular concrete gravity structure. The unwanted junk consisted mainly of old scaffold fixings, reinforcing steels and enormous redundant towing eyes. On one occasion we had to remove a towing shackle that probably weighed well in excess of a couple of tons.

We secured the shackle from above with steel hawsers and stationed the cradle just above it, so when cut free it would not drop with killing force on us. We ignored the possibility of it breaking free to sink any boats 160 metres or so below. A 2-tonne deadweight dropping suddenly, even barely a metre, will undoubtedly stretch the steel wire cables, guaranteeing it would swing slowly but meaningfully while spinning gently with deadly unstoppable force. Plans of mice and men!

The taut hawser cable caught our suspended cradle, tossing it violently about. We just hung on with arms wrapped around the side frame rail as it first swung out, then came crashing back into the concrete side of the rig. Definitely not good for your heart or your pants!

On another occasion, I noticed that one of the gas cylinders had started leaking from the valve attachment when it started to spurt flames. Not a bonfire blaze, more like a very big Bunsen burner. Remember these 4-foot cylinders are filled with highly inflammable acetylene/oxygen flame that burns at about 3,773 K.

The cylinders are securely tied on to the cradle, so they cannot fall off, however, any halfwitted health and safety person would recognise the danger and stop working or be the first to dive for cover.

Jumping over a hundred metres into the sea was not an option. I am just not brave enough, so I started to desperately beat the burning source at the cylinder head with my thick leather gloves and was soon joined by Jack, who turned the gas off. Wow, at least the flames had been flaring on the outside, thankfully no blowback! I am still here today, not blown into many indistinguishable parts, splattered all over the rig, into the sea with the rest of me scattered into the upper atmosphere. It was not fear and blind panic but self-preservation that saved all our lives that day.

Precision of timing is achieved by nodding, shouting or hand signals; our unison was not guaranteed. I was working with a quick-tongued Scouser, who always had an answer and who had his eyes rigidly fixed on the distant horizon. This is only OK when you are stationary!

There are lots of nasty obstacles, big and small, poking out from the side of the giant one-legged concrete rig that are there to ambush your cradle; it is for your own safety you need to watch your progress. Approaching a snag you push the cradle out and away from them. On more than one occasion my co-operator failed to notice said snags and certainly upset the balance, rocking our precarious platform from side to side. We were lucky not to have the cradle flip over and tip us out into the North Sea.

Not surprisingly, when you are looking at a 200-foot drop, rocking, swaying and see-sawing have a different meaning and effect – especially on my bowels. The Scouser snagged the 12-foot cradle badly at his end. He had kept his grip on the dead man's handle in a supreme moment of madness, either he froze or his brain just stopped working – he even stopped speaking. The moment I saw what was happening, I released my dead man, because it was obvious there was a serious problem.

His brain-fart had enabled four or five feet of cable to speed through before he released his grip on the dead man's handle, kicking in the automatic brake. As I started towards his end to sort out the problem, he now engaged a brain-storm and kicked out against the side of the rig, which pushed the cradle off the snag. Immediately his end sharply dropped 30 degrees and I was all but catapulted off the cradle. As I flew past the Glaswegian, I managed to grab the safety rail and save myself from a long fall into the

North Sea. Now it was my turn to have a moment of insanity as the red mist came down.

The temperature at that time of year was well below freezing and the winds that blew our cradle about created a serious wind chill, so we were well wrapped up, with the obligatory hard hat perched on top. All you could see of each other was a pair of eyes and a nose. Yet what I could see in front of me was a huge target. In a few short seconds I regained my footing and quickly I closed the gap between us. I let go of a right hander my old trainer and Joe Frazier would have been proud of. It hit the target right on the button, back went his head and the legs just collapsed under him – plenty of claret!

Did I care if he was hurt, or worse had gone over the cradle's safety rail, to drop the 200 feet into the sea and probable death? At that moment the answer would have been no.

That evening, back at the camp, I had a quick swill n' splash and headed off to the bar. I had downed a couple when I spotted the Scouser, with his newly broken nose, noticeably flanked by a couple of shiners. I remember being pleased with my work, but not so happy at the sight of the posse flanking him and heading my way. They didn't look a jolly bunch – then the verbal started. A big-mouth piece let everybody within hearing range – which was the whole bar – know that I was going to pay in blood for nearly killing his mate. The odds were not good – there was nowhere to hide or run to.

Just as we were facing off, Jack the Glaswegian with a couple of his mates showed up, adding to the party. Oh shit, now I'm in really big trouble. To my amazement Jack stood in front of the posse and pointed at the Scouser and shouted that it was the bampot's own stupid fault, sparing no detail as to his lack of balls and crazy actions that had nearly killed him and me. Walking away he vehemently spat out that it was a shame the Jessie hadn't gone over the side. (Bampot is Glaswegian slang for an idiot; Jessie for an effeminate man.)

As Jack stepped away in disgust, I moved in and threw a couple of vicious punches, devastating the already mashed-in nose – down he went, squealing.

When I was involved in the crazy subculture lifestyle of drink, drugs and violence, I just went along with crazy practices because they were the norm at that moment in time. As is often the case with me, the enormity of the stupid risks I took only became real to me years after the event, when the cold and clear thinking of common sense and acceptance cuts out all the macho bullshit. Today, over forty years later, with my feet firmly planted on the ground, I attempt to console myself by asking myself a question: which was worse, his momentary loss of balls and rational judgement, or my moment of insanity?

CHAPTER 9

Walking into Darkness

I know that entering into the unknown is a frightening experience, but with the right preparation almost anything is achievable. So when returning to Exeter from Kishorn didn't work, I went back to my old hunting ground – the Smoke – and picked up my old lifestyle.

Looking back, I enjoyed a certain level of confidence in all I did. I equipped myself with survival skills, listened and learnt from experts, good and bad. Good was when I set out for the North Pole, which is scary for anyone who has enough common sense to recognise the awesome challenge Mother Earth can provide. Bad is the crazy bravado of my early life, when my own head encouraged me to do crazy, some would rightly say stupid, things, without any thought of consequences or repercussions for me or others.

If you were at Earl's Court Underground station in the 1970s, you may have seen scaffolding spanning the platforms, high above you; one of my 'fill-in' jobs was erecting it at night. One night I found myself worse for wear, drinking in the formerly named Nashville, also known as F3K – the Famous Three Kings, a large Edwardian pub standing next to West Kensington underground station, one Tube stop away from my place of work, Earl's Court. One evening I popped in for a couple of beers on the way to work and stayed a little longer than planned. At closing time I came out of the pub with a head full of madness and a belly full of beer. When I realised the time I rushed off to the station to catch the Tube, one stop to Earl's Court Underground station and, as nobody was about, I jumped the barrier in haste, then hung around waiting impatiently for my train. I remember becoming aware there was no one about, it was very unusual for both platforms to be deserted.

I had a dodgy light-bulb moment and decided to walk to Earl's Court Station ... through the tunnel! I believed – or rather assumed – that the power was turned off after the last train had gone home, because that's when we started working through the night erecting scaffolding, creating a secure working platform high up in the gantry so the maintenance people could do their work in safety.

I quickly hoofed it to the end of the southern platform, heading east, sidestepped the end-of-platform warning sign and ran down the ramp. I walked on crushed stone ballast railway track for approximately 300 metres to the tunnel entrance, which is about 3.56 m wide. Staying on the right-hand side I shuffled along, deeper into the Tube tunnel; I could see nothing. Whether my eyes were open or closed made absolutely no difference, I was immersed in total darkness. My only senses were of the uneven stones under foot and my hand touching the rough bricks of the tunnel walls as guidance.

It was definitely not brave or clever, it was alcohol-fuelled insanity. Booze takes away all common sense and inhibitions.

I recall thinking that some passenger and maintenance trains might run through the night. They can't swerve or stop quickly, so if one comes, I'd just dive down between the rails, in the full knowledge that the underground rail tracks were electrified and live. If I touched a rail, I would stick to it and fry! Could there have been more wrong with Roger the Wacko, than just drink? Could drinking and drugs have been just a symptom? I'd drunk just enough to believe I was immortal!

I remember coming out of the tunnel into the light at Earl's Court Underground station and bawling out a cocky mouthful of bull to my work mates. Strangely nobody responded. There was total silence; the whole crew were gobsmacked, they just stared! I was sacked. Dark tunnels and a light at the end have a different meaning for me now. Did I learn from that experience? Not for a long time! Putting myself in dark places was so often stupid, totally thoughtless and dangerous but at the time none of it seemed important. Many times over the years I have woken, covered in sweat, haunted by the vivid memory of that stupid walk to work. To this day I can still 'see' the absolute blackness.

CHAPTER 10

Another Day, another Tunnel,
another part of the World

In 1979, and again in 1982/3, I was hired as the labour trouble-shooter for contracts in the Middle East. To say my CV, references and interviews were bizarre is an understatement. For example, in 1979, an 'employment interview' started totally by chance while I was drinking in the Cross Keys, in Lawrence Street, Chelsea.

I got into a conversation about nothing special, just the usual bar bullshit with a random guy who seemed interesting. After a few beers we decided to change pubs.

As we walked up Oakey Street (in the Royal Borough of Kensington and Chelsea), I eyed, standing by a pillar box on the corner of Margaretta Terrace, three 'Jack the Lads' I vaguely knew. They confronted me, it's possible they thought I was an easy mark, or they had some kind of personal beef with me. Whatever! Nonetheless, for some silly reason they also felt the need to part me from my money.

My new friend watched as I exploded and landed a few lucky shots. Little did I realise, but this ruck turned out to be my interview! Recruiting techniques for choosing suitable talent back then were a far cry from the bits of paper that are needed in today's world. Even for unconventional employment.

Strange, how booze takes away not just fears, but common sense and consequences, both for me and my new employer. On arriving at a different pub I was getting ready for a serious session when his tone changed, and he began talking boringly about his work.

He said he was looking for a 'Rottweiler' to work on a specific contract in Abu Dhabi, UAE. I was dubious, trust in people was not a strong point of mine. Over the years I have heard plenty of bar bullshit and been made all sorts of offers, from the bizarre to the downright stupid. He suggested we meet next day in the bar of the Cross Keys. To my surprise, he turned up. This put him a couple of notches higher in my estimation, so I listened. The work entailed being the link and mouthpiece between him, his Arabic clients and a multinational labour force at a desalination plant in Abu Dhabi. I was only half listening, drinking his money and nodding; suddenly he triggered my full attention when he spoke the magic words: tax free money.

What I didn't find out until a couple of weeks before arriving in Abu Dhabi was that the skilled lads were all Geordies. A team of rugged and seasoned Shot Blasters, who had learnt their trade and honed their skills in the shipyards in the north-east of England. The labourers, drivers and general gophers were mainly from the Indian subcontinent. We lived in a camp in Portakabins, with outside toilets and a shower block. The well-equipped kitchen came with the biggest and toughest 'mother' on the contract, an imported Geordie cook.

Our place of work was an enormous desalination plant at Abu Dhabi Power Station. Desalination is a process that converts seawater into fresh water for drinking, irrigation and industry. The contract, for which the labour force was hired, was to shot blast the inside of desalination tanks, using iron grit. Asian semi-skilled labourers, under the watchful eye of a Geordie charge-hand, shovelled or poured iron grit of specified grade into the machine hopper, which was linked to a powerful air compressor. Iron grit blasted by compressed air and projected by nozzles delivered at about 130 psi – a minor blunder would be enough to make your eyes water.

It is imperative to clean the metal, removing paint, rust and scale to a high standard, in order that coating of corrosion protection can be applied. This was done by the specialist team, again from the north-east shipyards. It's hard, dirty and dangerous work, made worse by the stifling heat. The UAE is an extreme physical environment to work in. The climate is arid but subtropical, with humidity exceeding 85%, and on the coast up to 100% in summer. In winter the temperature range is between 17 °C and 20 °C, while in July the shade temperature can reach 50 °C or more in the desert.

A highlight of the three-month tour was a special Xmas dinner, planned by the UK agent's wife, the only lady we had seen not in a hijab, and cooked by our Geordie chef. Trestle tables, graced with colourful paper placemats, cutlery and glasses, were all laid out in a large extended square. Once seated, we were given and expected to wear colourful paper party hats. All started well, scrumptious Christmas dinner and beer flowed. It proved to be a quaint but stupid idea!

Under a burning sun, looking complete muppets, sat a bunch of hot, sweaty, tired hairy-arsed men who were away from their families, wives and kids. A build-up of frustrations, tiredness and alcohol led to cracks appearing. Friendly banter began to turn to piss-taking. Lads were getting 'mortal' (Geordie slang for drunk). More beer flowed and surprise, surprise – it kicked off.

Our Christmas dinner party became a drunken battlefield, everyone fighting anyone, with no referee! The place was totally wrecked, no tables, no chairs and only a couple of the lads left still upright. Most of us suffered a variety of bruises, a couple of loose teeth, a few had minor cuts, but luckily there were no serious injuries.

Overall, it was what it was, a tough assignment for all, however, they were a great bunch of proper tradesmen there to 'addle brass' (Geordie slang for earn money). Their work ethic and general attitude, although gruff on many occasions, was 'proper mint'. Or, in southern English, really good/cool.

The contract was coming to an end; the daily work schedule slackened, leaving only a bit of snagging to be done by a small maintenance crew. Most of the lads enjoyed, or endured, a 48-hour bender. A few of the worst offenders, including me, were shipped back home. To this day I have no recollection of boarding the plane. I came around at some point during the eight-hour flight. I was sitting next to the Geordie cook, who looked as rough as I felt. He filled me in on what had happened, or at least as much as he could remember. We all shuffled off the plane, through customs, miraculously without further trouble, said our goodbyes, and that was it, a great bunch of guys. I never saw them again.

In the autumn of 1981, I was hired by a different contractor, to go back out to Abi Dhabi to do a similar job, but this time with a fancy title, general foreman. By this time I was nine months clean and sober; whether clinically sane was certainly questionable. After all, up to that time in my life had I done anything to suggest I ever had both oars in the water?

My role was much the same, controlling and supervising the multinational labour force. They were tasked with repairing joints from the inside of 1.5 m diameter seawater intake fibre pipes. The original contractors excavated deep trenches, and dropped in the fibre pipes, which were then slotted together. However, the flaw in the system was the heavy-handed method of backfilling the trenches. They used bulldozers to heave large quantities of soil, sand and rubble back into the trench, smashing down onto and covering the big pipes. This clumsy work deflected the fibre pipes and distorted the sealed joints, allowing the water to leak out, thus making the pipeline ineffective.

The cost of digging up the pipeline and re-laying it was not commercially viable so we were to repair it from the inside. Or rather, that was what the multinational workforce was paid to do. My role was to make sure the paymaster's wishes were met. The workforce was a far cry from the professional teams I had before. The recruitment agency just collected warm bodies from all parts of the UK and a couple of Europeans. As with my last contract in the Middle East, the majority of the workforce was from the Indian subcontinent, on the whole, they were a hard-working bunch.

Amongst the UK workers there were no tradesmen or professionals; there was an ex-SAS territorial, a convicted bank robber, a few Glaswegians and some blokes who looked like rabbits caught in the headlights. This contract was different to the one in '78, mainly because of the quality of the workforce. From the moment some of the dicks stepped off the plane they started to bellyache. If it wasn't the searing heat or the accommodation, it was the food, if not the food it was the work.

Above ground, in a shack – the Indian workers' cafe – we ate hot, strange-tasting curry that had a greenish hue to it, until one lunchtime a rat ran over both my feet then up the leg of the bench we were sitting on. It stopped and turned and looked at us then started to clean itself, all while I and my Irish colleague was eating – we were scooping out the curry with naan bread as there were no forks or spoons. This registered the level of hygiene we had up to that moment unconsciously reached, or rather sunk to. Gross!

The ultimate bosses were Abu Dhabi nationals and the main contractor was Scandinavian. Neither seemed to be good at handling labour, politically or physically – they gave the orders but never directly. On one occasion I was told to cut the bottled water ration because it was costing too much. All the guys worked in torturous conditions, excessive temperatures of over 40°C and 100% humidity. They spent an eight-hour shift, working only by the light of their handheld lamps, while crouched over and standing ankle-deep in brine. Overexposure to a high-concentration solution of brine can create havoc with the skin, and did. The worst affected parts were hands, feet, bums and boys' dangly bits. My job was to ensure the bosses got their money's worth. I went to the office and told them that cutting back on drinking water was an unacceptable, penny-pinching instruction; it would create ill will, health hazards and undermine my drive for positive results and reaching our targets. It was not enforced.

Self-catering during an eight-hour shift, while inside a pipe, underground in stifling heat, was not much fun. The Europeans ate various concoctions of foods. Indian and Sikh workers had their own individual tiffin lunch boxes, filled with cold curry, rice, naan and chutneys. These underground pipes were full of hard-working, sweaty men who didn't hold back on venting various bodily functions, including cold curry farts. Consequently, the rank, sultry air was so heavy you could chew it.

I had a little trolley made from a spare piece of the 1.5 m fibre pipe, caster wheels and a handle, so I could lean my weight forward on it and travel distances down the pipes to check on progress. I would descend via an access point and charge along, sometimes with a lamp on and sometimes not, you could see the lamps of the gangs long before you reached them. Sometimes you would find them sleeping, then they got a serious bawling out.

On one occasion my trolley was being repaired, so after descending I started a crouching jog. Some way in, I came across a large bundle of clothes that I promptly kicked out of my way. The bundle erupted, exploding into life, and my lamp was knocked out of my hands. In the darkness and in the constrictions of the pipe, an unknown opponent and I fought. I could not see where and what I was hitting and nor did I care, each of us was fighting for our very life. I used everything the streets had taught me, aggression and will for survival was the winner that day – as it often is! He was working in the worst of conditions, but we both had a job to do. It was a shock for both of us, but his bruises would heal and he continued to send money home to his family. There are old proverbs like 'let a sleeping dog lie' and 'look before you leap', none of which quite fitted. As much as I tend to jump into situations with my eyes wide open, I do try to 'see'.

Which was still bollocks thirty years later, otherwise why would any sane 61-year-old with a stent be walking 400 miles in conditions cold enough to freeze the balls off a brass monkey and in danger of being a polar bear's Dish of the Day?

Arguments and whingeing on site and in camp were frequent. No one had been press ganged into coming, and they were all being paid good money. On a good day, I agreed that some of the conditions were diabolical and tried to help where possible. On the other hand, I ignored the bellyaching.

My job was to enforce the instructions that landed on my lap. Unsurprisingly this made me very unpopular. I had one Indian who was a good worker, yet for whatever reason he always seemed to take pride in messing up, even grinned and gave me the Indian head wobble. Enough was enough; to grasp his full attention I picked him up by an ear, so he was on tippy toes, and I bellowed down the other. Out of the corner of my eye I saw the Scandinavian site manager with two Arabs in robes appear from around the corner, momentarily witnessing my behaviour; they turned on their heels and were gone. Later that day I met up with him, and instead of receiving the expected bollocking, I got a thumbs-up for keeping firm control of the workforce under harsh conditions. I reckon he was happy he had a buffer – me – keeping him at arm's length from the sharp end!

Of the many confrontations during this contract one stood out; it was with a large Glaswegian. I think he was surprised I stood my ground, not backing off an inch. Before the fighting started, as we were standing nose to nose, I told him I had spent time in his local prison – Barlinnie. He looked at me in a new light! The outcome was that I shipped him back home to Scotland on the next available plane. Four years later I bumped into him in an AA room. He was as surprised as I was. However, his surprise was not for the reason I expected.

'I thought you would be dead by now,' was his opening comment.

'Why?' I asked.

Looking me straight in the eyes, he said, 'Me and some of the boys were planning to knife you and bury you in the desert.'

During the contract I did ship workers back to their home countries when they stepped over a line drawn in the sand. The contract was tough but paid well, so you had to man up. Anger and occasional violence happens, but letting your mates down through unacceptable behaviour (bullying, lying or laziness for example) is – well, unacceptable.

CHAPTER 11

The End of Life as I knew it!

During the winter of 1980/1981, unknown to myself, I was nearing the end of my drinking. At this time, I shared a flat in Hayes End with another doorman. I wiped my face constantly to remove the giant spider's webs. I watched 'things' burrowing out of the walls. I'd wake to witness creatures that tried to gnaw my feet. Alone in my room the physical and mental withdrawals were getting bad. The DTs (delirium tremens) visited me more and more frequently.

These were alcoholic withdrawals, for which I had developed a 'cure'. There was a pint mug next to my bed that I would pour about an inch of spirit into and add three or four inches of water. Even with the shakes I could hold the half-full mug without spilling. I needed the excess water because I would gag, and I didn't want to waste any booze. Once I got the booze into me the shakes stopped and the hallucinations magically disappeared. While this was my immediate cure, it was temporary, serving only to offset the dreadful daily cycle of my desperate craving for a drink.

I still did a little dealing and was still occasionally working the doors; I was more often taken to different venues, generally busy pubs that usually had music and, as it happened, I was being used as a troublemaker. A role that, given a few drinks, came naturally to me.

I would kick off, and cause problems so the crime family I was working for could approach the landlord sometime later offering their 'services'. I can confirm, based on my own personal experience, that drug and alcohol abuse has the potential to increase angry, irrational and violent behaviour. Admittedly, when I punched someone I use to get a rush of adrenaline and as much of a feel-good sensation from the violence as I did from booze.

Most mammals, including normal humans and me, are naturally aggressive in some way or another. It had its benefits as we humans evolved; you defended your territory, your mate, your kids and family. In today's societies such aggression is no longer acceptable. My behaviour had become far more irrational and totally unpredictable. I was unreliable in every area of my life. The most civilised comments made about me that I can remember ranged from 'a royal pain in the arse', to a 'real arsehole … a real drunken arsehole'. I had been called an awful lot worse on many occasions, yet they now seemed to take on a new meaning. My reflective bell rang, for the first time I secretly thought perhaps they were right.

When asked how much I drank I replied that I never counted my drinks, I just drank …

Was this a crossroads in my life where I was mentally building up to, or collapsing to, a point where I could accept reality? I guess I was so out of touch with the real world and in so much denial that I didn't know even when I was lying. I recall searching the flat for a bottle, I put my hand into one of my secret caches, felt something solid and pulled out a sawn-off shotgun. I have no recollection of how or when it got there, the 'why' wasn't important. First and foremost, there was no bottle.

Such was the power of the subculture I lived in, where drink and violence were acceptable parts of daily life and everything else, sawn-off shotguns, beaten-up people, pissed-off friends and family, were all mere sideshows in the drama of my psycho compulsion!

Working on the door or collecting debts there was always plenty of posturing, some pushing and shoving, and of course there were occasionally punches thrown. Over the years, people did get damaged, although surprisingly, rarely did it get totally out of control. On the other hand, aggression against other villains or gang members would often get very messy! The subculture/bubble I lived and worked in accepted booze, drugs and violence as a daily reality; I had become desensitised. I fought in temper and worst still in cold anger. I have used weapons with intent. Anytime, anyplace, when a fight broke out it was like a magnet to me; the stimulant of violence acted like a drug. I was attracted and lost sight of consequences. I have been asked to be more open and graphic about my past life, I do find that difficult. I feel great shame for my unacceptable behaviour.

Late one evening in February 1981, I returned to the sanctuary of my reclusive room after some drinking, though not to the usual excess, having been in yet another scrap – not a bad one, just a few punches thrown – a relatively quiet night for me. However ...

Deep down in the very core of my being, I was sick and tired of being sick and tired. As a consequence, I experienced a truly pivotal moment. For the very first time, I saw myself for what I was. There were no bright lights, no voices, just a moment of absolute clarity. A life-changing concept formed inside my head. Maybe alcohol wasn't my friend after all! If I stopped drinking – perhaps for a week, or possibly for a month or two – things might get better.

It was a long, long night. I was rattling from head to foot, yet somehow I escaped my usual hallucinations without my 'cure', only to experience the powerful shakes and the night sweats. Somehow, I didn't take a drink. Up to today I still have not taken that first drink.

I had no idea what to do, physically feeling all mushed up, mentally in a brain fog, barely capable of deciphering my own name. Eventually I slowly got myself together. A few doors away was a doctor's surgery, so I walked falteringly to it. I guess the receptionist assumed I was very sick or didn't want a scene, so she let me go straight in to see the doctor. I have no recollection of the encounter other than being told I must go to Alcoholics Anonymous and being given a telephone number. I had vaguely heard of AA but the way I felt I just didn't care, pride and worrying what others might think of me was long gone!

I made the call. To this day I have no idea who I spoke to or what was said. I must have given him or her my home number (this was the pre-mobile phones era). I received a call and, although I was expecting it, it was still a surprise. All I can recall is that the man told me I must go to an AA meeting and I agreed. He told me where it was and how to get there by public transport. He would meet me and walk me to the meeting place. So I started telling him what I looked like: 6'2", big build, lots of dark hair. I remember him stopping me mid-sentence to say, 'It's OK, I'll recognise you.'

My overblown ego assumed he knew I had a reputation. My view of myself at the time was so distorted, I suppose it can be compared to the blurred world of today's reality stars, where the self is all important, and truth and integrity are irrelevant.

Oh yes, he did know who he was meeting; a big, sweaty, red-eyed lump who was barely off the piss is not difficult to spot! At the meeting my first thoughts were negative, the tight bastards handed me half a cup of coffee. Complete strangers spontaneously approached me, welcomed me and introduced themselves.

Someone told me where to sit. I have no idea what was said during the next ninety minutes. It all sounded like gobbledygook, but nobody fronted me up or was in any way challenging me and I spilt no coffee! I began to feel comfortable and in a strange way became aware of a sense of identification and inclusion.

On the way back to my flat I collapsed at the side of the road and was taken by ambulance to Ealing Hospital. I had gone into serious withdrawal. I remember lying there, seeing the support rails up as if I was back in a toddler's bed, and with a strap over my chest. I believe I was a patient for a day or two when a doctor and a social worker visited me to discuss my drinking. Physically, I felt spent with nothing left in the tank; mentally worse, frazzled and drained. They told me there was a place next to the hospital that would help me. I couldn't really compute what they were talking about, but it sounded like the easier, softer option and would give me time to recoup, so I said I wanted to go. I assumed it was a treatment centre or rehab. Yes and no – it wasn't poetically named like The Priory, Clouds or Primrose Lodge.

I arrived at Uxbridge Rd, Southall, to be greeted by an enormous signboard stating St Bernard's Mental Hospital! A staff member escorted me into a locked ward, specifically for alkies and addicts, and allotted me a bed. In addition to group therapy and occasional individual counselling sessions, we were given responsibilities in the form of minor tasks and jobs. I was allocated the responsibility for the dry stores, a large walk-in cupboard that contained commercial quantities of coffee, tea, sugar and hot chocolate, for the use of all of us residents. Unfortunately, old habits die hard, and it follows that there were consequences even in a mental hospital where they were trying to help me. It was not long before I began to 'borrow' heavily from the dry stores and pantry of Southall's loony bin. I created a black market, selling my acquired stock to fund my nicotine habit!

CHAPTER 12

Difficulty with Re-entry

Putting down the drink and drugs happened over night. The mental transition, however, took an awful lot longer, as did the terminating of my criminal activities and also the physical life choices that are so necessary to enable an addict to re-enter the normal world. The reality of the 'normal' world, despite being very difficult at times, eventually turned out to be far more exciting, interesting and fulfilling, in complete stark contrast to the hell I had left behind.

I can remember looking out of my window from my first floor flat in Hayes End, seeing people busily getting on with their lives and wondering if they were going to work or coming home; my body clock was totally out of sync. My thoughts concluded they were all losers. How wrong was I?

Now that I have made peace with the 'normal' world and the people in it, I have experienced many personal blessed moments that I will to take to my grave.

In more recent times, while high up on a mountain, in the Atlas range, Morocco, I can vividly recall the marvel of opening my tent flap to see a clear blue sky reaching out forever, looking down at the rugged rocky terrain that I and friends had trekked up the day before, seeing the layers of mystical cloud far below us, enshrouding the lower slopes and valleys. I felt fresh, clean and so alive!

Taking pleasure in the novelty of waking with a clear head, a mug of coffee in a steady hand and walking out on the small deck of our safety boat, seeing the greenish blue water of the English Channel, with white splashes stretching out to the horizon where the sun was just beginning to show itself. Just a few yards on our port side (my left, when looking towards the sharp end) were seven of my colleagues busy rowing our Thames Cutter, in a few minutes we would swap over, and I would be taking my place for my stint, taking us three hours closer to Paris.

During a trek across the Northern Sahara, I was rudely awakened early one morning by a camel poking his head through my Bedouin tent door flap. Beauty is in the eye of the beholder! Only a camel's mother ...

Looking up from Everest Base Camp in Tibet to see the morning sun hit Mt Everest and turn it golden.

Cradling my beautiful baby daughter, Georgina, in my arms and, just over two decades later, cradling my gorgeous granddaughter, Mya. What wonderful gifts!

In darker moments I have wondered, is it worth the effort and the struggles?

Yes, it gets better!

Forced to change

In 1983 after being clean and sober for two years, I was still holding on tightly to the old ways. My reaction to most situations was to attack first. I had yet another fight, or rather I had exploded and inflicted unnecessary pain, spilling the blood of a fellow member of a 12-step group that was helping me better my life. The violence happened in front of a number of friends, people who knew me and had befriended me, but this time they no longer supported my behaviour. I sat alone in a cafe next to Shepherds Bush Tube station, in a dark empty void. For the first time ever, I accepted there was more wrong with me than just drink. All invariably linked back to past childhood traumas and to alcohol misuse. My options were very limited, bridges were already burnt. The desperate nature of my circumstances became crystal clear.

My whole life was hanging by a thread. I was between a rock and a hard place. I could easily say f**k it and run, go back to my old life, or I would face up. To face up I knew I would have to change. Through emotional pain and desperation, I made an immensely significant decision, as only the dying, maybe, are willing to do. I am Roger and Roger had to change. That moment of inspiration took away indecision.

I wrote myself a list of resolutions:

- Stay away from the first drink and first drug – one day at a time

- Stick with the winners, and I'll have a better chance of becoming one too

- Give up swearing and learn to bite my tongue

- Take off the gloves and keep my hands in my pockets

- Give up smoking and try to live a healthy lifestyle

- Obviously it was eating meat that made me violent, so I immediately became a vegetarian!

Inflicting a veggie diet on myself was not anywhere as extreme as the radical Catholics and monks of ages past called flagellants who dressed themselves in itchy, rough horsehair shirts, beating sin and sexual desires out of themselves with nettles before breakfast as an extreme form of mortification. I, on the other hand, as a vegetarian and piss-poor cook, endured a highly flatulent veggie diet for twenty years. After a couple of decades, I began to question my diet. Was I doing the right thing, health-wise, in view of my body's requirement for additional protein to support my increased training and endurance challenges? The decision to eat meat or stay vegetarian was not taken lightly; putting aside the temptation of bacon butties with brown sauce, it was far more a psychological dilemma.

Was I taking a step back to my old ways? I queried myself, what if I am subconsciously chipping away at or diluting my resolve? I had desperately needed to change to remain sober and to live a new, interesting and productive life.

Still today, after so much water has passed under the bridge, I laugh at myself for blaming the eating of meat for my aggression. Primarily, the discipline of being a veggie was an important building block, acting as a constant reminder to me of my former violent behaviour.

These were important resolutions I made in 1983, and apart from vegetarianism, sticking to them helped me change. The proof is, I have remained 100% clean and sober from 02.02.81 up to today. Two years later I became tobacco free as well.

CHAPTER 13

Trying to Live a Healthy Lifestyle

Gym work

I have sweated, on and off, in various gyms over the years. In the 1960s and 70s the gyms I used were mainly for boxing training. I am not embarrassed to admit, I rarely adhered to a proper training schedule until more recent times. To do so is not as bad as asking directions or reading a map when not exactly sure where I am or, as my ex used to wrongly insist, 'you're lost'! (Modern technology can be a blessing, I love my satnav.)

I became a member of the Serpentine Running Club in 1983, and I gained a running partner and a lifelong friend, John Hadley. My new pal, John also belonged to a gym in Balham that he invited me to. Unlike today, you didn't need a gym induction or, if you did, it was ignored. You just parted with cash and became a member. Not unlike those after-hour drinking clubs no one ever admits to going to, let alone being a cardholder of.

John invited me and the first time I walked in, I was assaulted by the vision of very powerful men surrounded by heaps of weights, barbells, sets of dumbbells and kettlebells varying from big to enormous, with a scattering of free weights benches. None of the neatly regimental lines of fitness machines of today, certainly no posers, just a waft of stale sweat, Deep Heat, horse liniment and rotten shoes.

Many of these buff guys were in the process of creating the perfect bodybuilding physique. They believed the best method was as hard core as it could be, the old-school training, a simple, brutal, taxing training style. So if you want pure, raw, natural beef, take a tip from the old school, and put in good old-fashioned hard graft. Thankfully there was no Lycra on these lads, although occasionally some wore short shorts and wrestling singlets, displaying the goods! The star attraction in Balham gym, besides the manager, 'Wide George', was its sauna. George earned his nickname because he was as wide as he was tall and there was no spare on him, nothing wobbled.

In the sauna, the heavily muscled big boys chewed the fat. Intermittently one of them ladled water, liberally scented with eucalyptus, splashing it over the hot sauna stones, intensifying the heat – deliberately upping the already extreme temperatures to inflict still more pain on their sweaty bodies. There was an unspoken attempt to outlast each other, the 'elephant in the sauna'! The Balham gym had a colourful mixture of members; besides sporty and fitness freaks, many of them were involved in all manner of 'interesting' activities, possibly in various shades of unofficial work their bulk suited.

John Hadley and I were treated a little differently; after we pumped iron we went out on the street and ran a few hard miles. On one occasion I was attempting a bench press, while John was spotting for me, (taking the bar off when I did get it up and/or if I got into difficulties). Two lads came from each side and slipped huge extra weights on the already heavy bar. I couldn't move – I was pinned down and gradually began to change colour. Oh, how they laughed! Before I was completely crushed, they lifted the overweight bar off me. It was a strange way for the regulars to show they had accepted me.

Over the following 30 or so years I have witnessed gyms becoming big business; it is an industry, more open and acceptable to all, which is good.

It is with the help of equipment and exercise machines in today's gyms, mixed with running off-road that I have been able to build stamina, and effectively train for extreme challenges. Training and workouts have changed.

However, to my surprise, when in 2008 I contacted most of the major health clubs by phone and followed that up with emails, explaining that I was training to trek 650 km to the North Pole for charity and asking if they would like to support me, only one ever responded – LA Fitness, who were first rate. Most mornings, on arrival at their gym in Cheam, Surrey, while training for the polar trek, I did a 10,000-metre row on the Concept 2000 in a steady 40/42 minutes, followed by a solid 60 minutes on the cross trainer. Then, due to the new rowing challenge, my focus changed. On the Concept rowing machine I did a minimum of one hour daily, and twice per week I increased this to a two-hour session, plus an hour of good cardio workout on a cross trainer. I included general workouts using free weights, concentrating on multiple sets of reps rather than heavy weight training. I required endurance rather than bulking up!

In 2015, in preparation for the Atlantic, I increased my daily sessions to two hours and three hours on the Concept rowing machine. In 2018, building up for a possible adventure on a kayak, I rowed 14,000 km per hour on the Ergo rower and did upper-body strength/stamina exercises on alternate days.

I pamper myself after strenuous exercise by swimming a few lengths, followed by relaxing in the steam room and then a sauna. Boredom is my enemy when I'm pounding over extended periods on a running machine, stairmaster or rowing machines (though Lycra can be a welcome distraction). Conversation in modern gyms is minimal; while exercising, mimicking the hamster on its wheel, most of us are firmly plugged into our personal world, avoiding going totally nuts through pain-burying music, and limiting communication with the outside world.

I miss the banter of the weights room but I need to improve stamina, not my six pack, not that I ever had a great one! I have found that physical exercise keeps the body and mind in good shape, creating a positive energy bank you can draw from in times of great stress or adversity.

A jogger on the streets

One bleak and dismal Sunday morning in 1983 I was desperately trying to find a new direction, to separate myself from my bad old ways, when I had a light-bulb moment while watching the London Marathon on the telly. Yes! I would take up running and, of course, it had to be a marathon!

In 1983, I cannot recall ever seeing a jogger on the streets of Shepherds Bush, West London. Occasionally you would witness a body running, but we all assumed they were heading for trouble or more likely on their toes away from it. So there I was, at 6'2" and 235 lbs, pounding the roads of the Bush, in an old pair of plimsolls, a pair of baggy sweatpants and a top with the hood up (an early form of 'hoodie'). For some bizarre reason I believed that, with the hood up, I would not be noticed, in the same way as do the street kids of today. Movement, of course, always draws attention and trying to conceal this makes you stand out even more. Oh boy did I get noticed! On the first few outings I jogged in a circle around roads not too far from my home, because I had no idea how far I was capable of running. One evening, I was jogging around a set route of mine and on the third time of passing I noticed a couple who were eating each other's faces off in a darkened doorway. The guy jumped out to confront me, calling me a perv. Although I did verbally put him wise, I could see his point. I lengthened and varied my route, gradually getting more confident as my fitness grew.

My plimsolls soon got worn out and I needed a new pair. I decided to visit a proper running shop. I travelled all the way out to the Original Sweat Shop in Teddington. A member of staff introduced me to proper running shoes. To be more correct, a very fit young lady sold me a pair of extremely expensive trainers that she assured me were perfect for a big strong man like me to be running in. Blinded by a pretty girl, I paid a small fortune for a fancy pair of plimsolls. A simple man, thinking with his bits, not his brain!

I joined the Serpentine running club in Hyde Park. My fellow club members were a great bunch of people whom I still hold in high regard. We trained together twice each week, at Hyde Park on Saturdays and in Harrow mid-week. In the early days, on Saturdays, I would get the Tube from Shepherds Bush up to Hyde Park. On one memorable occasion I was walking to the station when a black car pulled up next to me, the window came down and an authoritative, bossy voice told me to get in. Was it my past catching up with me? Feelings of guilt hit me: oh shit, what have I done now? I am straight. I am clean and sober. This was followed by a flood of emotions – shame, humiliation, embarrassment and lack of self-esteem.

Ignoring the voices from the car and from inside my head I carried on walking. The car followed me and the voice got louder and more commanding. I stopped and looked, opening my mouth to tell whoever to f*** off. I saw the policeman was wearing a flat-peaked hat and I knew they are only worn by officers in a car; because he was in the back seat he must be an inspector or above.

Anger was building and about to explode to the surface when he removed his hat. It was that nutty Geordie, Police Inspector Peter Forster, from the running club. He really got a kick out of the ruse, and the stupid eejit was shaking with laughter. He got me good and proper – a 'you've been framed' moment. Even though he was a copper, he was a genuinely nice guy, mischievous with a crappy sense of humour that I like.

It was not long before I started to enter road and cross-country races of various distances, including 10 km, half marathons and full marathons. My first marathon was the Harrow Marathon in 1984. It was two races over the same course. The half marathon was one lap and the marathon two laps; the first lap was fun, lots of runners and spectators. As runners approached the halfway point, everybody in front and around me started waving their hands in the air, celebrating the completion of their race. I was waved on. The road ahead was empty; few runners and even fewer spectators. The second lap, running around the suburban B roads of Harrow, cheered on by one man and his dog, was a testing slog, physically and mentally.

I finished behind some good club runners and ahead of the main pack, and I narrowly broke the 3.30 hour barrier.

In the 1987 London Marathon, my official recorded time from the gun to the finishing line was a respectable three hours 15 minutes and 26 seconds.

As with the majority of the 21,485 runners on that day, we recorded our actual time on our personal Timex/ Casio digital watches from the moment we crossed the starting line to breaking the tape on the finishing line.

Chip timing of today eliminates the time spent in a logjam caused by the funnelling of thousands of competitors through the start gate. Queuing in 1987 added seven minutes to my actual running time.

I am an admirer of 10,000 metre runners; the way these wonderful elite athletes don't just have exceptional levels of aerobic endurance, but also have the ability to think and plan tactics, while running 25 times around a track. For me, a one-pace runner, it's just repetitive and relentless, I totally lose the lap count.

Serpentine Running Club held a 10 km race on the Battersea Park running track, exclusively for club members. John Hadley and I were on the last lap, and he was a little ahead of me; independently we both started to sprint early, which actually meant upping our pace a tad. John hit the line with his arms raised and pumping, celebrating, having achieved an excellent time, only to be waved on by a chubby little man with a clipboard shouting loudly, 'Two more laps to go.' John was noticeably pissed off.

I had also miscounted the laps and was waved on. This felt disappointing and deflating, but for me, the edge was taken off by watching John's grumpy antics! We weren't smooth, elegant runners at the best of times, yet, as endurance athletes, we would always man up and dig deep. It's by taking one stride at a time you can eat up the yards, and the miles will take care of themselves. The lousy feeling of deflation was overtaken by mental and physical tiredness during those last two extra laps; at the same time pride and self-esteem drive you on to the finish line, even knowing your time is going to be a bummer. It was like breaking out in a sweat while racing to the toilet, in a brisk penguin shuffle, only to discover it was just wind!

Crossing the line... finally!

CHAPTER 14

Pregnancy and Mr Respectability

I met Gloria in 1987 and we married in 1989. We created a home and a few months later she bushwhacked me with the reality of starting a family. Responsibility and acting like a grown-up at the tender age of 42 is a big leap; however, I was fully up for practising. Yet the possible consequences of no contraceptive pill and 'leaving it in', was a step into the unknown for me.

Despite being willing participants with spirited commitment, our efforts passed without hearing the pitter-patter of tiny feet. Tests were done and medically, everything appeared normal and positive. Then I had an amazing idea: a distraction was needed – I decided to buy Gloria a horse. I found and bought an Anglo-Arab horse, named Apollo, from the local Conservative MP's wife. Apollo was a good-looking beast. However, temperament-wise, it very quickly became clear he didn't like men. At every opportunity he showed his feelings towards me with either his teeth or hooves or both!

One winter's evening when Apollo was out in the large paddock, bounding around, enjoying some exercise, I thought I would join him and attempt to befriend him with the help of tasty treats. I had walked a few yards in when he spotted me. He paused for a moment and then broke into a gallop towards me. Luckily, bribery prevailed. I was rooted to the spot, with the palm of my hand held out, adorned with wobbling sugar lumps. It worked, his sweet tooth was more important than kicking the crap out of me.

Six weeks later Gloria was pregnant and had to give up riding. Apollo had failed as a diversion from the pregnancy quest, he became redundant and was retired off to a grassy field. Gloria gave birth to our beautiful daughter, Georgina Louise Anastasia Davies, on 16th December 1990. Two people were born that wonderful day, Georgina as a baby and Gloria as a mother. I do truly believe that during the first six months, when Gloria was being a full-time mother, she was the happiest she had ever been in her life; indeed it was probably the very best time of her life. It was so beautiful to have been a witness to that.

After six months, when her maternity leave came to a halt, she went back to work and her life changed. While she was an amazing mum at home, from dusk to dawn she maintained an incredibly successful career in a man's world. I have the utmost respect and admiration for her. Even as her ex-husband, I will happily stand toe to toe with any man who thinks otherwise!

So 1993 found me eleven years sober, straight and to all intents and purposes Mr Respectable, with a good wife and a beautiful daughter. We were suburban homeowners to boot. To get to this position I had grafted throughout the 1980s. I started at the bottom, working eight-hour shifts, six or seven days every week as a bricklayer's hod carrier. My job was to support a team of bricklayers by mixing mortar, carrying bricks, stones and mortar, and over the weekends erecting or dismantling scaffolding. Within two years I was tendering for brickwork contracts and employing my own bricklayers. After a couple more years of sweat, blood and tears, I had built up a small pot in the bank and I decided to start up my own fully-fledged business. I hired a qualified civil engineer to cost and estimate building contracts for me. Using his figures I tendered for various building projects, including new builds and refurbishments.

In the early years I remained connected with my past contacts with one foot still in my old world. Many old faces purportedly required people they could trust. On a hand shake you would be willing to accept a bag of cash and in return, you could arrange for a quiet refurbishment, build a secret storeroom, supply and fit a hidden safe, or convert a house into undisclosed multiple dwellings.

By 1992, I was running a small but profitable and legit company called Marathon Builders. I had an office in Marylebone, London, and employed a team of men and a phone book full of sub-contract tradesmen I could trust. I owned vans, power tools and general construction equipment; somehow I opened a few trade credit accounts.

A householder, Mr W, of Grafton Wood, which was no more than 800 yards from my home, contacted my company; his bungalow was suffering from subsidence. It required underpinning. After detailed discussions we agreed a price acceptable to him and his insurance company.

After a few weeks of hard grafting, hand digging under the existing foundation in sequenced bays to a depth where firm strata existed and replacing the excavated soil with mass concrete, Mr W approached me to build a second floor! We agreed a new work schedule and price. I started by partial demolition; the first job was to take off the roof so we could prepare the building for supporting additional vertical loads and services in readiness to create a second floor. Work was progressing well on the underpinning and the new building works were on track when, totally out of the blue, I received a fax to my office: 'Stop work on extension' – no funds!

I had by then learnt to resist my instinctive reaction, which was to get right into the face of Mr W with the aim of causing maximum damage. Maybe that's just as well for Mr W's health. Gloria, who had a very responsible, high-powered job in the City, reminded me I was now Mr Respectable, so I went to a lawyer. First mistake of many. I hadn't a clue how expensive, frustrating and complicated the legal process could be for a novice to the system. Not only was I up against a professional knocker but also, circling like vultures, were a scattering of greedy professionals hiding behind bits of paper that gave them a licence to steal.

I was instructed by my lawyer, for a stiff fee, that I was legally contracted to complete the underpinning. Against my gut feelings and common sense, we completed all the underpinning works. Surprise, surprise, no money was ever paid to me. I contacted Mr W's insurance company who told me they had paid Mr W in full. Two weeks later another building company proceeded to complete the second-floor extension. It was not rocket science to understand that the new builder had been paid with the insurance monies. Mr W had no money when he employed me, yet now he had a new extension for free.

Friends from the old days offered to collect what was due to me. I was extremely tempted. I had to pay money up front. Lawyers are grand fellows: a grand for this and a grand for that. Costs soon mount up. Mr W received Legal Aid. So I followed his example and when I applied I needed to show I could not afford to pay for this help. My application was rejected.

So how did Mr W, man of property, owner of a bungalow with swimming pool and now a brand-new extension, owner of an import/export business with a retail shop in Clapham High Street, qualify for Legal Aid?

I was fighting against an almost bottomless pool of money, while he could employ quality lawyers and later a barrister with absolutely no cost to himself. But my pride would not let me walk away. I was clean, sober and honest. I had done everything according to the book. On the other hand, I didn't know how to play the game. Oh how I wanted to take the gloves off. I ploughed my own money in and borrowed more; tied the debt and costs to a property. Time marched on and on. After some years, I got my day in court. Mr W never appeared, however, I was told to present papers before a new court date was set.

Some months later I arrived in court with all the requested papers that the judge had asked for. Yet again Mr W never showed. In court, a chinless barrister, representing Mr W, ambushed me with a technical time issue, otherwise known as a load of bollocks. The judge openly apologised to me in the courtroom; he could see

I had been stiffed, but there was nothing he could do – legally, his hands were tied.

Leaving the court building, Mr W's barrister attempted to apologise to me. I wanted to put his lights out. I dipped out financially big time. I almost turned to bankruptcy, however, I limited myself to an Individual Voluntary Arrangement (IVA), eventually losing a property valued at £500k. I never received any payment for all the underpinning and works that I had dutifully completed. My original actual debts amounted to only 20% of the final total costs. The overall result, including paying off my IVA in full, was that the suited and booted vultures who legally had their noses in the trough – lawyers, barristers and insolvency practitioners – picked my financial carcass clean. At least Dick Turpin, probably the most famous highwayman of all, had the decency to wear a mask when he was robbing you.

There are many bankers, lawyers, barristers, insolvency practitioners and businessmen who need a high income to maintain their lifestyle, so it's as well to acknowledge that you're not their friend, merely a meal ticket. What have I learnt from this experience?

- If you want justice don't use the law. Law is the law – it is not justice.
- If you're rich, you can buy justice.
- If you want moral justice confront the debtor yourself.
- Justice is never served until you do justice to yourself.

Today, I don't necessarily advocate violence or shaming for the best results; however, proactively taking action and coming up with a plan can lead to a positive resolution.

CHAPTER 15

Mistakes of Youth, Winners and Losers

I did some stupid things and bad things as a young man, usually fuelled by alcohol, sometimes drugs and occasionally both. When I look at the youth of today I can understand their actions to a point; I can't judge or point the finger and I tolerate them to a degree but definitely do not agree with many of their actions.

The reasons for carrying knives and guns need addressing. If I ever had a message to give them it would be fight, sure. I have no problem with that, it's what boys and young men do. But have the courage to use your fists, do not act as a coward and hide behind a weapon. Respect is earned. You do not deserve respect just because you think you do. I respect anyone who tries, no matter the outcome, as do most intelligent people. Perhaps, in your heart, you believe you haven't got respect from some and you are worried the mythical 'they' are not responding to you the way you want them to, or how you think 'they' should. You think you are weak inside and you are frightened others will recognise that about you and see behind the 'front'. I recognise these feelings, having had my own personal doubts.

Only cowards and weaklings will offer praise to someone who needs to hide behind a gun or knife. It requires real courage to stand up and fight with the knowledge you may lose occasionally. Win or lose, by standing tall, you will earn respect, this is based on my personal experience of my own violent behaviour, from the age of sixteen to my mid-thirties I certainly was not averse to exploding with fists or weapons, especially when fuelled up on booze. It was not the glamorous violence portrayed on TV and in films.

So many sad young men who thought they were tough and needed to feel they were respected end up on a cold marble slab. The lucky ones spend their best years inside a prison cell. Does anyone remember them? No – over time they are forgotten; everyone on the outside gets on with their own lives, living inside their own personal bubbles. The only place they think they are important is inside their own heads and I recognise that from bitter experience. I was one of the lucky ones, I escaped.

It is better to try being more concerned with who you really are. We are all unique, with our distinctive personal mental and moral qualities, but it's amazing the number of traits we share. To me a reputation is an image of what others believe you are – which can be far away from the real you. It is merely an opinion, what others think you are. In the sixties and seventies I wanted a reputation and I created one. Not one I am proud of today.

On one occasion I was the front-page headline in the local paper: Madman Attacks Police. I bragged, even waved the newspaper aloft in all the local pubs, I certainly made sure everyone knew. Today, embarrassment doesn't even touch the depths of my cringe moments.

CHAPTER 16

A Change of Direction

I'd had enough, actually a bellyful, of the building industry. I was working seven days a week and often unsuccessfully chasing debts by legal means. My head said get out, my heart kept saying, fight and damage the bastards. I bumped into a close acquaintance, Tom McCabe, who in the 1990s was a flamboyant telecoms entrepreneur. He started out by setting up a pseudo gay telephone dating agency, in other words, gay porn chat lines. He later moved on to create Swiftcall, selling prepaid telephone cards that enabled a user to make international calls far, far cheaper than, say, BT.

Visiting Tom's office near Tower Bridge, I witnessed an exhilarating telesales room buzz. Every call was money in his pocket. A wave of excitement tinged with a little greed swept over me, unlocking my thinking – it opened a new direction for me. I joined his sales team for a short time and quickly grew to understand the basic simplicity of the business model. Tom joined me in launching a business, Clearcall Ltd. We opened a telecoms shop in Edgware Road, a busy road in a district in North London known for its diverse and multicultural makeup. The southern end of Edgware Road, where we were located, was almost entirely taken over by Arabs. Very quickly we were busy with clients who were eager for the opportunity to make cheap international calls.

After purchasing our Clearcall prepaid card, you used it

by dialling our access number. You were then prompted to punch in your own personal identification number, as listed on the card you had purchased, and then just dialled the telephone number you wished to call. Every call a client made put money in my pocket!

In the shop we sold prepaid international cards and adapted mobile phones. A gifted artist, Brian Looney, decorated the interior walls with murals; we provided private telecom booths with comfortable seating and supplied free coffee. All to encourage the clients to relax, stay longer and spend more!

With our specially adapted mobiles, you could dial in your 4-digit code and the phone automatically linked to Swiftcall's network, so our clients could dial directly internationally at 30% to 50% of BT costs. The discount telecom business was new and innovative but still a grey area, and all went well for a while; the business grew and within a few months of trading was turning over £25k per week.

In 1997/8, our telecoms business was attacked by fraudsters at a cost to the company of about £200k. I called in the CID. Anthony Carter (our techie) had all the details and records of the fraudulent transactions, including the telephone numbers of the thieving fraudsters, making them easily traceable. After all our investment in time, money and working for relatively low margins we had been hit by theft and accounting skulduggery. It all seemed too much bother for the Old Bill, they showed no interest in a so-called victimless crime, leaving me with a bad taste in my mouth. Off the record, they said, 'If it was a £2 million fraud that would be a far more interesting bust.' The police turning their backs on our small company and a blind eye to the less than significant crime of fraud is worse than honest villainy. If I had robbed a bank and pocketed £200k, I would be looking at doing a sentence that could range from anywhere from five years to life imprisonment.

At the same time, Tom became far more interested in producing, financing and acting in a movie, The Tichborne Claimant.

It was directed by David Yates and boasted a quality cast of actors: Stephen Fry, John Gielgud, Robert Pugh, John Kani and

Tom McCabe. Unfortunately, the movie was never picked up and no distribution deal was ever struck. This left Tom with a big black hole in his finances. Tom was astute, he had accountants and tax lawyers who all knew how to play the financial game. He started to set off very heavy movie debts against Clearcall, questionably for tax reasons. I felt very uncomfortable, partly because I didn't understand all the financial shenanigans – I am sure they were legal. But I was the obvious fall guy if the shit hit the fan. Time for me to move on ...

During this period I met Ed and his financial/techie right-hand man, Stephen Milton. Ed wanted to get involved in the telecoms business. Steve and I created a working document setting out a business's future objectives and strategies for achieving what he wanted. He talked a lot, even introduced me to possible investors. It all turned out to be just talk. Twenty plus years later, Ed has long disappeared, but Steve and I are still in business together, which speaks volumes. Ed was a different thing altogether; he was, on the surface, a successful businessman but personally I found him too devious for me to comfortably trust. I always sensed he had an alternative agenda. I tried hard to do proper telecoms business with him, and even travelled to Europe on his behalf. Late one evening, after a particularly messy business meeting with him, he showed his true, two-faced self. I had a sense that things were not right, normally he was very secretive but on this occasion, he kept his driver/minder in the office.

The moment he made it clear he was attempting to screw me, I chased his excuse for a minder out the office and locked the door. I walked over and opened the second-floor window. I turned back, grabbed him by his labels and gave him a few gentle slaps to let him know I was deadly serious. Then I dragged the nasty little two-faced rat, squealing, over to the open window, intending to throw him out. For the first time in Ed's miserable life there was nowhere to run and nobody to hide behind. At that point in time, no amount of money would fix the problem and he knew it.

The growing wet patch on the front of his highly pressed trousers was proof he was actually being honest, at least with himself. He wasn't worth the trouble. I walked out with my head held high and went home to my wife and daughter. I left him in a miserable, damp heap on the floor; he may have cheated and stolen money from me but he had lost something money cannot buy. Experience has taught me that at all levels of society there are bullies. Be extra careful getting into a fight with the wealthy, even if they are in the wrong.

I learnt the hard way; they can afford to surround themselves with the best briefs and hire the cleverest lawyers money can buy. A well-trodden rich man's ploy is to threaten you, while hiding behind some judicial process and stretching it out for years. This is solely with the intention of destroying you financially. Time is the enemy of the less well-heeled. However, they are often fearful of the unfamiliar, especially when directly faced with any personal physical violence, real or imagined.

Blustering turns to whining and whimpering when they are confronted and they find they have no place to hide, especially with the possibility of being the target of retribution. Even if, figuratively speaking, it is only a dry slap or a broken nose, they bottle it. However, my favourite ploy was to use their inflated ego against them – use shame and embarrassment. I put on a suit and tie, and just appeared at their golf club, favourite restaurant or suchlike – it worked wonders!

At this point you might ask, had my changes gone deep or were they superficial?

A case in point, and a cause for further soul-searching perhaps: in 1995, on a quiet Saturday morning, I was enjoying lunch with my wife and daughter in Bella Pasta on Epsom High Street; the popular restaurant was busy, mainly filled with families and their young children.

A couple sat down at the table directly behind us. The man was talking loudly and his voice was rapidly increasing in volume. That was bad enough, but his language was more suitable in a downtown bar than a family restaurant. I left my seat and had a gentle word, suggesting for the sake of the kids and women all around that he calm the swearing. Blustering, he nodded. I sat back down and a few minutes passed until we and most of the other diners could hear him raising his voice again: 'Who the fuck does he think he is?' I waited for his courage to build. Just as I expected, he came to my family's table. Before he had the chance to shout abuse or take a swing, an automatic response took over in me. I can recall no thought process, I simply slapped him down on to his arse. To me, it wasn't a fight, just handbags. He left Bella Pasta with a few loud and colourful verbals thrown my way, followed by the threat of going to the police.

A dad carrying a tiny baby came over to us and said he had witnessed the whole incident and would be happy to give a statement that the guy was way out of order. Other customers agreed, and the restaurant's manager came over and offered us a better table. However, Gloria did not agree with my behaviour at all, in fact she repeated many times over the following years that I had handled the situation disgracefully. Looking back, I can see that in a way she was right. Importantly, what I did learn was that buried deep down under my cloak of respectability and years of sobriety, the old me still lingered. I needed to change even more.

CHAPTER 17

The Tough Guy Race was a Stepping Stone!

Tough Guy claims to be the world's most demanding one-day survival ordeal. I have conquered it five times, between January 1992 and 2008, and the ages of 47 and 61. Worryingly, before taking part, I had to sign a death waiver, to acknowledge the many risks and dangers, and which the organisers claim absolves them of any legal liability in the case of injury.

At the start of the Tough Guy Race you're corralled with 3,000-plus runners, reacquainting yourself with those familiar odours of liniment, feet and farts. Charge! You are off and running. It is then you realise you are witness to a lemming-like dash into the self-inflicted misery of a cross-country run plus the Mighty Killing Fields Obstacles. After a few country miles you reach the leg-sapping slalom, racing up and down eight or more times. That brings you to the Ghurkha Grand National, which takes you over a sticky muddy field into a thigh-deep ditch full of cold brown water. Out we clambered, jogged over another field and arrived at a river, with the surface decorated with 2-cm-thick slabs of ice that mutilated my legs – barely pausing we jumped in. There was a collective gasp when the water broke over the average man's nut height. Climbing out, my legs ran with streaks of blood, no pain – they were numb with the cold. Now that's bloody freezing.

Through the woods we continued, only to be ambushed by

2-foot high and 40-foot-long nets. Then we broke out into the open to see two 30-foot Tigers (commando-style climbing frames) to scale – and in between them electric fences that stung. Over the three Colditz Walls (two, three and four metres high). Next came the Behemoth, four 30-foot-tall platforms; we had to cross the voids between them using only ropes.

From the Battle of the Somme, with its fire and barbed wire terror, we progressed to wildly jumping and scrambling amongst the Fiery Holes, a series of mud filled ditches, followed by a number of burning bales of hay, where any exposed body hair was singed.

This was followed by crawling through a seemingly endless line of tyres – the Tyre Crawl. Into the swamp, where there was plenty of cold, dirty water supplied by natural springs and topped up by over 120 resident elderly horses that live, shit and piss anywhere and everywhere. It's a trip from ankle-deep, clinging mud to knee-high slime that gives off an interesting smell that lingers with you for days. On through the Vietcong Torture Chamber, concrete tunnels designed to effectively peel all the skin off your knees and elbows. Then on to the next climb, with netting and ropes as high as houses that people fell off with regular frequency – possibly due to hands, feet and wee bits being numb.

As we were scrambling over the 14-metre-high suspended commando climbing net, I heard a guy shout, 'I could go a beer.'

A northern voice answered begging for a hot cup of tea. Then a mud-covered, shapely girl, with mire-splattered blonde hair, responded in a very loud, sexy voice, 'I could do with a good shag.' This was met with silence. All the male heads went down. (Well, you have to understand how critical it was for us to concentrate on feet placement!) Really; there was not a man amongst us with the balls to respond. She had called our bluff – and we lost!

The next obstacle was the uninviting dark brown waters of the icy lake. Pirates of the Caribbean has nothing on walking across planks towering over the murky depths of the lake. I held my nose, why I don't know – there was already plenty of sh*t up there. Off I jumped, plunging deep under the freezing brown water to swim, paddle and waddle manfully to the side. Back into the water, this time the Underwater Tunnels – the cold bites deep when the head goes under the freezing brown water – the ice cold shocks you each time you attack the tunnels and pop up into one of the two small, dark, air pockets in between. It certainly takes one's breath away.

Out we floundered, covered from head to toe in slimy river silt and more, much more; by this time all sense of smell had gone. We slogged onwards to reach and scale the seven-bale, 40-foot, near vertical wall, named the Brandenburger Gate.

Maybe I should point out that there were relatives, sadists and frogmen grouped around these water features, clutching thermos flasks, chomping on sandwiches, offering gems of advice and cheering at particularly good examples of the art of submerging oneself.

More water obstacles next, as if we weren't already carrying half our body weight in mud, slime and dirty water. Then the Death Plunge – planks of wood extending out over a lake. This was followed by Jesus Bridge, a rickety bridge of barrels and planks of wood; off I toppled, and nearly drowned myself. Dan's Deceiver, up into the air and over cargo nets. Traverse the Dragon Pools via a series of monkey bars, unstable ropes and slippery planks. Of course, I fell into the dirty water, again! Of the few harsh challenges left, the Stalag Escape was the pits, you lay face down in the mud and belly-crawled for 40 feet under barbed wire.

On tired wobbly legs, we had a painful path of randomly laid tyres to stumble across, correctly named the Tyre Torture. I tripped a couple of times. Next came a series of knee and elbow peeling concrete pipes, followed by the dreaded Anaconda's hanging electric wires. On exiting, before me were the Viagra Falls, a steep muddy hill-slide beneath hanging electric eels ready to shock you.

The finish – at bloody last! A horse-brass was hung around my neck and I chugged down three cups of hot chocolate. I sported abrasions, gouges, bruises, an overdose of lactic acid, muscle cramps, pulls, strains and a temporarily shrunken penis.

In the 2000 Tough Guy I even had to carry a heavy wooden cross from the start over a good part of the course. Over the time

I have competed in the Tough Guy Race, the course was shortened in length, but Billy Wilson , better known as , Mr Mouse expanded and varied the sadistic 'Killing Fields'. Still it was good training, in case a person was crazy enough to, say, trek to the North Pole!

Before ...

... and after!

CHAPTER 18

Insurance Undercover

Dodgy claims

During the 1990s I was discreetly contracted by specialist cargo underwriters on behalf of the world's biggest insurance market, based within the City of London's financial square mile. London is home to the world's leading insurance platform, a unique indoor marketplace. Accommodated under its umbrella are the very best of the best specialist underwriters, men and women who are at the cutting edge of the world's fifty-plus primary insurance companies.

The underwriter needs as much information as possible to make a professional assessment as to risk; to me, they are akin to bookmakers who set the odds. There are over 200 insurance brokers registered in this market, employing two types of brokers: those that go out globally to find insurance business, and the placing brokers who facilitate the risk transfer between clients and underwriters.

Or, in plain language, a broker pitches his risk to underwriters in a number of syndicates.

Syndicate underwriters glean info from all types of sources, not believing everything the placing broker says; after all, a broker is just a suited and booted salesman.

My first assignment was to covertly visit, observe and report on the rice trade in West Africa. It sounded so simple! I hadn't realised that rice is a staple food for a greater part of the world's population; every year, according to Skuld, a world leading marine insurance provider, about 450 million tonnes of milled rice is produced. It is a billion-dollar industry, controlled and run by savvy businessmen. The majority of cargoes of rice that were shipped to Africa were insured through syndicates probably in, or connected in some way to, the City of London. It seems some of the more astute cargo underwriters smelt a rat. They were seeing a trend that was failing to achieve historically known profit percentages. Coincidentally, the insurance premiums received by the insurance companies closely matched the losses paid out in insurance claims to the clients. Thousands of tons of rice are imported into West and Central Africa each year. The value per metric tonne of rice in 1996 in the international data portal 'IndexMundi' was in the region of $300.

In the 1990s rice was normally transported as break-bulk cargo in bags, usually 20–25 kg woven polypropylene bags, allowing for easy handling and stowage. Bagged cargo is susceptible to a number of problems, including wet damage, tearing and theft. Hence, the true value of my eyes on the ground.

My first outing for a leading City of London Syndicate – Benin 1995

I tend to walk into potentially life-threatening situations with my eyes wide open. Trekking 650 km over immense, desolate, frozen terrain with the constant threat of polar bears and the danger of open water could easily fit this description. However, on my way to the Port of Cotonou in Benin, West Africa, I had little idea of the dangers that lay ahead. Here, ships unloaded vast tonnages of rice, after which the bags of rice would begin their inland-bound travels to destinations far and wide across West Africa, by various modes of transport.

My job was to check out a huge warehouse in Cotonou's port activities area, from where it had been recorded that tons and tons of rice had gone missing. When I walked through the door, into a vast space where you could easily park a couple of Boeings, I could see thousands of white polypropylene woven sacks of rice stacked up the left-hand side, and on the right-hand side, thousands of jute/hessian sacks which I guess were also filled with rice.

Walking down over the left – diminishing – tiered stacking was a queue of men carrying white sacks, while walking back up the stack on the right – which appeared to be growing – there were more men carrying brown jute bags. Directly in front of me was another group of tough-looking men, some with shovels and a few with machetes. In the few short moments as I walked towards them I could easily see what was happening. They had a system.

A white sack, carried down from the left, was thrown down onto a flat area. Then a machete slashed down, spilling the greyish-white rice, adding to the pile already there. The split polypropylene sack was thrown away onto a growing heap. A man held the mouth of the empty hessian bag open while others shovelled in the spilt rice. A couple more stitched up the newly filled hessian bags. Back then, cheaper white rice in polypropylene sacks became premier rice when it was re-packed in jute sacks, so I am told. Lads carrying hessian sacks found themselves joining the queue on the right-hand side of the warehouse.

Everybody stopped and turned to face me the moment they became aware of my presence. I smiled and waved. 'Hi, how are you doing?' I said boldly. 'I'm from the insurance company, I've got to look at the warehouse's structure,' I continued, speaking in a confident way. 'It looks pretty solid, if you ask me.' I began knocking on the side walls, as if it would make any difference – I would have had trouble denting it with a sledgehammer.

One of the guys, with a wicked-looking machete in his hand, walked towards me, oh shit – he was a big lump – 6-foot-plus in height and matching width. I continued walking, closing the space between us, with my hand held out for a handshake and a big smile on my face. It seemed to confuse him! Or was I just hoping …

Again, I rambled on about insurance, and how big and solid the building was. Not much risk of fire or flood. A question came to the front of my mind: can he speak English? If not, I'm in deep doo-doo! I asked him if he could show me around. Yes, he understood and waved a slightly younger but bigger version of himself over. Nobody else had moved.

Quite suddenly he smiled, gave what I suppose was instructions to the black giant and walked back to the pile of rice, continuing to shout instructions to all around. The workers started working again. I made a big play of studying the doors and wandered around, even going back outside, banging on the enormous framework; possibly I was paranoid but I could hear them laughing and I am sure I was the butt of the joke, a crazy white man. I wasted no time in getting back to the safety of my hotel in Benin.

As I understand it, in Nigeria from 1986 to 1995 there was an embargo on the import of rice. I had arrived during the transition back to normality, when the quantitative restrictions on rice importation were being lifted. I can only speculate at the possibility that large-scale smuggling and insurance scams were still at work. If you stood on higher ground near the border, you could see scores of men, each with a bag of rice on his head, walking along paths leading from Benin over the border into Nigeria. They looked like long strings of ants taking food back to their nest.

Rice seems such a cheap and mundane commodity, however, when a metric tonne of rice costs US $300, and you multiply the value by hundreds, or thousands or more, it immediately creates a vastly different ball game; insurance market vs international criminals, with me in the middle!

On returning to the UK, I reported on what I had witnessed; they could make their own judgement. A few weeks later, I was given my next assignment. My instructions were to checkout strategically located warehouses in, arguably, some of the world's most dangerous tourist destinations including Kinshasa, Brazzaville, Pointe-Noire and the war-torn streets of Luanda.

During my flight to Kinshasa, I was seated next to a white American who told me in a long rambling account that he was a missionary, as was his brother and also his parents before them.

He, as with many people who have the calling, could switch from breathing fire and brimstone to glowing with a happy and joyous naive innocence. Unfortunately, a few days later I bumped into him on the street in Kinshasa when I was busy getting myself acquainted with this rather dangerous city.

The Democratic Republic of Congo, with its huge wealth of natural resources, is potentially one of the richest countries on earth, but crime, a subculture of violence and a homicide rate of 12.3 per 100,000[1], coupled with rampant corruption – seemingly at all levels – have turned it into the second-poorest country in the world.

I quickly realised I was being targeted, and while I knew I could make it back to the security of the hotel before these guys could nail me, this American missionary started to cling to me like a limpet. A big fellow, who was on foot, was now next to us and invited me to meet his boss, who was sitting in a car that had pulled up and was now parked a few yards away. I said thanks but no thanks and that I needed to leave. The missionary was a real plonker, all naive smiles, telling me it was no problem and it would be rude to reject such a friendly offer. What offer?

The car drew up close to us and the plonker got straight in. I was cornered, mentally more than physically. I couldn't leave him on his own, it was me they wanted. The big fellow moved to block my way, although I felt confident I could still hit and run.

Reacting like a total novice I climbed into the back seat and was immediately wedged between the plonker and the big fellow. The man in the driver's seat looked slim but wiry. Next to him, in the front passenger seat, sat a large, heavy man, the obvious leader of the little gang; when he turned to face me I could see by his wide-open bloodshot eyes and dilated pupils that he was certainly on something – local juice or drugs. This was serious, he was stoned and didn't give a shit. The car's engine was running and the moment the big fellow had sandwiched me in, we sped off.

---

1. According to: www.ceicdata.com

Boss man spoke in deep measured tones, almost like a drunk man pretending to be sober; he was attempting to reassure us. I asked where they were taking us. The plonker continually interrupted and started to really babble. Banging on about being a missionary in Africa, mainly Zaire, as was his brother, and how all was well. This carried on for a while. I was watching where we were going – looking for opportunities (for what, I am not sure), and I did not like the position I was in. Abruptly, the car pulled up to a stop in a quiet side street. The driver reached down and twisted in his seat, producing an AK-47 that had lain hidden at his feet. The way he was pointing the thing, I got the uncomfortable impression his optimal target was my head.

The missionary really started to act like a god-fearing man, praying, offering them prayers and salvation, even reaching into his little shoulder bag and handing them religious leaflets. My thoughts would have got me killed. I honestly wanted him to shut up. I was actually embarrassed; I thought, if we're going to die, let's act like men.

And never mind turning the other cheek or praying for them; no, I did not feel sorry for their difficult early starts in life. What's more, don't they know I am a nice guy in recovery from addiction who is now going totally legit? It would be my pride that was going to kill me, not the man holding the gun. I had fought down my pride when the boss man asked for my papers and pointed to my bum bag under my shirt. This was daylight robbery – both he and I knew it.

I recognised that he didn't give a shit about consequences but in my new life I did. The big fellow next to me started to assist me in pulling out my shirt so as to get to the bag and the wiry one was making aggressive gestures with the gun. I handed the bag to the boss sitting in the front passenger seat – he opened it on his lap so I could not see what he was doing. Moments later he handed it back and told me not to look in it, just put it on again. At that moment I knew he had taken the $2,000 US out. But had he also taken my passport? He was robbing me of what would be several years' income to them, ensuring the boss and his little gang would definitely go to any length to enjoy the proceeds!

He told us to get out of the car. This is when everything hit the fan. I was trapped and my way out was blocked by the big fellow on one side and the missionary on the other. Big Fellow was not to be moved. When the car stopped and the missionary opened his door for us to get out, I knew that would be the moment – once we were out of the car and exposed – that they would shoot me. Before the missionary's foot hit the road, using every ounce of my core and shoulder power, I rotated my body, hitting the big fellow in the stomach with an elbow strike. Hurt and winded, he instinctively reached for the point of contact instead of grabbing me. I kicked the missionary out of the car and sprang out, quite a feat for a 17-stone 6-foot 2-inch lump. I barged him out of the way, spun round to the blind spot at the back of the car and ran for cover. They didn't shoot. I heard them shouting at each other; all of a sudden, the driver gunned the engine and accelerated away.

There was nothing remotely subtle about my exit from the car – self-preservation triggered my actions. An onlooker would have seen neither the agility of a Ninja nor a stylish James Bond in action, more the finesse of a startled Gruffalo.

My surprise action created instant confusion, making crucial decisions an absolute nightmare. Shooting the missionary, without shooting me, was not a good option, that was lucky. Later I came to understand that killing the locally-well-known American missionary, or leaving him alive as a witness, would cause a lot of political trouble. It could be the kiss of death for them.

It was very strongly suggested, by powerful people in the know, that this gang belonged to President Mobutu's secret police and could not afford to be recognised. For my protection it was deemed necessary to hide me away until I was smuggled out of the country. While I was hiding in Kinshasa, the white American missionaries thought they were treating me like royalty by feeding me once a day on dried fish (called 'stink-fish' locally). Fish are a great source of rich protein, but unfortunately, once they are dried, you can multiply the smell by ten and then it becomes possibly the most pungent source of protein on the planet. Dried fish is most definitely something of an acquired taste. My hosts had gone native and thrived on the local food and I did not want to insult them and their kindness by rejecting the food they put in front of me, but it was a very close call. The smell grabbed me by the throat, creating a gagging reflex. Just writing about it is making me heave.

First step in my extraction was to cross the mighty Congo River to Brazzaville, capital of the Republic of Congo; that was followed by an internal flight to Pointe-Noire and a plane home. But that's another story!

Roger cocked and loaded

Rice – Benin and the local butcher

Another assignment sent me back to the small West African nation of Benin. This time, after getting off my international flight at Cotonou, I travelled on the Benin-Niger railway; replicating the manner in which thousands of bags of rice had been transported from the port of Cotonou, 273 miles to Parakou, the largest city in Northern Benin.

Over time, Parakou has served as an important hub in the distribution of all manner of goods throughout Africa, including, in years gone by, African slaves.

Soon after arriving I located the precise warehouse, the supposed ultimate destination for a mountain of rice. I searched every nook and cranny of the vast empty warehouse. Probing and rooting through heaps of decaying waste and general refuse was to no avail, there were no empty plastic or jute rice bags. Not a single grain of rice could be found anywhere!

During this time, I witnessed the 'running' of a bull through the streets of Parakou. While watching, everything and everyone was dusted red from the sand, carried by the hot, dry, dusty harmattan wind, blowing south off the Sahara. The bull strode magnificently, his head held high and horns flashing, spirited yet not aggressive. The herdsman flaunted his bull's enormous testicles by constantly pointing them out to anyone and everyone. I was graphically informed that size is important! His owner or master goaded him onwards through the township; the bull was building up a real sweat on his body and getting the blood rushing through his veins. I was assured this was a popular custom.

Almost as a throwaway remark my local guide told me the bull was heading for the butcher to be slaughtered. Or could it be a brutal element of the voodoo religion that includes sacrificing animals? I was expected to be a spectator to a ritual. The assassin, or rather the local butcher, stood quietly waiting; he was standing on a very shallow, flat rock basin waiting for the arrival of this proud beast, and the crowd of people gathered were celebrating.

When the bull arrived he stood, head held high, blowing and stamping his feet, proving his lineage and exhibiting his freshness, which was much admired by the people. He was quickly and efficiently butchered. His throat was cut in one swift and decisive stroke. The once proud beast sank to his knees, collapsed and died. The blood was drained through a channel into vessels, I guess to be mixed with meal and to be consumed. This then, was the ritual, not voodoo; there was no singing, dancing or drums as I had anticipated.

Later that afternoon I was shown what I was told was the meat of the bull on a wooden slab on the side on the road. As I got closer, I observed what looked like a huge shivering black mass. As we drew near, the butcher suddenly waved his fan and a gross swarm of black flies flew off, revealing a large, fleshy pink hunk of meat. Humans, especially Europeans, acquire serious infections after being bitten by the disease carried by the black flies of West Africa. Yet, the locals promised me, it was fresh prime food of top quality, just minutes rather than hours old. On balance, I prefer my food sanitised, a fresh cut of rump from my local butcher or a frozen sirloin steak from a supermarket.

There were no clues as to where the vast quantities of rice were being stored. I wasted the first couple of days wandering around the town, with no success, until I heard rumours that the Benin-Niger train made frequent unscheduled stops en route. Allegedly goods, including sacks, were quietly unloaded at these secret locations. This was a light-bulb moment when the mysterious fog that shrouded the disappearing rice began to lift. I very strongly suspected the missing tonnes of rice had been quietly transported off, one bag at a time, on the heads of local labour to new owners in unknown pastures!

A pile of money

When I visited Freetown, Sierra Leone in 1996, to discuss rice, again on behalf of insurance companies, I made contact with the biggest and most powerful traders: a Lebanese family. I was escorted into a large building, and led through the reception area into a secure room where, set in the middle of the empty room, was a large iron cage, measuring roughly 12 foot by 12 foot square and 8 foot in height. Seated on top of the cage was a guard armed with an AK-47 that tracked me around the room. The guard warned me that if anyone, other than a family member, stepped inside the white line that circled the cage, they would immediately be shot. What was even more eye catching was the enormous pile of US dollars neatly stacked inside the cage.

Missing rice and the fallout

I wrote up my personal experience of hundreds of missing metric tons of rice from various West African countries into reports. My reports created a multimillion-dollar hiccup. Large cargo losses of rice were having a significant impact on the marine insurance sector. Total losses ran into many tens of millions of US dollars. Allegedly, my eyewitness accounts had a surprising effect on the market, and leading syndicate underwriters altered their positions. More far-reaching questions were asked of insurance brokers, many risks were declined and premiums were increased. As a consequence, the financial balance was tipped back in favour of the legitimate business.

Traders became very concerned. The word on the street and in the global insurance market was 'where is the information coming from?' It was obviously not coming from the worldwide network of agents or sub-agents covering more than 170 countries and territories. They all reported directly back to senior underwriters, and even directly to boardrooms of the City of London's financial square mile. Insiders suspected that the working life span of a local agent might be limited if they trod on the wrong toes; based on where I visited and what I saw, that point of view is definitely viable. Highly dangerous, questionable businessmen, whose wings had been clipped, were looking for the source of their woes – me. Serious money was being spent in the search, and a bounty was on offer. Suddenly, my services were no longer required by the

London Market. No golden handshake for me; my existence was totally deniable. It was strongly suggested I just piss off quietly.

It was time to walk away with my head held high and still on my shoulders!

Any risky or unexpected undertaking I treat as an adventure. I believe I needed to grow a pair, to let go of the familiar, and to accept change by embracing, even welcoming, the unknown. Letting go of the comfort of the familiar can create feelings of insecurity. With growth you get achievements, gains, occasional hiccups and moments of priceless peace. Don't undersell yourself. Ask for what you want – precisely what you want, not a bastardised or diluted version of it – and negotiate until you get it. Life takes you where it takes you. You and I can look back over our lives and see where life has taken us so far.

You can simply set yourself free by not worrying what others may think, and by literally turning your own hopes and dreams into actions. The outcome, for me, is that I am willing to own the person I have become; therein lies my freedom. In my experience sobriety has opened far more doors for me than it closed. Sobriety is an adventure just as much as climbing a mountain.

You can gain real inner strength and wholesome self-esteem from 'out of the box' adventures – this is what my experiences have shown me.

CHAPTER 19

Lifting my Mental Shutter

In 1996, at the tender age of 49, and fifteen years sober, I started waking in the middle of the night covered in sweat, experiencing chronic nightmares. I felt I was being brutally hurt, punished. The essence of the nightmare was fleeting. Years in recovery had made me aware of myself and taught me to 'clean house', to examine and improve my thought processes and emotions. This includes letting go of the past, and accepting that not everything bad or uncomfortable about my past life could be changed. So I was convinced that my subconscious was blocking something from the old drinking days, and I was paying the price for many of the unsavoury deeds I had committed.

This went on for some weeks, every night, until the early hours, before my waking mind took over. Then one night, for no apparent reason, I was awakened from the nightmare and my subconscious mind seemed to open up, revealing that I was reliving the beatings I had received forty years earlier at St Columba's College. Now I knew what was happening to me: the mental shutter I had dropped down over the traumas, the humiliation, shame and the fear of disappointing my parents was being lifted. It is said that a good thing about getting sober is you get your feelings back. Also, the bad thing about getting sober is you get your feelings back. That's what I was experiencing. It is over twenty years since I first experienced these dire nightmares, unfortunately they occasionally still occur. Providentially, my desire to exact revenge has lessened a tad.

From weakness I acquired strength, but when wrongly directed I became a bully, creating pain and havoc in others as well as myself. On the positive side, in later years I believe these terrifying experiences enabled me to develop the ability to cope well in adversity. It's not about being without fear, but having the determination to go on in spite of it.

My polar perspective or flip-side of fear is freedom. I realised I needed something that would help me to get through this, and that's why I sought out professional help. I made an appointment with the Westminster Pastoral Foundation. I acknowledge that drink, violence and a bad attitude had led me to open my own personal gates of hell and now, after all these years, I had walked in. As I have said, there were many traumatic causes and they need to be faced head on.

Shit happens; there is nothing that can be done to change the past. I needed to accept the things I could not change and have the courage to change the things I could – meaning me, Roger. I had to change.

They were very kind and professional in their approach and found me a counsellor. I think what confused her was how open and honest I was. I regurgitated the whole story on our first session; I could see real fear in her eyes and body language. Her main comment to me during our first session was that if I was violent I would have to leave. She didn't immediately grasp that it was the nightmarish consequences of the violence that I needed help with.

I was informed my counselling was likely to be a long-term affair. The majority of their clients drag it out over years. I repeated all the details over a six-week period – and the nightmares ceased; I had exorcised my demons. All it took was total honesty, courage, saying everything out loud on my part and having someone to sit, not in judgement, and just listen. Simple analogy: it's comparable to entering a smoky room and opening all the windows.

The dark thread...

Traumatic experiences from my school days were buried from consciousness as a protective mechanism. Unexpected stimuli linked to recovery and change triggered acute flashbacks – nightmares. This is a hallmark of post-traumatic stress disorder (PTSD). And in fact, I was diagnosed with complex PTSD.

At 7 p.m. on the 5th June 2019 I was sitting with Lesley, my wife, in the White Rock Theatre, Hastings, enjoying a coffee and chocolate cake, while waiting to go to our seats and be royally entertained by a real ivory tickler – Jools Holland, and his Rhythm & Blues Orchestra and Friends – the 'friends' included my favourite singer, Ruby Turner. A random couple came to our table and asked if they could join us on the two spare seats. We all made friendly small talk – had they seen Jools before? – Yes but only once. Had they travelled far? – Yes from Hertfordshire.

I mentioned I had lived in Hertfordshire and been to school in St Albans. Which school? St Columba's College. What a coincidence, our son went to that school. Were you there when it was full of those dreadful monks? That question was asked in a tone of undisguised disgust. She continued, 'They all got shipped out and it is run by proper teachers now!' There was a pause, and then she said, 'I suppose you utterly reject religion.'

That was the first time in over fifty years, outside of a therapy session, that I have ever spoken of or heard anyone speak about the brutality inflicted on the young boys at St Columba's College in the early 1960s.

CHAPTER 20

The Gentle Art of Fly Fishing

The last gift I received from my mum, before she passed away in 1997, at the age of 72, was a fly-fishing rod, reel, and a special fly line, along with casting lessons. An all-encompassing gift, which to me has become much more, it's a legacy that has opened the door for a lifetime of special days for me. My mum must have remembered the fun I had experienced fishing as a young boy 45 years before.

I caught my first fish in the late 1950s. Since then, fishing has held a fascination for me. Why or how I don't know, it doesn't seem to have come from the genes. Dad was a top-class rugby player, scratch golfer and a very capable cricketer but had no time for fishing. He thought this phase would quickly pass. No chance! I was bitten by the bug. I started humbly, a long bamboo stick with a line tied directly on one end and a hook attached to the other.

My fondest memory as a young boy was being totally absorbed watching my little cork float upright on the Grand Union canal near Leighton Buzzard. After much pestering, Dad bought me a two-piece bamboo cane rod and reel with line, float and a hook on which a small lump of white bread was pinched – I was now the mutt's nuts! Those clever little fish ate my bread without impaling themselves on my cunningly concealed hook, or with the wisdom of hindsight did my bread bait absorb water, go soft and fall off the hook?

I had little success until I asked an older, experienced angler (who was probably all of twelve or even thirteen years old) for some of his maggots. I baited my hook with a particularly wiggly maggot and cast out. Once that float bobbed under the water, I caught my first fish – an outstandingly beautiful 3½ inch perch. I was truly and absolutely hooked for life.

An important lesson I learnt in early sobriety – that ultimately saves time and avoids picking up bad habits – was to take the cotton out of your ears and stick it in your mouth. Listen to learn and learn to listen from the very best. So it was that I listened very carefully to Robin Elwes.

Robin is one of England's top fly-casting instructors, and he taught me to cast a fly. Not only did he teach me to cast but over time he introduced me to the art of fly fishing. I am proud to say he became a good friend and fishing partner. We've spent some great quality time flicking the fluff over the last two decades on many different waters including dry fly for trout on his stretch of the River Test, Hampshire, salmon in Norway, sea trout in Tierra del Fuego, carp on fly in Surrey and wild brownies in Ireland.

Fishing gives you the opportunity to welcome tranquillity, to see nature in the raw with all its hidden surprises, and appreciate the beauty of our world. Robin and I were fishing the River Itchen, Hampshire, when for the first time I witnessed a blue flash splitting the air as a kingfisher streaked across the chalk stream; it was magical. Later the same afternoon I had the rare sight of escapee mink sitting pertly on a branch looking out over the stream. To Robin's amusement, I have also experienced the river in full flow, from the trout's perspective, after falling in fully clothed, clutching my rod in one hand and soggy sandwich in the other.

I had always imagined that fishing, more especially fly fishing for trout, was a relaxing pastime; after a day on the water you would be refreshed and revitalised.

Not a bit of it. When stalking a trout I am totally focused, especially on dry fly when everything is visual. Casting to a rising fish is the epitome of fly fishing. All your senses are on maximum alert.

CHAPTER 22

En Route to the Top of the World – The North Pole

There I was, at the ripe old age of 61, with 28 years of sobriety behind me, standing shoulder to shoulder with my teammate, James Trotman (a sprightly 34), ready and willing to race (our team of two against four determined teams of three, all of them polar adventurers) in the world's toughest race – the Polar Race.

We were to set off from Resolute, on Resolute Bay, (74° 43' N and 94° 53' W), in the territory of Nunavut, Canada, to walk/ski for 648 km (403 miles), pulling our food and equipment on sleds (traditionally called 'pulks'), bound for the Magnetic North Pole.

Insanity? No, I've learnt that insanity involves doing the same thing twice and expecting a different result. Having never attempted to race across the most desolate terrain in the world before, I had no idea what to expect. As well as the tough conditions, there were a dozen other determined competitors to beat, all of whom were much younger than me and none of whom had recently recovered from major heart surgery, as I had. So how did I, in March 2009, reach this crossroads? As with so many things in life, it started with a harmless off-the-cuff remark.

Gloria, my ex, worked in a syndicate at Lloyd's, in the City of London's rarefied atmosphere, as a cargo and specie market leader; she spent her days rubbing shoulders with similarly successful high-flyers, whose conversations usually led back to money, power and prestige. However, on one occasion Gloria started to brag about a work colleague who had pulled a sled to the North Pole. I knew I couldn't compete with their manor houses and fancy cars, but this kind of thing levels the playing field. I was fit and strong; if they could do it why couldn't I?

I asked Gloria who the organiser was, and demanded his number. She made a call and gave me the home number of Jock Wishart, a maritime and polar adventurer, best known for his world-record circumnavigation of the globe – and for organising the occasional race to the North Pole.

I called him and said, 'I understand you are looking for a good man to go to the North Pole.' Jock's immediate response was a hearty belly laugh; then we talked and he briefly outlined the race. It was a captivating conversation that ended with a request for a £1000 non-refundable deposit. I was on his doorstep, the following morning, holding a brown envelope filled with the cash!

The Polar Race is divided into four sections, with checkpoints flown in by the race organisers at pre-agreed locations where we could stock up on fuel and food and catch up with fellow racers before heading out again. The Magnetic North Pole moves and rests on sea ice, so there is no real value in a map, nor could you be guided by the stars – it was summer, which means permanent daylight.

Every team carried a Garmin GPS, about the size of a mobile phone, for finding our way. We also had a satellite phone to check in with base when we set up camp, giving them our position in case we had a problem, such as an injury or polar bear attack – not for calling your mates back home or checking your favourite football team's results! In case we got lost, or if there was a life-threatening incident, we each had our own Emergency Position Indicating Radio Beacon (EPIRB) which transmits signals to a satellite and alerts search and rescue services (SAR).

I stepped off the plane at Resolute Bay Airport to be greeted by a chilling wall of deep, raw cold with blasts of icy wind that made my teeth hurt. The frozen air reached down into me, shrinking everything from my lungs to my scrotum. We had been warned that cold air can be irritating even to healthy lungs. We had first class kit and had received excellent training; all we had to do was implement what we had learnt, and all would be well. On went my hat, face mask, snow goggles and up went the hood. At arm's length, even my own mother wouldn't have recognised me.

Resolute is one of the coldest inhabited places in the world, a little town of two hundred residents. During our training and acclimatising week we stayed at South Camp Inn, run by Aziz 'Ozzie' Kheraj. Ozzie came to Canada from Tanzania in 1974 and stayed.

James Trotman, my teammate, was the Polar Race paramedic; given my age, what a strange coincidence! James is multi-passionate. Everything and everyone interests him. This has led him to travel to some fascinating places, including the Nepalese Himalayas, the Peruvian Andes, the Moroccan Atlas Mountains, the jungles of Borneo and the Namibian desert (and the North Pole, of course). Paramedic officer, crisis management adviser, operational delivery manager, expedition leader and lifeboat volunteer: these are a few of the things he's been known as in the past. These days he's a coach with a particular interest in helping people develop the realisation that they can actually do what they love and that they don't have to be stuck on the corporate hamster wheel. He holds a master's degree in resilience and emergencies, a bachelor's degree in archaeology, and is a member of the International Coaching Federation. But most importantly, he's a loving husband and a doting dad. You can find him roaming Brighton's coast and surrounding countryside in his spare time, if he has any.

Training, out on the ice, was when reality really hit home. Attempting simple tasks, like pitching a tent, operating a stove or fitting bindings to skis, in sub-zero temperatures are difficult and challenging. Most of the time you are wearing bulky gloves, and anything that needs to be done must be achieved with much-reduced dexterity.

Over time I have slept in tents at the opposite ends of Earth's temperature spectrum, from the North Pole to 10,000 km south of it, on the equator. Along the way I have enjoyed and endured lots of interesting, enlightening and occasionally awful bivouacs dotted across the world. After our first practice night out on the ice, I can confirm the Arctic is the coldest! A dress rehearsal, hauling a pulk on foot and wearing skis, was an eye opener; it's nothing like the infamous tyre-hauling training in UK. My body harness was attached by rope and bungee cord to a heavy load with no braking system, and the pulk had a mind of its own when being manhandled over sea ice rubble! A big learning curve was clothing and moisture management. It was -40 °C so I layered up substantially. Not long after I started hauling I knew I was wearing far, far too much. Being too warm in the Arctic creates extremely uncomfortable results. Sweat freezes. In preparation, Jock had warned us that two of the most debilitating problems that can spoil your time in the Arctic are toothache and piles. The extreme cold will quickly and brutally find a weakness. So I had to get myself checked out.

I dragged myself reluctantly along to my local dentist in Sutton, a very nice man. I explained what I was doing and said whatever needs to be done must be done. He was very enthusiastic about my challenge and equally enthusiastic about the local children's charity I was supporting. He immediately found work to do. I had three fillings, and an X-ray showed a mysterious dark 'cloud' on the root of one of my front teeth. The diagnosis was infection. The remedy was to remove said tooth, along with any infection, and replace it with an implant costing approximately £3,000. When I discussed the cost with his chief receptionist, I was told I did not need to have it done – I could become goofy or live with a plate. Assuming that was true, it was certainly not what I wanted to hear.

I explained that £3,000 was equal to £4,000 of earned income; anyone working 40 hours per week on minimum wage would have to work for three months just to pay for one tooth. My pleading fell on deaf ears. I did attempt to suggest that the prestigious practice could sponsor me and my local children's charity – each member of his dental practice would have to raise a mere one pound per mile if I pulled the sled to the North Pole; this was greeted with smiles, nods and lots of empty words.

Tipsy teeth: a digression

I feel no pain, but much shame, when I think back to the distant and dark days of the early 1970s, and an after-hours drinking session. Our affable drinking accomplice was in pain with severe toothache. He decided, after getting well-oiled on rum (as we all were) that the tooth must come out. We all agreed.

Playing the fool, I put on the dirty old cellarman's off-white coat, the equally tipsy landlord handed me a pair of rusty pliers, and I went to work. Today, on reflection, I do not believe anyone, including me, thought it was any more than a charade. But as so often happens when drink is involved, situations get a momentum of their own and I, for one, go too far. Alcohol mixed with mad macho males – often leds to deranged and dangerous behaviour. Sensible judgement flies out the window and the bizarre becomes normal.

Once his mouth was open, the offending fang was obvious for all to see. I pinned him down with hand and knee, clamped on, then just yanked! For me, it was all very swift and pain free. I can't say the same for my 'patient', he definitely needed a few more stiffeners from the top shelf!

A well-known hard man from South London was reputed to pull out rival gang members' teeth with gold-plated pliers. How he did it stone cold sober I can't imagine.

Piles!

From north to south (anatomically speaking), reputedly every healthy person has piles (haemorrhoids) including the rich and poor, famous or forgotten. In the sub-zero temperatures of the Arctic, having an itchy bottom is a major problem. You are wearing numerous layers of clothing: thermal underwear, power stretch pants, trail trousers, all topped by your windsuit, and your hands are protected by inner gloves and mittens. A serious barrier for a good scratch!

Keep your toothpaste and pile cream warm, in your pocket, and at night in your sleeping bag – you don't want them to become ice pops. Put a little tape around your toothpaste to identify it as a mistake can burn or taste awful.

Quote from my diary, 5 April 2009

On the eve of our departure, I feel a tension, knowing my physical ability is that of a fit 61-year-old, not that of the healthy 30–40 year olds who surround me. A spate of frenzied and methodical packing of 14 pulks is going on all around me in the 40 x 40 ft room that Ozzie has let us use. Each of us felt unsurprisingly antsy, ranging from excitement to an understandable myriad of the jitters.

We slowly move from organised chaos to almost military precision in our attempts to squeeze all our kit, from lip balm to a three-man tent, spare socks to the stove etc., into our own pulk.

Jock had taped a map – not just any old map but 'The Map' – on the wall showing the route. When I first looked at it, it held no real meaning until I split the distances marked into days to be walked/skied. Then the full force of the task ahead became clearer. There was much talk and debate regarding such questions as:

What is the best route?

Do you set targets of time travel per day or by distance?

How long between breaks? One hour travelling with a five-minute break for a drink of tepid water and dive into your munchy bag, or 90 minutes with a ten-minute break?

Answers to all these questions and many more became very apparent in a very short time once we had got underway.

The Route: waypoints

The first leg, a four to five days' polar plod, took us from Resolute round the coast of Cornwallis Island. Marching northwards, following the coast of Bathurst Island (through Polar Bear Pass National Park) to a waypoint just north of Bathurst: CP2 (Check Point 2). On the next leg there were no landmarks as we headed further north across open ice to CP3 (Check Point 3), near King Christian Island. The final leg took us across the Noice Peninsula on Ellef Ringnes Island to the 1996 position of the Magnetic North Pole at 78° 35' N and 104° 11' W.

We inserted these waypoints into our GPS and checked and double-checked before we started! Getting lost in the Arctic's polar area of 14.5 million sq. km/5.5 million sq. miles (roughly 1.5 times the size of the continental US), is not a clever option!

Years of practical experience and modern technology have made great strides in clothing and equipment. It proved to be a bonus for me in 2009, when I experienced the same intensely cold temperatures experienced by the Scott and Shackleton expeditions of a century ago.

I feel the need to make reference to the infamous pee bottle, a much ignored, but very necessary piece of kit. There is no way you want to leave the warm sanctuary of your tent, even less crawl out of your sleeping bag, when the temperature inside the tent is at best -35 °C, so you use the cosy pee bottle. It has a screw top, with a watertight seal and good capacity; it takes a lot to fill it. However, always be alert, you don't want spills!

No need to worry about the diameter of the pee bottle opening, even big boy porn stars will fit comfortably with some wiggle room. Normally guys assume the kneeling position, however with a little practise, rolling over onto your side will do the job. This way you are still tucked up snug and warm inside your sleeping bag. The pee bottle's importance grows as one gets older! Ladies have the equivalent – Shewee – a female urinating device: on which I cannot share any personal experience, only guess.

Boxers, thongs or briefs?

Boxer shorts are breathable, with plenty of ball room, but rather lacking in support, best for casual wear. Thongs, also known as 'cheese cutters', may look good on some, some of the time: they may look good on others all of the time, but they never look good on me at any time. Practically speaking, they are not designed to keep the 'bad boy and his two chums' properly tucked in. They mercilessly chafe and ruffle where they touch, or so I've been told.

I wore my lucky, merino wool, snug-fitting boxer briefs every day, for the whole of my 25-day polar plod. They always kept the crown jewels warm and (astonishingly) remained odour-free under demanding pressure. As a backup, I did carry a spare pair, just in case I had an incident with a polar bear or a particularly nasty follow-through!

Toilet paper or wet wipes

Toilet paper is light but bulky and must be protected from getting wet; no one wants soggy tissues.

Wet wipes are the best innovation for personal hygiene and gentle on your bits during adventures.

Some brands are very eco-friendly, for example Opus Innovations Genie Wipes are 100% biodegradable and totally plastic free. Also, they are tiny pellets that take up almost no space, and are light and easy to carry in your pocket or bag. However, when you add just a few drops of water, they expand into a large, strong, hard-wearing reusable wipe.

As with all supplies you carry with you, they are rationed. You are issued with three sheets per dump: one up, one down, and one to polish!

Poorly feet can spoil your adventure

Your feet are your foundation, they take the weight of your whole body, so foot problems can quickly lead to discomfort, and affect the way you walk, which can in turn cause knee, hip and back pain. Foot maintenance is important. Keep your feet clean and dry and exposed to air whenever possible. Change your socks often. Watch out for bugs.

A small but important preparation that is often overlooked, usually by us men, before embarking on an adventure – trim your toenails! Be shoe savvy, they are an incredibly important investment and your closest friends.

Smells and body odours

I add a note not to justify or explain, but we did not wash for the whole Polar Race – all 25 sweaty days! The experience was remarkably odourless, other than stinky feet. James's socks won prizes for dedication and commitment for their ability to undertake marching patrols around our tent by themselves. The highly technical reason for this is that he wore plastic bags on his feet! I kid you not – bare feet encased in a layer of socks topped by plastic bags, creating an impermeable membrane – all of which are inserted into the boot inner lining then planted into the big Baffin boot. The feet had no chance to breathe – nor did his tent companion, who was too busy gagging when the naked tootsies were exposed.

On the other hand, you don't notice any fully developed, over-ripe body odour, which is partly due to the strategic use of wet wipes, our sole source of intimate cleanliness. We divided fat commercial packs of scented or unscented wet wipes into small plastic bags, ready for use.

Of food and farts

Clay and James made up 575 munchies bags with a total weight of 460 kg to be shared amongst the 14 novice Arctic challengers.

Whether you are adventure trekking on the polar ice cap, desert or ocean, pouring hot water into a packet of freeze-dried food, mixing, then eating the contents is the supreme high spot of the day. They can be delicious – ambrosial and hot! However, I will never eat them again when back in civilisation. I savour the moment when I can feast upon real nosh, and devour any meal cooked in an oven that does not have the consistency of baby food!

A practical observation: when living on a diet of freeze-dried food, never trust a fart. Many a blast was that violent and skanky it physically attacked all your senses – smell, taste, hearing, and even eyesight – especially when expelled within the confined of a down sleeping bag!

Snow goggles and sunglasses

These provide protection from glare of the sun and the reflection off the snow that can cause snow blindness; they are also a safeguard from the intense cold winds. Snow blindness can be brought on by even a brief exposure to the sun's glare on the snow. Symptoms start with the eyes losing the ability to detect variations in ground level. As the condition worsens, the eye becomes inflamed, sensitive and painful, even when exposed to weak light. Treating snow blindness involves several days of complete darkness.

The Inuit create their own form of snow goggles designed to reduce the amount of reflected sunlight off the snow. Traditionally they are made from driftwood and bone, walrus ivory or caribou antler; they are wide enough to cover both eyes and have narrow rectangular slits cut in the wood. Simple and effective!

Personal items

An old friend, nicknamed Belfast Archie, suggested I take the Big Book with me to the top of the world. It is the story of how tens of thousands of men and women have recovered from alcoholism. The basic text was written in 1939 by Bill W, with support from Dr Bob. It's more than merely a book. It's more a way of life. It has served as a lifeline to millions of drunks worldwide, helping them to recover from alcoholism. It is a fellowship of men and women who share their experience, strength and hope with each other, so they may solve their common problem and help others to recover from alcoholism. Our primary purpose is to stay sober and help other alcoholics to achieve sobriety. It has undoubtedly helped numerous recovering alkies whenever they've found themselves in a lonely place.

This particular Big Book was sent to me from the USA by Tim M, an old and very close chum, signed by himself and his wife Lucy. Not only did they sign it but they also added a few supportive and warm comments. Many more of my friends here in the UK also signed it, wishing me well and adding uplifting comments and some clever illustrations. Amongst the friendly gang of contributors were Michael B, Jimmy M, Archie C, Gerald G, Miss B, Kate, Pete M, Geoff T, Ian K and many more. The plan was for me to carry this unique, customised Big Book all the way across the frozen waste, over pressure ridges, through huge mounds of ice rubble, dragging myself and my pulk with its precious cargo northwards, regardless of white-outs, ice storms, the constant threat of polar bears and probably over a thousand miles from the nearest fellowship meeting. On reaching the North Pole I was to leave my Big Book in a specially prepared sealed container, a seriously naive but well-intentioned gesture.

Once I was out on the ice, major stumbling blocks became apparent:

- The Magnetic North Pole is not marked by a pole conveniently stuck in the snow.

- The North Pole is situated on the Arctic sea ice, which constantly moves and melts.

- The area Arctic sea ice covers averages, in the springtime, approximately 14.43 million square kilometres (5.57 million square miles) – plenty of room to get lost.

I had become physically, mentally and emotionally attached to my Big Book.

Luminous orange was the colour we decided for the container, so when anyone visiting or if someone just happened to be 'passing by' they would immediately spot it and enjoy the opportunity to read it.

Who the **** will be passing by?

6 APRIL 2009: START DAY

Jock made an agreeable effort to send us off full of fighting spirit. Bursting with oomph, he recited a poem called 'The Quitter', which struck the right uplifting tone. On finishing his recital, he fired his pump action shotgun to start the 2009 Polar Race. We were underway, in front of us a 650 km/400 mile trek in the most desolate terrain on earth ... Living the dream!

After a 12-hour day pulling our pulks, we needed somewhere to cook, eat, sleep and survive the night. James and I were issued with a Terra Nova Tent that was proven to withstand Arctic conditions, without adequate shelter we would never survive. It was reasonably lightweight even when frozen, as well as being tough.

Pitching a tent while wearing gloves, in 'oh shit' freezing conditions, is far different to the practising we did in ambient temperatures in the UK. Jock suggested strongly we colour code the poles to indicate the collapse points. We had threaded the poles while at Resolute and they stayed in position, so all we had to do – technically – was to roll up the tent and attach it to the top of the pulk with bungees.

At the end of each day we attempted to find a fairly level sheet of sea ice, then removed any obvious lumps and set up camp, a routine that we stuck to throughout our journey. We unrolled our little home, and matched up the poles, making sure the front door flap faced the wind and the cooking flap vent was in the lee of the wind. I would grip the tent tightly as James jumped inside, preventing the real possibility of us watching as the wind dragged it off across the frozen sea towards Russia or Alaska.

Under normal conditions I would secure the four corners with our skis, even though I was not wearing mine they did have an important purpose. If there was no snow or high wind I used ice screws. Through the door I'd pass James the MSR XGK stove ready-fixed to a baseboard, essentially for our survival; it's the most reliable extreme-conditions stove over the last three decades. Then I handed in cooking pans, dehydrated food pouches, a shotgun and our personal kit. If needed, I would top up MSR fuel bottles outside and hand them to James so he could get the burners going. Then I would cut snow blocks to be melted for drinking and cooking.

I continued to secure the pulks, shovelling snow to cover the valence, to help keep the draughts to a minimum and also stops snow being blown up between the inner and outer tent in high wind and blizzard conditions. I then dug a little cold air trench in the vestibule space between the tent's inner and outer door. This allows space for cold air to sink below the platform on which you are sleeping. Every little bit counts. It also gives you a very handy place to sit, half in the tent, with your booted feet in the trench, making it easier to take off and put on your Baffin boots. In addition it helps to prevent you carting ice into the tiny living area.

When all the outside work was done and before I could get into our little house on the ice, my final job was to hand in the rest of our essential gear: sleeping mats, therm-a-rests and sleeping bags. Once in and snugly tucked into our sleeping bags, we stretched out a good 30 mm atop of a solid lump of ice floating, on average, 1,038 m (3,406 ft) over the ocean bed.

James was busy setting up our home, pouring any water still left in our thermos flasks into a pan which he sat on the burner to heat, then topped up with ice. Once the ice melted and the water was boiling he created the highlight of the day. A mug of steaming hot Trotman Special Soup. Ingredients can include cup-a-soup (any flavour), a sprinkle of chilli flakes and a knob of cheese. After twelve hours or more of physical effort in extreme conditions, it's staggering the amount of elation this hot tasty mug gave us.

One cold autumn evening in Surrey, some months after our return, I tried the same Trotman recipe. All I can say is it was outstandingly icky and 98% of it disappeared down the toilet. Occasionally, we spoilt ourselves, varying our routine and enjoying a mug of hot chocolate. Our short evenings were spent constantly boiling water for drinks, to reconstitute our freeze-dried food, thawing boots (while the stove was also drying clothes) and defrosting our sleeping bags.

After supper, we filled in our personal logs and called base camp on the satellite phone to let them know that we were alive and exactly where our GPS said we were. Only when all tasks had been completed, and just before getting into the sleeping bag for the night, did we enjoy the luxury of a few minutes off. It was during this precious quiet time I felt the urge to look at the comments my friends had added in my Big Book. I flicked from one comment to the next, picturing each contributor in my mind's eye as I read. I could not read them all at one time, the few I read were as much as I could absorb emotionally for one night. I was totally humbled by what my friends had written. Each evening I read a few more messages, absorbing mental and emotional strength from them to help me through the next gruelling day.

Waking early on the first morning, my dreams had been very vivid, not of the future but of the past, of persons distant in time but seemingly not forgotten.

Distance covered on first day: 7.5 miles

DAY TWO

My eyeballs were sweating!

I had great difficulty seeing when my goggles steamed up, as you would – well, I suppose that's not quite correct. In the first couple of days, every time I leant forward and exhaled, my hot breath created a mist over my goggles, so by the time I had become upright, moments later, they had completely frozen over and I was blind. At times, looking out through my frozen goggles resembled peering through obscure and twisted shapes of old-fashioned frosted-glass bathroom windows with the lights on.

Rubbing ice off goggles during the first few days was endlessly exasperating. Most of the time I was peeping out at the world with my vision limited to scraped peepholes. Later in the trek, the goggles magically de-iced themselves; my theory is that I got fitter and started moving at an economical race pace that suited my body. Once this balance was achieved, looking through an unfrozen screen was a luxury.

Distance covered: 15 miles

DAY THREE

We were getting into a routine.

I indulged myself by taking a small can of illy instant coffee, it was my one luxury item. I cannot tell you the pleasure it was to enjoy a hot cup of coffee on waking in -40 °C.

After a delicious breakfast, we would break camp, load our pulks, and set off to walk/ski. Generally our next hot meal would be twelve hours later. On a long day, during the trek, I would occasionally dip into the munchies bag and treat myself. We stopped every hour for five minutes to drink from our flasks, and that's when I really attacked the munchies bag. All the contents had frozen together, you would break a bite-size piece off the goody clump. Pop one in and it slowly thawed in your mouth. Every mouthful was a surprise: for example, mango followed by cheese, then a salted walnut, or a dash of Pepperoni, followed by a frozen cube of vanilla fudge. The eclectic mix caused wonder and havoc to your taste buds. We all suffered occasionally with strange food cravings. In the tents at night there was a lot of bartering. Arabella is reputed to have swapped three wine gums for a single piece of fudge. I liked chocolate!

I fell and pulled a muscle in my back, and it became inconveniently painful. It often meant I had to relieve muscle tension and spasm by stopping to stretch it out. The injury slowed me down some. That's when James confiscated my skis and made me walk the best part of 600 km in order to stop me injuring myself, him and causing lasting damage to the environment! We saw a number of polar bear tracks while walking through the rubble fields and over the pressure ridges.

Environmental hazards in the Cold

A harsh reminder came to me during a particularly vicious storm, with wind speeds of 60 mph and a temperature drop to -49 °C (56.2 °F) with the wind chill factor causing the temperature to drop to -80 °C (117 °F). Wind chill, simply explained, is the air temperature and wind hitting the body, causing heat loss. The heat is carried away by convection; wind chill can be deadly. There is no universally agreed formula for wind chill, but the one used by Canada and the US is becoming a standard. As a rough guide, -0 °C will feel like -5 °C in a 12.4 mph wind and -8 °C in a 31 mph wind.

Frostbite is caused by freezing, i.e. change in the skin and underlying tissues to a solid! It occurs on exposed skin within 30 minutes below -30 °C; one minute below -51 °C, and 30 seconds below -59 °C. Frostbite is not painful and this can be a problem because it's easy to go unnoticed. The absence of sensation and numbness can occur without a person knowing it.

Marching forward, leaning into my harness in order to drag the pulk over the most difficult terrain, I was wearing only a single base layer of merino thermals beneath my vivid orange expedition windsuit. When we stopped, even just for a few minutes, to avoid losing body heat, on went our duck/goose-down jackets before the intense cold could bite.

Distance covered: 13.2 miles

DAY FOUR

This was the toughest day to date, digging deep into the realms of the extraordinary. Wind chill reduced the temperature to -46 °C; fortunately we had the wind at our backs. We still made the normal five-minute pit stop for refuelling ourselves. I travelled a few yards behind James, not to be antisocial – it was just impossible to talk. So much of the 12-hour day you lived inside your own head – for me, a most dangerous place at times.

In these extreme circumstances I can overthink and lose sight of what is right in front of me. It's good to take a momentary mental pause, clear the head and refocus on what I can control, and keep going forward, one step at a time, in the polar plod.

Later in the day we caught up with Team Oman, and walked with them for an hour or so. Mutually, we decided to make camp by helping each other erect the two tents in the appalling weather conditions, making life a little easier. Nabs (Nabil Al-Busaidi) stood watching us, shivering, complaining he wasn't used to the cold because he was an Arab from Oman – as if I and the rest of us were! JP, his minder, often got frustrated with him, suggesting strongly that if he joined in it would warm him up and the task would be finished sooner! The advice fell on deaf ears ...

There's simplicity to surviving out on the ice, where half measures can guarantee serious injury or even death. I must have done something right because I still have all 21 digits in place and all in working order. I do listen and adhere to advice that's based on experience; I have little time for opinions. Opinions are like arseholes, we all have one, and nobody wants two!

In life mistakes can be catastrophic. This crystallises for me the importance of sticking close to a simple programme and friends who are fellow travellers, whether on the same adventurous road to recovery, climbing a mountain, rowing across an ocean or trekking for miles across sea ice rubble. Set apart from normal living, free of modern life's distractions and with time for reflection, made everything seem so fresh and poignant to me. I'm almost embarrassed to admit, it was as if I had opened the Big Book for the very first time.

Three hundred and fifty miles later, I became reacquainted with the spiritual essence of a new life and established a real link with the fellowship that had helped me move on with my life – entrenching within me a bond that no amount of physical distance or hardship could sever. I'm always willing to share my feelings and experiences with anyone in this miraculous fellowship, or someone still searching. Maybe enjoy a coffee and a chat with you. However, this signed copy of the Big Book is now mine; it is far too important to have left it floating around on a sea of ice in the forlorn hope that some random passer-by would find it. As my good friend Michael B often reminds me, even now, after 40 years of sobriety, I have yet to fully grasp the meaning of sanity!

Is sanity ...
Enjoying the ability to adjust to reality?

Seeing things as they really are?

Living in harmony with reality?

If so, given some of my antics, I could be regarded by some as mental, but not necessarily ready for a straightjacket. I remain a harmless, wacky nutter, who enjoys prolonged periods of rationality and balance. If I were rich, I would be referred to as eccentric.

Distance covered: 12 miles

DAY FIVE

We reached Camp 1 at 4.15 p.m. We travelled with Team Oman in poor visibility and by the afternoon the wind had increased, adding a cutting chill factor. My back injury was debilitating me, I was getting painful muscle cramping and spasms, marring the experience. My mind was closed and focused on pain management. Team Northern Lights went off in the wrong direction and did 26 miles in 18 hours – 15 wasted miles! While off-piste, they had an incident with a polar bear. It examined one of their pulks, posed for photos, then ambled off.

Pain and tiredness with extremes of temperature saps energy and my age was obviously a handicap. Steve Pinfield and Clay Smith, the highly experienced safety crew, arrived ahead of us and set the camp up, including a fun toilet! Unfortunately, between constructing the frozen privy and us arriving, the wind direction had switched and the windbreak was facing the wrong way. It became a wind tunnel rather than a windbreak.

Distance covered: 10 miles

DAY SIX: IN CAMP

Housework: airing, drying and repairing kit. The weather was dire; a monster storm with the temperature dropping to -50 °C and sustained winds of 100 km per hour. Taking advantage of the relatively warm, communal dome tent, we chatted and swapped stories with the other challengers. The Pole in One team were a trio of intrepid golfers, Iain Whiteley, who plays at Brocket Hall, John MacPherson, a member of Royal St Georges, and Australian David Stanton told us they had brought a couple of golf clubs with them and intended to play at the North Pole. Which they did!

The lads entertained us with army stories and by trying to convince us that a warm golf ball flies farther than a cold one, and to do that you keep a ball you're playing with in your pocket, add another and rub them together to keep warm! What a load of ... but fun. The problem with taking the opportunity to drink lots of tea, coffee, hot chocolate or cup-a-soup, was getting the balance between hydrating the body with welcome hot drinks and facing the Arctic wind when a pee was needed. The challenge equated to the level of urgency.

Much of our time was spent in our two-man tents, hunkered down, avoiding the boreal maelstrom around us. It was cold but bearable with the stove lit, alternatively, you could cocoon yourself in your sleeping bag. Often I chose not to read or play my iPod but to listen instead to random thoughts, similar to what I did while walking. I believe I was looking for inspiration and redirection to act upon, on my return.

It was comforting to rub shoulders and swap stories with fellow competitors. You got the opportunity to relax while the main adversary, Mother Nature, was outside, patiently waiting.

During our brief overnight stay at the checkpoint, Lucas Bateman, an experienced adventurer, availed himself of said WC. Lucas had relaxed and shed some of his clothing, as had the rest of us. He walked just a few yards towards the WC, into the stiff Arctic wind. With insufficient protection, the wind chill hit him hard, face on; he rushed his business and started the short walk back. By the time he reached the main dome mess tent his hands, only covered by liner (inner) gloves, were beginning to freeze solid. Due to the howling wind we could not hear his calls. Luckily, he jammed his thumb into the tent flaps loop opener.

He staggered in. Iain Whiteley, being the closest, immediately realised the seriousness of Lucas's situation. He opened his down jacket, tucked each of Lucas's hands under an armpit and hugged him tightly, sharing body warmth. In the extreme cold we were encountering, any exposed flesh will freeze, only a couple more minutes and Lucas's fingers would have been lost. Just a few minutes longer could have proved fatal. Lucas had relaxed and let his guard down – Mother Nature had not!

DAY SEVEN

The race restarted at 12 p.m. in rough Arctic weather; a fierce, frozen wind blasting directly into my face, forcing me to keep my head bowed. Constant tripping and bruising falls made me wonder what I was doing. Questioning myself, I was doing it firstly for myself, not for medals or glory and not only for my own self-esteem, but with the potential that I could carry a positive message of hope and inspiration to someone who may find it of help at a bad time in their life.

How? I had no idea, yet!

But who?

- Naughty lads, lassies and bad boys, who are where I came from!
- Those troubled in some form or other, to see there's always hope.
- I can show age is not necessarily a barrier.

Why? I want to encourage them to try stepping out of their comfort zone and give it a shot!

I was glad we stopped at 19.30, I had found the day particularly punishing.

Distance covered: 9 miles

DAY EIGHT: -30 °C

Heading into a north-easterly wind; very hard going over ice rubble. The sea ice misshapement is the results of ice floes being powerfully driven into and smashed against each other. We were still travelling with teams Oman and Magnetic Attraction. Walking with a large group, we tended to get strung out. However, the stronger ones kept an eye out for any stragglers. There was not much chatter. During our hourly breaks we were happier, when the group had a chance to talk with one another. Nobody likes to feel as if they have to face, physically or mentally, any desolate terrain alone. It's good to have mates. Personally, I was unaware of any special treatment but I do know that most of the group treated me either as a bit of an oddity or an older uncle – I was a similar age to their dads.

We were a mixed bunch; most, in the ordinary world back home, were professional people with solid careers. We had three high-level bankers, all with army backgrounds, that showed in their thoroughness and regimental approach. Otherwise there was a barrister, a physics teacher, a property developer, a businessman, PR, marketing, an international yachtswoman, a nanny, Nabs (who was being filmed for Oman TV as he became the first Arab to reach the North Pole) and his minder, JP, who was a serving British Army Officer. Then there was me!

Distance covered: 11.1 miles

DAY NINE

Bright sky, a noticeably lighter wind – it actually felt warm.

For the first time I travelled without my balaclava and wore a simple Heckler face mask with the mouth cut out. I found the going tough with the constant back pain, and it was difficult to relax and enjoy the peace. When I say peace, in these circumstances it was when I was in a constant state of tough experience with no mental input – on autopilot; it leaves the mind a blank page.

Optical illusions and visual phenomena in the Arctic are caused by exceptional atmospheric conditions, or so says science. On a private and personal level, I had a bizarre experience which is interesting in hindsight. In the early days while walking north, pulling my sled, I was convinced I was constantly walking uphill. My eyes were telling me one truth, my mind another, and often there was conflict. Attached to my pulk for twelve hours every day, I would automatically be leaning forwards, straining against the sled harness, with my head tilted at a suitably matching angle, so when my eyes looked straight ahead all I would see was the ice rubble, a few short yards in front of me.

To see any appreciable distance ahead required me to tilt my head uncomfortably backwards. In this position I would lose sight of my footing and act as if I were peering over the top of a pair of reading glasses – peering was the best option. Later in the day, when I was getting tired and leaning more heavily into the traces using my body weight, not just my leg strength, my overall posture was that of a man trudging up a steep hill, as if I was scaling the North Pole.

Distance covered: 13.5 miles

DAY TEN: -20 °C

We woke to a bright sky and no wind, and broke camp actually looking forward to another day in harness. After twelve hours of hard slog, we ended the day amidst some serious sea ice boulders. At Airstrip Point, Isachsen Station, going north, we encountered enormous lumps of bluey-green ice, some as big as a three-bedroom house. Some had cracked open. We found a level spot and set up camp; the site was shaded from the sun – not one of our better decisions. Lounging on a sofa in a centrally heated home, this may not sound important, but in a tent in the Arctic, any extra heat, no matter how minor, is gratefully received.

Today I listened and learnt from those who shared their experience, the guys who had done the extremes of the Poles, mountains and more. Our very lives depended on being able to shelter, rest and eat in our tent. It was our home, the only place of safety, warmth and comfort for hundreds of miles.

At one end we had our cooking stoves, fuelled by very flammable liquid. Topping up of fuel was done outside to avoid spillage, but still you treat the stove with respect because others have left themselves in desperate plight by underestimating the volatility. Sudden soaring jets of flames from the stove have destroyed tents in moments.

As for blowbacks, as a boy I never gave a thought to the possible consequences while entertaining my younger brother, Brian, in the magical art of igniting farts!

Distance covered: 15.2 miles

DAY ELEVEN: -22 °C

Although we covered 11.8 miles as the crow flies, you can conservatively add many additional miles, thanks to Lucas Bateman's navigational skills we zigzagged and meandered through a particularly massive boulder-strewn ice field. We took turns at sinking down to depths varying from knee to hip deep into snow-camouflaged fissures; it was tiring work struggling in the soft snow. I am sure we passed the same enormous blue ice monolith at least twice!

Distance covered: 11.8 miles

DAY TWELVE: -20 °C

We stopped half an hour earlier than usual and put up our tent in an ideal location, by coincidence close to where polar bears hunt for seals or ...

We chose not to go forward, due to too much rubble and the dangers of open water, it was best attempting to cross in the morning when we were rested and fresh. Three teams crossed a pressure ridge then onto an area of unstable ice field. JP got a boot full of freezing water.

I understate the obvious, that a boot full of liquid ice was very uncomfortable. The consequences of an extreme cold dunking would have led to serious problems – survival time is measured in minutes. JP handled himself correctly, emptying the boots and quickly changing into dry socks, in doing so avoiding injury. Many a jolly evening was spent holding boots upside down over cooking stoves in an attempt to dry them out!

As a concession, and to limit the possibility of disaster, we put our skis on to spread the load and crossed as quickly as possible, one at a time. I had no way of confirming how deep and stable the newly frozen surface of the sea was.

In the back of my mind was the knowledge that directly below the few shallow inches of ice under my boots lurked a 12,000-foot deep plunge of cold dark water.

Distance covered: 11.5 miles

DAY THIRTEEN: -25 °C

North wind blasting straight into our faces; a gruelling day, with little mileage to show for the effort. The first two hours were spent attempting to ski in the slush. The idea of me going back on skis was to avoid putting my foot through into -4.5 °C sea water. I thought I had an optical problem when I kept seeing a black dot where it didn't belong. It was appearing every so often in the desolate expanse of an ice field. Getting closer, we observed our first sighting of ringed seals. We had chanced upon a hole in the ice which the seal keeps open by regularly surfacing to breathe and scraping the ice with their powerful claws; this is necessary to prevent it from freezing over, or as an air-breathing mammal they will drown. Polar bears like to ambush seals; to do this they need solid ice for a hunting platform, while they silently watch over a seal's breathing hole.

The sighting of the seals ought to have alerted me and the team that breathing holes located along the broken ice edges among the pressure ridges are the ideal hunting ground; this is where seals are vulnerable to hunting polar bears, just as we are. We went on and once we were back onto thicker sea ice, off came the skis and we were back to trudging through an immense jumble of angular ice blocks with no clear passage or easy walking. By the end of the day we were a knackered group of friends who were very pleased to set up camp.

Fear: it alerts us to the presence of danger or the threat of harm. It was on this thirteenth night on the ice that James and I were rudely awakened by loud, hostile noises coming from the Magnetic Attraction team's tent. The volume and tone seemed even more extreme given the normal absolute silence out on the ice. We knew there was some serious situation at hand. We were correct. They were busy beating off an intruder, led by Julie Jones bashing it on the nose with a saucepan. This was backed up by lots of loud shouting from Julie and Lucas, along with a string of high-class blaspheming from Arabella. The ear-bashed intruder was a massive polar bear.

James and I opened the tent flap and eyeballed the supremo of the ice world at a distance of just ten feet; he was majestically fearsome. The polar bear is the largest land predator in the world. These big boys stand up to ten feet tall and can weigh up to 650 kg, and the girls up to eight feet and 250 kg.

Peering out from our little tent he seemed even bigger – an awful lot bigger!

The polar bear paused, turned his head and his dark brown eyes looked straight at me. I believe, for a moment, there was a look of yummy, scrummy. Both of us dived for the gun. James reached it first; he loaded it with solid shot, quickly slipped his jacket on and, gun in hand, he cautiously left the tent.

Fortunately, the big boy slowly moved off. In case he returned, James stayed outside on guard. Dressed only in his thermal long johns and down jacket, it didn't take long before the intense cold (-40 °C) started to bite and his core body temperature started to drop. He very soon began to shiver. The shivering became a rattling. What if the bear had come back? James was shaking so much he couldn't have hit a polar bear's arse with a shovel.

We contacted Jock, back at the base in Resolute Bay, by satellite phone and reported the incident. His instructions were brief and to the point: stay on the lookout in case the bear felt peckish and returned. Cold, fatigue and the physical comfort of the sleeping bag outweighed the fear of a second bear attack.

Later, after some dozing, we visited our colleague's tent and witnessed the large slash made by the bear's claws in their tent wall. When we were checking out the size and amount of polar bear tracks in the snow next to the tent, it hit home just how lucky we had been.

The picture over the page shows the relative size to my hand

Polar bear paw print comparison

outstretched, and part of my forearm; the paw was about 12 inches/30 cm, and each toe had a thick, sharp, curved, non-retractile claw – ideal for grasping prey.

Distance covered: 10.3 miles

DAY FOURTEEN

We started out tired, walking with the cold Arctic wind biting our faces. Within an hour of starting, JP began acting like John Cleese in *Fawlty Towers* when he gave his car a damn good thrashing with a rose bush! JP beat his pulk heartily with his skis; with Nabs silently looking on, not daring to breathe least the wrath came his way. I learnt later that JP had vented his frustrations on the pulk rather than on Nabs.

Continuing forwards, we attempted to work our way through a maelstrom of enormous ice rubble, but to no avail; we were forced to backtrack and take a new direction that led us to an ice-covered shoreline. With James Trotman leading us over the frozen Arctic sea we came upon a wide expanse of bluish-green ice where the ice had fractured and created a large opening between multiyear ice, which is up to 4 metres thick, and the land. Limiting the possibility of disaster, we put on our skis to spread our weight and crossed as quickly as possible, one at a time over the frozen sea ice crust that flexed gently as each of us travelled across. You could see undulating ice waves, bending without breaking. I thought it was scientifically impossible, yet I was witnessing the phenomenon with my own eyes. To all of us, it was an astonishing and perilous hazard to face.

I learnt some years later that new or 'fast' ice is where the frozen sea ice is 'fastened' to the coastline. To us it was unexpected, alien to our experience, and in our way. Walking on new fast ice is not recommended!

I had no way of confirming how stable the newly frozen surface of the sea was, and there's not much margin for error. In the back of my mind was the knowledge of what was directly below the few shallow inches of ice I was crossing and the consequences that potentially could kill me and my fellow trekkers. Following the frozen shoreline became our objective until we spotted a less dangerous route.

Three teams crossed that dangerous new ice field, in single file, as quickly as possible. Unfortunately, Julie sank into sea water over her boots; JP went to help and he also got a soaking, it was the second frozen footbath for him. Both of them handled themselves correctly, immediately emptying the boots and quickly changing into dry socks to avoid frostbite. Drying out completely is almost impossible. However, Julie and JP wore plastic bags over their clean dry socks, creating a barrier from the wet boot; the makeshift solution temporarily solved one problem but was no protection from the killer cold. They looked forward to spending a jolly evening holding boots upside down over cooking stoves!

Distance covered: 7 miles

DAY FIFTEEN

The north wind had picked up, gusting at 30 to 40 mph. We crossed a number of pressure ridges. I regularly nosed-dived into pockets of soft snow hidden amongst tangles of sea ice. After an extremely tough day we arrived at Camp 2. Bruised and knackered, for a fleeting moment I wished Camp 2 was the North Pole, but after savouring James' Trotman Special Soup I was back on track.

That night, I reflected on the first time I felt really cold. I can't remember how or why my kid brother, Brian, and I were playing on the frozen Grand Union Canal at Hemel Hempstead in the late 1950s. I would have been about 11 or 12, and Brian was about eight; we were young and having fun sliding about on the ice.

As an older brother I should have been more watchful; there was open water next to the locks, where the water is usually at its deepest. In hindsight that was a magnet to my little brother, and as an eight-year-old boy you just don't see the dangers. He didn't go to the very edge of the ice. In fact he was a few feet away from it when he suddenly went crashing through! He was dangling waist-deep in the icy waters and slowly slipping down, screaming from the shock of the ice giving way and the sudden cold. I can honestly say I never gave it a second thought – he was my brother. I ran over and grabbed him, pulling and dragging him up on to the safety of the solid ice, but the next moment the ice gave way and I went in too. I was almost completely submerged. I can still feel the impact of the cold water taking my breath away.

For some bizarre reason my main concern was that, as the older brother, I was responsible and now I was in serious trouble, not that me and my brother might have drowned in the icy waters. I managed to fight and scrambled out, dragging my little brother with me. I am unsure how, I just did! I was soaked up to my neck and the cold hit me, deep into my very core. My brother cried because his skinny legs and feet must have been painful. I had to get him warm.

We walked to the phone box and called home. We were both rattling with the cold and our clothes were freezing on us. I cuddled him. Naturally my dad came and picked us up as I knew he would. The drive from our home on Pancake Lane, on a Saturday afternoon would have taken about 10 to 15 minutes, but it seemed like forever.

Yes, he was angry, but luckily his anger was diverted from what happened to us, because I had disturbed his watching an international rugby match with his pals. I recall the warmth and safety of my dad's car and the pleasure of taking sodden and stiffening clothes off when we got home. I don't ever recall telling my parents what happened that day or ever telling them how grateful I was to them. If my dad has looked down on me during an adventure or other challenging moments, I hope he is proud of me. If I have a moment of doubt or weakness I pause, look up and I am refreshed.

Distance covered: 12 miles

DAY SIXTEEN

We spent the morning in Camp 2, drying, repairing kit, replenishing fuel and chatting. The race restarted at 3 p.m. Off we went, up over the ice-covered headland and straight into trouble – dramatic cascades of ice rubble as far as the eye could see. There was no rhythm to be had, either walking or skiing over the difficult terrain, during our entire journey. Unlike doing a marathon or an ultra-race, there was no getting into the zone and certainly no chance to relax.

The treacherous icy rubble beneath every step of the way was an accident waiting to happen – and it did as not only did I have the bruises to prove it but a pulled muscle or tendon in my side. It was a short, six-hour day; we stopped to make camp at 9 p.m. Sometimes there's a difficult balance between the number of waking hours spent walking and number of hours of sleep for recovery. It's comforting to spend a little quality time relaxing, eating and talking to your buddies.

Distance covered: 6.5 miles

DAY SEVENTEEN

A beautiful day, sunny with a light breeze, only -20 °C, almost shirtsleeve weather. It's at times like this that you must not drop your guard or the natural forces will teach you a brutal lesson. It was a long hard day with plenty of rubble and a number of steep-sloped pressure ridges, some rising up as much as ten feet. We had started at 7.30 a.m. and eventually found a suitable Arctic campsite at 8 p.m.

Sharing a small tent with another man is difficult at times. There was only just enough sleeping room if we lay parallel. The options are head to toe or head to head, each has pluses and minuses. My personal preference suggests it is better waking and seeing Mr Ugly close up! However, at -35 °C inside the tent, the beanie-covered head is tucked snugly inside the sleeping bag. Only the nose and mouth are partly exposed; throughout the polar night breath freezes, creating a personal frosty covering.

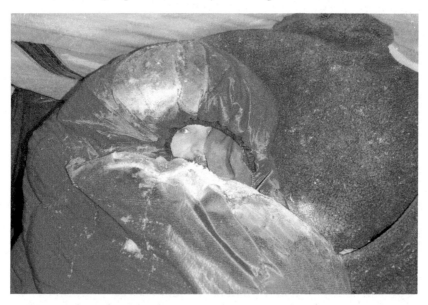

As our beards grew longer and a warm shower was a distant memory, you just accepted a familiar face. This is marginally better than receiving an unintentional kick in the head. No matter how well you know your partner there are always surprises. I was convinced, from the strange noises emanating from deep within James's sleeping bag, that he had a pet duck.

Each night we erected our tent, it became our home. James and I quickly became a team; just as well, because the personal space is very limited – you had to be organised. Whatever square inches we secured could become a target for territorialism and were fiercely protected.

We checked in with Jock at base using our sat phone, as we did every evening. We gave him our new position and I mentioned that covering fifteen miles was very difficult and we needed extra time to recover. He just chuckled!

Distance covered: 15 miles

DAY EIGHTEEN

The idea of a surface that we could ski across with ease, covering the 15 miles with no problem, was far from the surface we were experiencing. Stretching out ahead, the ocean swells had broken up newly forming ice that had herded together into a massive rubble ice field.

Travelling over the ice towards the Pole was such a far cry from when my then-wife Gloria and our eight-year-old daughter, Georgina, enjoyed riding in a reindeer sleigh on Rudolph's Reindeer Run to visit Father Christmas in Lapland in 1998. We found Santa and his two helpers in a little snow-covered cottage, hidden in a magical wood.

After a long hard day in the traces, James and I were ravenous. The meals we consumed were very high in calories but abysmally low in taste, leaving us constantly fantasising about real food. However, there is a hidden benefit to high-calorie, freeze-dried food while engaging in extreme activities in the toughest of environments: it's a great way to diet. I lost 42 lbs in 25 days pulling my pulk to the North Pole; Lucas Bateman lost 24 lbs. Arabella, though, lost none!

Distance covered: 15 miles

DAY NINETEEN

Twelve hours of punishing walking for me, and James is still on skis. I imagined there would be nothing new to see, but you can never get bored of the Arctic's unique nature, its incredible and bizarre formations of ice and snow.

James made the evening call to Jock, on our sat phone, to be told there were polar bears heading our way. That was the last thing we wanted to hear, since we were already tucked up nice and cosy in our sleeping bags, with full tummies. We rigged up a booby trap to create noise that would wake and warn us of an intruder. We also loaded two solid bullets into our pump-action shotgun, put the safety on and kept it close to hand. We were ready for action.

It occurred to me that there is a strange, obscure benefit to being out on the frozen terrain, where time has stood still since before man inhabited the planet, which is that you are never joined by any unwelcome guests – apart from polar bears. I appreciate that polar bears are predators and would welcome Roger as a tasty alternative to a ringed seal – 'Today's Special' vs 'Dish of the Day'. A polar bear can devour up to 150 pounds of food in one sitting; so there would be still 25% of me left! To feast on me would surely keep them going for a few more days. I am told they are shy and prefer to avoid humans, however, I kept a watchful eye out against being stalked by a hungry bear.

In the worst-case scenario, I was equipped to deal with them. My gun made me feel secure, exploded with loud angry bangs, and if all else failed and it was him or me, a bullet would end the bear's primitive survival need for my flesh. I felt certain that after surviving any such an extreme experience, I would don clean underwear and spend the following few hours processing adrenaline.

Out on the sea ice, with the lack of body hygiene – no bath or shower for a month and the same pair of merino boxers – I would be a prime target, a positive haven for bugs. But those tiny little things that wish to bite me, suck my blood and slowly eat me – they don't live around here, and how good that feels.

I am extremely popular with female mosquitoes, oh how they love me, showing their undying affection by the very size of the irritating bite, then they suck my blood, leaving me with a large itchy swelling that matures to the size and texture of half a golf ball and the possibility of malaria. The worst bug for me was often referred to as the No-See-Ums; as their name implies, you rarely see the dreaded ninja sandfly. When I was working in Abu Dhabi in 1979/80, I was very badly attacked one night by these silent flyers. This tiny, two-millimetre-long bloodsucker caused me to experience enormous facial swelling, due to an allergic response, which became very, very itchy.

The boys on site reckoned from a distance I resembled a pumpkin in size, shape and colour. The local Asians suggested rubbing half a lemon over my bulging face – the stinging was nothing to the overpowering torturous itch. As I am writing this I am beginning to feel prickly. I am eternally grateful that bugs don't like the cold!

Distance covered: 15.7 miles

DAY TWENTY

A gruelling day, twelve hours marching, with an occasional breeze. The goggles were off, to be replaced by new Cebe sunglasses; comfort with clarity. Yesterday's message from Jock was spot on, there were plenty of fresh bear tracks. The ice underfoot was comparatively flat, but out here on the ice nothing is what it seems.

It's easy for me to focus on life's troubles and out on the ice there's nowhere to run or hide. I needed to remind myself to watch out for my natural enemy, my own mind! Any negative feelings of indecision, self-doubt or lack of confidence cannot be tolerated, the consequences can be fatal. Reduce 'thinking' to the present, take everything one step at a time – not just on the ice!

The side sprain was still painful, as were both my feet. Oddly, when I stopped walking the pain in my feet got worse – so the answer was just keep walking!

Of dodgy feet

With a pair of dodgy feet since childhood, functional shoes are vital to me. Consequently, it is important for me to pay more attention to practical issues than make a fashion statement.

Trekking to the North Pole I walked for twelve hours a day over the rugged, uneven terrain of ice, rubble and snow in enormous

Baffin boots. They are not as stiff and uncompromising as ski boots, but they are solid and secure, with a certain amount of flexibility. They are actually comfortable if sized properly and worn on the correct feet! Baffin boots have a removable layered, inner boot system. The micro-cellular waffle foot-bed traps air and manages moisture.

In the Arctic, Baffins kept my feet warm, dry and comfortable in the harshest climates we experienced; even when the temperature dropped to -60°C my toes remained toasty warm. They have a comfort-rated inner boot down to -100 °C – now that is cold!

In practical terms the foot is cradled in a protective, waterproof shell, so when my feet leaked into my socks, the smelly liquid sweat cleverly escaped from the inner boot to the honeycomb inside of the outer boot, where it promptly froze. Don't wear cotton socks in extreme cold weather, they negate much of the insulation properties of the boot; cotton socks hold water – that's the last thing you want, frozen toes – that way frostbite lies. A quality smartwool / merino wool winter sock is the answer. Although my feet stayed warm all day it was very difficult to remove the honeycomb inner boot, which was firmly frozen to the outer boot.

One of our chores in the evening was to fill a pee bottle with hot water and balance each of the inverted boots over them in the hope of defrosting them, and enabling me to pull out the inner boot and complete the de-icing process ready for the next day. The inner boot stayed close to the stoves and the outer was put in the tent's vestibule. A daily build-up of ice inside the boots, if left, would soon leave little room for my feet!

Distance covered: 16.1 miles

DAY TWENTY-ONE

After travelling over six miles in the morning and seven miles against a searing wind in the afternoon, we spent two and a half hours in Camp 3. Sadly, during this time it was decided by Julie and the medics that it would be better for her to pull out. She had been nursing a leg/hip injury. Continuing could create serious implications.

There was another blaring, one-way uproar in camp between JP and Nabs. It seemed he'd rather stand and shiver than help JP and Claire!

Steve P and Clay S travelled with us now. Lucas and Arabella came to our tent. Arabella was struggling but she is a tough cookie and just needed a little support, as we all do at times. Hot chocolate, a chat in good company and all is well with the world …

Distance covered: 13.6 miles

DAY TWENTY-TWO

Cold wind and no sun. I spent twelve hours walking, tripping and falling.

Flat light is defined as a condition where snow and clouds compromise visibility: sunlight bounces through the clouds, all scattered and diffused, seemingly coming from all directions at once. Yet, spookily, features seem to blend into each other, producing a flat featureless vista – there were no shadows on the snowscape.

I even took off my goggles, risking the effects and possible damage from exposure to reflected sunlight from snow and ice. This happens even on grey overcast days.

Without the bronze tint of the goggle lenses, white-out and/ or flat light becomes even more disorienting and confusing. It is an uncanny feeling placing each footstep trustingly onto the unknown; my eye told me that everything was white, peaceful and flat. Contrast helps you see all the lumps, bumps and troughs of hillocks of broken ice both in and out of shadows. It's daunting, trudging through snowdrifts and over frozen sea rubble, with no sense of perspective.

Distance covered: 15.2 miles

DAY TWENTY-THREE

A long, arduous twelve-hour day. Pulling my sled in such extraordinarily strange, diffused light conditions I lost all visual indicators of shape and depth of field. Combined with my poor balance it was inevitable that I would endure numerous stumbles and tumbles – not without bruises and a few choice comments! I got weary and didn't recover as quickly as I'd expected myself to.

We had supper in Lucas and Arabella's tent, planning tomorrow's route. We are all gaining an incredible understanding of our environment and are a little more relaxed, but not complacent – Mother Nature has a mind of her own! Enjoy nature's constant, life-giving connection, including the bruises.

Distance covered: 14.5 miles

DAY TWENTY-FOUR

The day started with a climb over the Boothia Peninsula, up hills and down into valleys all created by glaciers. We were battling a severe wind, gusting directly into our faces. As we were nearing our northern goal we experienced another period of white-out.

The combination of clouds moving in, with snow whipped up by an escalating wind, resulted in very poor visibility. We reassessed; our amended target was to get within six miles of the Pole, camp overnight and continue in the morning, hopefully in better weather.

However, when James spoke to control at Resolute Bay during his routine medic call, he was told that they wanted us to keep going and head on to the North Pole.

En route, at 7 p.m. we received a surprise call asking for an update on our position; this must have been due to deteriorating weather conditions. With James leading, followed closely and in single file, keeping in close sight of each other, we ploughed forward as the Arctic blizzard increased in its severity, guided only by a bearing on our GPS. With 2.5 miles to go we pressed on; the tension during the last two hours was immense, high cold winds in our faces and the white-out. James, struggling to see, swapped places with Lucas for the last hour.

I suddenly saw Lucas and Arabella hugging each other, and that's when I spotted the faint outline of tents, and I realised we had arrived! It was 8.47 p.m. on 29 April 2009, and we had arrived at the Magnetic North Pole, 78° 35' 724" N, 104° 11' 915" W. We had covered the last 16.8 miles in 13.5 hours.

James, Lucas and I joined in boy's handshakes and girly hugs with Miss A. There was a lone figure standing in the camp, in the midst of the Arctic storm. It turned out to be John MacPherson, the 'engine' of team Pole in One. Was he intentionally there to greet us or just enjoying a quiet smoke? I didn't know or care. It was great to see him and be greeted by him.

Claire and JP (team Oman) came to greet us and help us erect our tent, which was kind and very helpful. Shortly after we were joined by Steve P and Clay S, who were woken from sleep by the noise and came out. They were happy to see us but shocked, as we were not expected until the morning of the 30th, with the prevailing weather conditions and our physical state. We enjoyed heartfelt camaraderie, the wonderful spirit of good friendship and loyalty among all the members of our group.

The Arctic is never boring; quietly it emits a raw power. It's still hard for me to grasp that I trekked across the Arctic Ocean to the North Pole, on constantly shifting pieces of sea ice, covered with ice rubble of fanciful shapes in a range of impossible sizes. I recall comparing the frozen seascape to a field of giant, rough-cut diamonds scattered by an unseen hand. The desolate landscape has a stark savage beauty that exceeds the expectations of all who witness it. Out there I am just a speck on the most desolate terrain on the planet.

And the results (it was technically a race, after all)? Team Pole in One came first, followed by teams Northern Lights, Team Oman, and Magnetic Attraction; Team Standard Life (including yours truly) came in fifth. The winners covered the course in 15 days and seven hours; we managed it in 19 days and 21 hours. It didn't feel like losing at all; we made it!

Rough Rog!

My arctic home

Our kitchen

The great expanse

CHAPTER 23

A New Challenge – Rowing

London 2 Paris Rowing Challenge 2010

I was enjoying a chat with my old friend Jock Wishart over a cup of coffee one fine morning, reminiscing about the North Pole race and the possibility of future adventures, when the conversation took a bizarre twist. I recall Jock chuckling as he said, 'I know a team that is looking for someone and you're just the man, I'll make a call.' Like a prize knucklehead, I nodded and that was all he needed. Briefly he explained in the very simplest terms about an interesting paddle to Paris from London. I said I had never rowed anything, anywhere, at any time. The nearest I have come to rowing is watching from the river bank and seeing various types of rowing boats gliding up and down our rivers. Crewed by guys and girls, young and old, effortlessly rocking backwards and forwards in rhythmic unison.

The only time I have ever witnessed the possibility of real strain and stress was watching Steve Redgrave, going for his sixth gold medal. It looked like a piece of cake; I lived to eat those words. Jock made the call, at this point I had no idea what he had said or what I was to expect.

Jock called a couple of days after our meeting in the coffee bar and told me I should show up at a particular jetty next to Richmond Bridge where I would meet the team and commence training. On arrival I saw for the first time the old wooden rowing boat; it looked harmless, bobbing gently on the calm water of the Thames. The first instruction I received was to go to 'number three'; I hadn't a clue what they meant. Which end of the boat do you count from, front or back?

Once seated, I was handed a bloody great big wooden oar thing to play with. Off we set and immediately I was bashing the guy's oar in front then the one behind. Steady down, it's all in the rhythm, you just lean back on the oar at the same time as the man in front of you. I thought at first that rowing required mostly upper-body strength, but it's actually the legs and hips that do most of the work, creating real power during a rowing stroke. You begin driving with your legs, engage the muscles in your back, then your core and finally with your arms. In addition to all the above, it's one of the best cardiovascular exercises you can do.

In reality, rowing is more akin to a duck swimming; the seemingly gentle movement, with a hint of tranquillity, on the surface, hides the fact that below the water, a pair of legs are frantically paddling. Oh boy, that beguiling movement plays you for a sucker. For me, after every rowing session I was always fairly knackered – and I thought I was fit. After a few weeks training on the water, I slowly began to feel more comfortable, less tense, with a slightly better understanding of what they were all on about.

It was from early on in my rowing career that my poor balance became an issue. I had been rowing a Thames Cutter from Richmond Bridge with friends most Sunday mornings for about eighteen months and over time a standard warning cry emerged: 'Roger, sit down!' When boarding, I always stepped carefully from the solid, secure jetty onto the boat, and immediately plunked my bum squarely on my allotted seat. One day I arrived a little earlier than usual and it looked as though none of the crew were about yet. I decided to help get our cutter ready, so I walked down onto the pontoon where Mark Edwards (master boatbuilder) had one of his lads tying up a boat.

I pointed out our cutter, which was attached at the end of a string of three. The lad sprang effortlessly across the gently bobbing moored boats one, two and three, making it so deceptively easy that

I followed him. Some of me more or less reached the second boat – but it moved. Caught astride the first and second at the same time, I involuntarily did a personal rendition of jitterbugging followed by an early bath in the River Thames, fully dressed. I surfaced with no specs, a bump on my head and a drowned mobile, all to rapturous applause from fellow oarsmen that I wasn't entirely anticipating. A dance never to be repeated!

I concentrated on improving my fitness level by spending extra time in the gym on the Concept rowing machine. Occasionally, after setting myself a particularly difficult target on the rowing machine, an inner voice started telling me, halfway through the routine, that it was going to be impossible, but thankfully my body defied my head and kept going.

Most of the team had rowed at university; they already had the skill set and techniques that they were now toning and honing. Nice bunch of guys. Overall, they were a relaxed group, except on the water, when they became serious. I was so often in trouble, not for lack of enthusiasm or effort, but because I was interested, even a little nosey and liked to see what was going on around me. Rowing is a very robust, sustained, repetitive motion, not unlike the focus needed when boxing or street fighting, when a moment's hesitation can cause you serious grief.

Metaphorically I was talking when I should have been listening. I would get in sync with other rowers, but I was easily distracted by a passing boat, a pretty girl, a fisherman, or indeed the general panorama, when a shout would go up from the cox or bow, jerking me back to attention. 'Roger, get your head in the boat!'

On 28th April 2010 between 7 a.m. and 7 p.m., members of team 'Outloars', including me, each rowed a 3-hour session on the Ergos rowing machine at Great Ormond Street Hospital, fundraising in aid of GOSH Children's Charity. We used this effort for charity as part of our training schedule. This was followed by sea trials in Ramsgate and night rowing trials in choppy coastal water.

The 2010 race would start in the morning of Sunday May 9th and finish at about 8 a.m. the following Saturday. The key

factor that dictates these dates is the need to row the tidal section
of the Seine (from Le Havre to Rouen) in daylight and with the
tide. Although the oarsmen had different backgrounds and a
variety of reasons for signing up for this gruelling jaunt, which
would challenge the stamina of the very strongest, the one thing we
all shared was an enthusiastic sense of adventure.

The London 2 Paris is open water rowing at its hardest. I
looked forward to an interesting and punishing journey from Big
Ben, down along the River Thames, across the English Channel
to La Havre then up the Seine to the finish at the Eiffel Tower, a
distance of 440 nautical miles, or 500 landlubber miles. We were
rowing our old-fashioned, traditional Thames Waterman Cutter,
34 ft long, with a beam of 4 ft 6, clinker-built from timber.

There was no modern rowing technology or comforts; it had
fixed seats for up to six rowers plus room for a coxswain and
passenger. The cutter is rigged for sweep rowing (one oar). The
stroke was the oarsman at the blunt end of the boat directly in front
of and facing the cox. He would be responsible for the stroke rate
(how many strokes per minute), and all you had to do was replicate
the same rhythmic movements time after time after time. It is very
hard core on the back, hands and especially the bum!

The cox would shout instructions and encouragements; in my
early months of training, half the time I had no idea what he was
talking about. I just got on with the job and tried to follow the
oarsman in front of me. If the cox was in a good mood he lightened
his tone with comments like 'just stroke it', 'just pull it hard', 'rowing
makes you handsome'. If we were working hard his favourite quips
were 'sweat is just pain leaving the body', 'sweat is just fat crying'!

We started from Big Ben, London, rowing our Thames Cutter
towards the sea. We had rotating teams of six rowers and a cox
over six days, this including brief mid-race pauses to allow for
tides, bad weather, and locks, and we only rowed in daylight on
the River Seine. You observe things differently from the water. For
example, the Thames Barrier was much bigger than I expected;
the four large central gates are 20.1 metres (66 ft) high and weigh

3,700 tons each. As we rowed down river there were an astonishing number of grey seals and harbour seals, sunbathing on the muddy banks of the lower Thames. We rowed on to the mouth of the Thames Estuary and into the English Channel, where we were met with a whole heap of rough water. It was great fun.

You dipped your oar in where and when you could as close to the stroke as possible, put pressure on and squeezed the oar; the fitness and technique of all the oarsmen became somewhat ragged, so I was now a little more equal to everyone else. I was bobbing up and down, splashed by the cold sea water – it was not long before my ill-advised attire, i.e. jogging bottoms, soaked up the sea and weighed heavily. Adding to my discomfort, out on the English Channel and during mid-shift I was caught short; my excuse was it was my age, but perhaps a surfeit of energy drinks had something to do with it.

The wind picked up and the waves we were encountering got bigger. However, I was too busy worrying about my seasickness and trying to paddle in time with the rest of the crew to be concerned. The cutter is surprisingly buoyant, it bobs about on top of the waves. Occasionally you get a wave crashing over the boat. As a team, we found it was becoming even harder to row through the angry water and settle into any kind of steady rhythm, you either had an incredibly heavy oar to pull on or your oar missed the water completely. Crossing the English Channel in an open rowing boat left me cold, wet, tired and with a very different viewpoint!

It all started to go wrong when the Gravesend boat took on water and began to sink off Herne Bay. Fortunately, all the crew were OK. Back to Gravesend and into a B&B for the night and off to France next morning. Back in the water we made it to Le Havre, then we had a 3 a.m. start, rowing into the mouth of the River Seine.

Rowing from Le Havre up the lower Seine to Paris was most interesting. We rowed passed some beautiful sights and places: Pont De Normandie, Rouen, St Etienne du Rouvray, Amfreville, Notre Dame, Mericourt, Vernon, Andresy and Chatou.

Rowing the Seine - Bridge (Pont) Mirabeau with just 2km to go

The Seine is a major transport artery for a substantial fleet of high-capacity barges, push-tows and cruise ships. At one point a French barge came chugging towards us at a much higher speed than we had experienced on the Thames, creating a bow wave of up to a metre; they are commercial and have the right of way, so we just had to look out.

Rowing is not allowed on the River Seine at night. We rowed in daylight in three-hour shifts, steadily up river via a series of locks, towards the finishing line at the iron foot of the Eiffel Tower. During one section our cox was over-enthusiastic; he steered too close to the bank on a bend and unintentionally ignored a fisherman whose lines we had crossed. That was the first time, and I hope the last time, I witnessed a French man 'mooning' – exposing his bum as an insult to us – not a pretty sight. On entering the Parisian suburbs, we picked up a shadow, an intimidating patrol boat (RIB) crewed by an elite squad, armed and dressed all in black; members of the brigade fluviale (Paris river police).

On 15th May, my friend Michael Broderick was at the Eiffel Tower finishing line to greet me with a white fluffy bichon frise tucked under his arm. I learnt that the dog's name was Bichoo and she belonged to Michael's flatmate, Cora Sue Collins. Known to her friends as Suzie, she is a renowned and respected Hollywood actress; she was in over 100 films in 1930s and 40s. My reception did get strange looks and sideways glances from my hairy-arsed crew mates!

Our team finished in third place, and we completed the trip in a very respectable 57 hours, 9 minutes and 27 seconds (but who's counting?). More people have stood on top of Mt Everest than have rowed the English Channel from Dover to Calais, and only a very few have rowed the distance between London and Paris.

A surprise compliment

I have done and experienced many interesting things. Yet nothing quite prepared me for the complimentary reference Jock gave about me, when introducing me to the crew of the Outloars: 'Roger is solid and reliable.' At 62 years old, and 29 years sober, I had never acknowledged the man I am today.

No good looking in the mirror. As I get older, not only do I see my dad, but the reflection only sees my outside. I verified his outrageous claim by calling my adventure and endurance athletic friends, who would not be afraid to give an honest answer. They questioned my sanity in querying it. They all agreed, apparently. I had long felt that growing old is unavoidable but growing up is optional. I may be a questionable oarsman, a dodgy climber with balance issues and growing older ungracefully, but I am reliably informed by – real players – that I am solid and reliable. That made me feel good, but the shadow of my past life obviously still lingered in my subconscious.

Rowing events I have enjoyed

The Thames Diamond Jubilee Pageant was a parade on 3 June 2012 consisting of 670 boats on the Tideway of the River Thames in London, as part of the celebrations for the Diamond Jubilee of Queen Elizabeth II, celebrating 60 years on the British throne. The pageant started from Cadogan Pier, Wandsworth; we paddled our Thames Cutter, 'Tiger', crewed by eight oars and Roger Gould (owner and cox) under 14 of London's Thames bridges, ending at the world-famous Tower Bridge.

The procession of boats, 7.5 miles long, was formed up in sections, each led by a 'Herald Music Barge' carrying ensembles playing music of different genres. The procession took approximately 90 minutes to pass. I take my hat off to two tough OAPs, Queen Elizabeth herself and Prince Philip, who despite the cold and rainy weather were standing on the top deck of The Spirit of Chartwell waving to us and all who passed!

Thousands of spectators were spread along the entire route supporting and cheering us from all sorts of vantage spots, lining the embankments, standing on rooftops, hanging out of windows and even a few sitting up in trees. I understand that some real enthusiasts, guaranteeing to bag themselves a hotspot, even managed to bivvy-up overnight. Tens of thousands viewed the event on large screens, in pubs and other venues, millions worldwide watched from their homes on TV. We were on show to the public for about six hours, hence peeing during this event was something of a problem. Girls in some of the boats developed a wonderful system. An extra-large full-length dress was passed to the girl in most urgent need, she put it on over her rowing clothes and squatted demurely over a bucket. For us boys, without practice it is a little difficult removing your bad boy from layers of clothing, while in a sitting position, and pointing accurately. For discretion, a towel was draped over the lap, or since it was so cold a flannel would suffice!

We were decked out in a very fetching team kit, generously supplied by Jimmy Mulville, a good man, CEO of a well-known TV production company, consisting of blue shorts, a matching T-shirt and a baseball cap. It was a long, cold, very slow row, rather a more gentle paddling than rowing. I had dressed for the occasion but not for the conditions, so why was I surprised I was freezing my nuts off?

Tudor Pull July 2012/May 2013

The Tudor Pull is a ceremonial pageant. The first time I took part in this historic event, we rowed our Thames Cutter in a flotilla that included the Royal Barge, Gloriana, 25 miles from Hampton Court to the Tower of London, with lots of pomp and ceremony. Our collective job was to deliver a stela to the Governor of the

Tower of London for safekeeping. A stela is a piece of wooden water pipe in a fancy glass case – a ceremonial token. Dress code for the oarsmen included knee britches, big colourful shirts and funny hats. In 2012, in addition to the stela, Sir Matthew Pinsent carried the Olympic Torch to the Gloriana, on which it continued its journey to London. It has been suggested that the origins of this festival lie in the commemoration of the sinking of Queen Eleanor's barge by London Bridge in 1256, with the loss of one of her courtiers. We Brits so love an excuse to get dressed up!

The New Waterloo Dispatch 2015

The New Waterloo Dispatch was the bicentennial re-enactment of the Duke of Wellington's report of victory over Napoleon Bonaparte at the Battle of Waterloo arriving to a fanfare in Kent. Major Harry Percy and Commander James White left Belgium carrying the letter/dispatch from the duke, but the ship had problems, specifically lack of wind, on the English Channel. So crew members lowered a gig and rowed the final 20 miles, finally reaching Kentish shores at Viking Bay, Broadstairs.

Three pilot gigs, one impressively crewed by young Ramsgate Sea Cadets, re-enacted the event by a 20-mile Channel Rowing Challenge in celebration of Percy's epic row, two days and 200 years after the battle on 18th June, 1815, carrying a replica dispatch and two Imperial eagle standards. Another wonderful British excuse for pomp, ceremony and dressing up!

Rowing on the English Channel is always interesting. Now you can see over 100 wind turbines consisting of 116-foot spinning blades atop 212-foot towers, rising up from the depths with a total height above the water of 328 feet. A powerful, majestic sight on the very passage of sea we both rowed our gigs across 200 years apart. I wonder what Percy would have made of the offshore wind farm.

Great River Race (GRR)

The GRR is the annual UK Traditional Boat Championship; it covers 21.6 miles from London Dockland to Ham, Surrey and is also known as the Marathon on the River. A spectacular boat race on the River Thames, it attracts serious oarsmen and charity paddlers alike. Over 300 crews from UK clubs and from across the world come for a challenging and fun day on the water. I have had the pleasure of competing in the GRR a couple of times, as a crew member in a Thames Cutter (Tiger). Pleasure may not be the best choice of word for the gruelling 2 hr 20 min row. We trained almost every Sunday morning throughout the year, meeting at 9 a.m. at the pontoon opposite Mark Edward's boathouses, just downstream of Richmond Bridge. Both times I was with friends, we were essentially a fun crew.

As training for the North Atlantic, in an old whaling boat, crewed by a mix of old and new adventure friends – Mike Johnson, Lucas Bateman, Mickey Pearce, Richard Wattam, Iwan Hughes and coxed by Lesley – we competed in the GRR of 2015.

Skiffing

The Thames skiff is a traditional, hand built, clinker-built wooden craft, which I am told evolved to suit Victorians taking pleasure outings on the Thames and other waters. The design has remained virtually unchanged for more than a century. Skiffing is sculling on a fixed seat with two oars per person. Skiffs are usually singles with one sculler, or doubles with two scullers (one behind each other) and a coxswain.

In 2012, I turned up at the Skiff Club at Teddington (the oldest such club in the world) and became a member. I was given two 8-foot long wooden poles with leather collars and traditional shaped spoons on the ends and I was expected to handle them with mechanical precision after an hour or three. A skiff is beautiful to look at and a pleasure to sit in but they do hurt the pocket, at £20k each, and a pair of oars costing around £500.

The first thing I was told was it's easy to handle a skiff; you just get into the rhythm by placing your blades in and out of the water at the same time as the person in front of you. Or in a double you follow the stroke, who is the rower closest to the blunt end of the boat and usually the most technically competent and competitive rower. The stroke can communicate with the cox to set the number of strokes per minute, which is necessary when racing. It all sounds so simple: the stroke only consists of fast movements and slow movements, in rhythm.

Mastering the basic technique was the problem, I had never held an oar in each hand, just one big one in two hands. I was told my hands must never pass one above the other. I was also told that one hand must always lead. I must have misheard that one; my version turned out to be that at least one hand must always bleed. After my second attempt at skiff rowing I was asked to wear gloves because the sight of blood from my torn knuckles was making the cox feel quite queasy.

The Great River Race, Thames

CHAPTER 24

Mount Kilimanjaro, 2010 and 2012

Kilimanjaro is on the northern border of Tanzania, 200 miles south of the equator. It is the tallest freestanding mountain in the world, rising out of the African plains to an impressive 5,895 m (19,340 ft) above sea level – not to be underestimated. Along with some friends, I embarked on a huge personal challenge, to climb the highest mountain on the African continent by the Machame Route in 2010. We were a mixed bunch, some had been with me to the North Pole, and others were enthusiastic novice adventurers.

The day started with a 50-minute drive from Moshi to Mt. Kilimanjaro National Park Gate. Machame (1830 m climb to 3000 m) is on the forest treeline, where there were a number of campsites in small clearings. Shira Camp (3000 m climb to 3850 m) is situated on the vast Shira plateau, which is a volcanic spill-off from the last explosion, some 100,000 years ago. It's a long open walk that is often dusty, with small, fragile plants scattered amongst the rocks, under the looming presence of the snow-topped summit of Kilimanjaro, a photographer's dream. The camp is sited in an expansive area with wooden sheds sitting over the long drops and ranger huts well spread out, making it easy to have some privacy. Mawenzi Tarn is very quiet and remote. However, as will be revealed shortly, the quiet was shattered by Dr Eileen's incident in the long drop!

Barranco Camp (3850 m climb to 4560 m, descend to sleep at 3950 m) is in a big clearing at the head of the steep valley which drops down into the Umbwe route, with dramatic cliffs around and right below the ice fields of Kibo, a stunning location for a camp. One of our young guides pointed out a streak of colour created by a darting Scarlet-tufted malachit sunbird that frequents open scrubby moorland and forest edges at higher elevation.

Karanga Camp (3950 m climb to 4200 m and descend to sleep at 3950 m) is a very open camp on a hillside with great views of the summit massif and vast African savannah below the mountain. Brothers Mark and Sam were best buddies and were also extremely competitive. We stopped for a short break when Mark was hit by altitude sickness and started to vomit; his younger brother Sam immediately burst out laughing, apparently his brother's plight was the funniest thing ever!

Many people go direct from Barranco to Barafu, so Karanga is traditionally a halfway stop, but still there are latrines and a ranger hut here. Barafu, (3950 m climb to 4600 m), meaning 'ice', is now no longer covered in permanent snow but it is cold, rocky and exposed. People definitely feel the altitude here and you can expect snow and sometimes high wind. The campsites are dotted among nooks and crannies in the rocks, perched on a small ridge.

On the day of our ascent to the summit we arose early, almost before our sleeping bags had had the chance to get warmed up. About 2 a.m. we were well on the way to the summit between the Rebmann and Ratzel glaciers. Heading in a north-westerly direction, we ascended through heavy scree towards Stella Point (5739 m) on the crater's rim. This is the most mentally and physically challenging portion of the trek. It is a 90-minute ascent along the rim to the summit, Uhuru Peak. To most of us, this was a once in a lifetime experience.

The cold and fatigue were briefly dismissed when we witnessed a breathtaking sunrise. Although, to be honest, I was too knackered to fully appreciate it. Descending was not without difficulties; I had trouble with my dodgy knee and tired legs. Unintentionally I began to gather speed going down a steep slope of black volcanic rock, but luckily for me one of our guides grabbed me before I took off over a ledge.

The Long Drop or Mountain Toilet

Each and every one of us needs a wee and poo-poo, a private and personal experience. When planning to climb Kilimanjaro with a group of strangers or friends, wandering minds turn to nightmares of filth, evil whiffs and creepy crawlies. On my first trip to Kilimanjaro the toilets were small wooden huts with holes in the middle of a slippery wooden floor for your business to plunge down into a black, bottomless pit, though if it's been busy, then the original long drop may be reduced to just a few inches! Squatting in the door-less mountain loos is, as you might expect, windy, and you will inevitably experience good and bad consequences. Wind dilutes the smells but plays havoc with the dangly bits. When you have mastered the art of squatting and perfected your aim, the long drop is hygienic because you are not touching anything. Unless you fall down into one, as did Dr Eileen Feeney!

We never asked her the obvious questions, such as how or why. We didn't need to ask, but by the tracking marks that ran from her toes to her armpits, Eileen had been lucky and ended up dangling! Julie J and Claire S masked up, donned rubber gloves and set to the job of washing off dark brown skiddies. Hair and makeup sorted, the finishing touch was a liberal dousing of local deodorant. What a trooper she was. Eileen was teamed up with the big, fit young porter who carried her day bag and generally assisted her, catering to her every need over the next couple of days. She had a broken collarbone, but she conquered both her injury and Mt Kilimanjaro.

My Knee

My dodgy left knee was getting worse. The tipping point had happened while getting my knee into awkward positions wrestling with a simple wheel change on my daughter's car, after which the ex-wife noticed me struggling to climb upstairs in our home.

Uhuru Peak

Lesley outside the long drop preparing for the evil whiffs
and creepy crawlies!

A couple of weeks later I was admitted into St Anthony's hospital, Cheam, Surrey where a leading orthopaedic surgeon, Mr Gerry Kavanagh, replaced the knee I'd had from birth with a metal one called Stryker Triathlon. I passed on the opportunity to watch and/or listen to the surgeon chopping off the ends of my femur and tibia and opted to sleep through the event. He neatly sliced me open, then drilled, screwed and hammered home a curved piece of metal into my femur. The end of my tibia was replaced by a flat metal plate, then tidied up.

The Stryker Triathlon Total Knee System was fitted to the newly secured metallic hardware, which triggers security alarms – I am a nightmare at airports!

Stryker's bionics has given me the opportunity to achieve two Guinness World Records by playing rugby near the Advance Base Camp (ABC3) 21,000 feet up the world's highest mountain, Mt Everest, in April 2019.

Mr Gerry Kavanagh did a superb job on my knee. He is a highly skilled consultant orthopaedic surgeon with hands as big as a blacksmith's. You may ask, what skills do you need to be a blacksmith?

- good hand-to-eye coordination
- practical skills and technical ability
- problem-solving skills
- creative and design skills, for decorative work
- good communication skills
- mathematical skills for measuring and making calculations

You may also ask, what skills do you need to be an orthopaedic surgeon?

- good hand-to-eye coordination
- practical skills and technical ability
- problem-solving skills

- creative and design skills, for decorative work
- good communication skills
- mathematical skills for measuring and making calculations

Mt Kilimanjaro (with my new bionic knee) in September 2012

I had my stent and knee replacement operations in St Anthony's Hospital, so when I was approached to help raise funds for the attached St Raphael's Hospice, it was a no-brainer. At an introductory evening at the hospice I was introduced to a very friendly and spirited bunch of people, who were supporters and fundraisers. As the talk and Q&A developed it was obvious the group were fledgling adventurers and for most of them, climbing Kilimanjaro would be the trip of a lifetime. Everybody goes to Mt Kilimanjaro with the ambition of summiting, of course, however, it is generally recognised only 50% will probably make it.

With this knowledge I saw my role as encouraging everyone to be physically prepared, as a group and individually. Focus your training towards hill workouts! I wanted my friends to smash it, and get to the top.

I shared my experience with the group. On Kilimanjaro there are some steep ascents and descents in a short period of time, hence you reach higher altitude sooner, making it far more physically demanding. In my experience, the 'summit day' on Kilimanjaro is harder than any part of the Everest Base Camp Trek. Don't underestimate Kili ...

In consultation with Gavin Bates (Adventure Alternatives), we selected to summit Kilimanjaro via the Rongai Route. It is quieter, offers trekkers a relatively unspoilt wilderness experience, and we were less likely to encounter rain. Before we knew it, we were on our way, flying to Nairobi Airport, Kenya.

Our transport was waiting for us, a canvas-covered lorry called Pumba, in which we endured a buttock-pounding, 330 km journey to Moshi. OT was our driver and has been with Adventure

Alternatives in Kenya since day one. He is their fleet manager, chief mechanic and the principal driver of Pumba. As a very experienced on and off-road driver with an extensive knowledge of East African road networks, he made sure that we arrived safely at our destination. He also understood the need for comfort breaks. I watched him chuckle as we men stood in a line on one side of the road, all pointing east, and the women hurried off in pairs amongst the shrubs on the other.

We spent a couple of nights in a hotel preparing ourselves. On the second morning we rose early, enjoyed breakfast together and boarded Pumba for the 3-hour drive to Rongai Gate. We walked for four hours, passing maize fields and through a delightful pine forest that offered us a better chance of seeing wildlife to our first stop at Simba Camp, at 2670 metres.

Looking out from camp there were superb views of Kibo summit (one of Mt Kilimanjaro's three peaks) and the eastern ice fields on the crater rim. Our camp was in a sheltered valley with the alien-looking giant Dendrosenecios plants nearby. Each porter carries up to 20 kg on their back or head! Their loads include our food, tables, chairs and the kitchen sink. It right-sized me, when they trotted past, wearing flip-flops or sandals made from old car tyres.

Next morning we set off to climb 3600 m, a long, 6-hour trek through moorlands to our second camp, near Kikelewa Cave. I think it's important to note that every morning our morning peace was broken not by a dawn chorus or cockerels crowing, signalling the start of a new day, but by Peter W (a senior oil executive in the UK) proudly owning an enormous fart. Every morning, the cooks and porters who were preparing breakfast and readying camp learnt to expect it and cheered!

Now we were trekking and gaining altitude. I worked quietly with the seasoned guides to make sure we gave everyone the best opportunity to acclimatise. The group mantra was 'poli poli' (slowly, slowly) and I also encouraged people to 'Stop, lift your head up and look around – take the opportunity to soak up the views – take plenty of pictures.'

I tried to keep an eye on everyone and remind them how critical it is to keep the body hydrated at altitude – you need to constantly sip water.

After a five-hour trek around Mawenzi Tarn across an alpine desert with a few steep sections, we spent a rest and acclimatising day taking walks in the area. Some of the group were starting to feel the effects of altitude. That evening we dined sitting at the base of the towering spires of Mawenzi, one of the three peaks of Kilimanjaro. The view was far more memorable than the dinner!

We reached Kibo Hut camp, after four hours trekking over a lunar landscape, devoid of any flora. The ascent to the saddle of Mt Kilimanjaro is between the peaks of Kibo and Mwenzi, and we got some great views. On arrival, it was important we settled down quickly to eat and sleep, as we had to wake in the dark, at 1 a.m., to start the final push through the pre-dawn hours. This was necessary in order to experience sunrise on the 'Roof of Africa'. So after a hot drink and nibbles we shuffled off into the night.

Summit Day was gruelling, zigzagging up through heavy scree for five grinding hours towards Gilman's Point (5680 m) on the crater rim. I recall passing another group of trekkers, bent over their walking poles, some panting like dogs. Occasionally the quiet was broken by the sounds of throwing up. One of our guides tapped me on the arm to get my attention and pointed back. Adam was staggering about like a young giraffe on brand-new wobbly legs. He was suffering from a loss of coordination and confusion, having succumbed to altitude sickness. Time was of the essence, he had to descend immediately. Two porters took an arm each and ran him 1000 m down the scree slope. Once down, he quickly recovered, thankfully.

At Gilman's Point we were able to look down inside the crater. Then we spent two hours plodding gently around the sloping rim on Kibo's giant crater, to summit Uhuru Peak, at 5,895 metres the highest point in all of Africa. Darkness was gradually replaced by a glorious morning sunrise. From the Roof of Africa we looked out onto a panoramic landscape of snow, glaciers and rocky peaks lifting out of the clouds.

After queuing and friendly jostling to get that all-important photo for the family album, we began the knee-jarring descent. It was a very long day, between the 6 km ascent and 17 km descent we arrived jelly-legged at Horombo Hut. The next morning we descended back to the forest and all the way down to Marangu Gate, where transport was waiting. We arrived at our hotel in the late afternoon – bath time!

Overall, the 72-km trek was a success. It was superbly organised, and our guides were amazing – a helpful and happy bunch. Every day we trekked at a pace suitable to all. The camps were well set up and the food was always surprisingly good.

First job before getting on our transport was to divvy up any kit we wanted to leave to our guides, porters and cooks. The cash tips generally came to £80 per visitor and this was given in local currency to Castro at the end of the climb, so he could distribute it fairly amongst his lads. (Some company's porter's wages are as little as $2–$3 a day.) I had explained this to the team and we all put into a kitty to stop any disagreements about money.

However, you so often get one novice who knows better. The oldest member of our group complained he was being harassed by one of the guides; surprise, surprise, against my advice, he had been giving this particular guide gratuities and promises. He had created the very problem I had warned him about. This was the same man who, at Nairobi Airport, freely gave a £20 note to a passing local, to just lift his suitcase off the ground and pass it to our driver, subsequently moaning that he'd been ripped off!

Some people never learn, or some people never learn to listen and some never listen to learn ...

CHAPTER 25

Love vs Hate

There are moments when emotions are so strong they can destroy rational thinking. Love and hate are the 'drivers' for me. I love my daughter unconditionally, so when she told me she was pregnant I accepted the reality with my heart and soul. She gave me a beautiful granddaughter, Mya (A'myra Sky Davies) in 2013.

To have a baby it takes two, no blaming or finger pointing, Georgina was equally responsible. On the other side of the coin was a disappointment that needed to call himself by a concocted street name. I invited him to sit at the kitchen table in my home along with Georgina so we could discuss openly what plans he had, if any, and what responsibility he was going to shoulder. I spoke as a dad, no raised voice, no threats – just in a business-like manner. I asked deep and searching questions: where are you intending to live? How do you intend to support mother and child? He just sat there looking like a tailor's dummy. Not a word came out of his mouth. Next day, Georgina told me he had had a real go at her, ranting that 'Your father emasculated me.' To me, to emasculate a man means ripping his balls off – I wish!

He showed himself to be totally untrustworthy when he broke Georgina's trust and accessed a bank account Gloria and I had set up for her and stole just over £9,000. At first Georgina didn't believe us. We monitored the bank account and a few days later there was another unauthorised withdrawal. Apparently, he had never held a proper job, and had no obvious source of income that explained his leisurely lifestyle. He intimidated my daughter, by confronting her with a couple of cars full of his mates. It seems he was a bully to women, but even then he needed backup.

Each of us humans has varying ways of dealing with problems and all are valid. At any hint of a problem, I was repeatedly told by Gloria and Georgina not to say anything, don't make waves, thus avoid the problem. However, I prefer to confront, deal with and hopefully solve the problem.

Neither Gloria nor Georgina showed any interest in dealing with the elephant in the room. They seemed totally unaware of the enormous conflict that was living inside my head. I am, like most dads, very protective of my child. So dealing with odious behaviour and bad attitudes could take me to a level where protection of my family totally outweighed any consideration of possible repercussions. On reflection, I was being driven past feelings of anger, resentment or hatred into a very dark and dangerous place. My real friends and the programme of recovery gave me insight, which opened me to experience a moment of clarity. That was good because, buried deep inside me, I knew if it kicked off I wouldn't know when to stop. For all his weaknesses he was Mya's biological father. During my life I have been a fighter in many different arenas, mental and physical. Fortunately for him, I am in a recovery programme that helped me to change; at the time he crossed my path I had been sober for over thirty years. The lesson I learnt from this episode is that I can still be a dick. The mental gulf between me on one side and Gloria and Georgina on the other had become a vast chasm that I was descending into. All this was happening, with a spectre floating in the background, whispering or shouting his demands to Georgina, who acceded, and Gloria backed her, all for an easy life.

I love Georgina and Mya to the moon and back; I still have great respect and admiration for Gloria. However, I didn't want to become the man I once was. A man neither Gloria nor Georgina knew. I knew deep inside me, I had reached a crossroads in my life. I had to leave the family home for everybody's best interests. If I didn't, that old version of me would surface and eventually sort out the problem for good, then go to prison or even worse – the same man will drink again.

Today, Georgina has a good man by her side, Don Porter. Mya has a caring and loving family, mum, dad, brother Duke and grandmother.

Saying goodbyes

For the first twenty months of Mya's life I was her main carer. I fed her, played with her, changed her nappy and bathed her. Some nights I drove for miles around Surrey with her in her little seat when she was restless, in an attempt to get her to sleep. My favourite time was sitting in the rocking chair with her snuggled up on me, enjoying her bottle, while gently rocking and quietly singing the Seekers song 'Morningtown Ride'.

I am so grateful for the last hug I enjoyed with my beautiful granddaughter Mya. I knew that it would most probably be our last tender little hug. I love Mya. Those cherished moments gave me a chance to be a grandpa, the most precious of gifts. I had such mixed emotions, sadness and longing for the grandchild I was about to lose, expectant pride and joy at the child and woman she was to become. If you, Mya, have your Grandma Gloria's brains, the world is your oyster. I wish I could be with you, Mya, on your wondrous journey through life. Georgina and Mya have a little of me in them, the good bit I trust.

The first step of a journey usually starts with a thought, an idea or even a dream. In my case, the dream was a living nightmare of dangerous consequences, extreme and terminal, that triggered the dire need to walk away from my world. I couldn't think straight, with so many crazy dark thoughts flying around. Inaction, balanced against my deep-seated need to react, created an enormous internal conflict. I likened the inside of my head to a glass of muddy water. If you put the glass on a shelf and leave it alone, let it settle, allow the muck to sink to the bottom, the water will become crystal clear. If you keep stirring, the water will continue to be murky and eventually something nasty will float to the surface. I made a decision to go to rural Kenya. Get away from all distraction. I needed time and space to figure out and focus on what was really important.

More than just stars and dark skies

Wherever I am, I often take a moment and look up at the night sky. It's as captivating as it is mysterious and I quietly soak up the serene enormity of the universe. During all of my hellraising and drinking years I never knew it was there! Night just meant I could hide in the darkness.

In March 2002, I was fly fishing for monster sea trout in the Rio Grande that flows through Tierra del Fuego (Land of Fire) at the very southern tip of Argentina. The fishing day is split into two sessions, the first is from late morning through to afternoon, when you eat a luxurious packed lunch followed by a siesta. You start fishing again from the evening, continuing well into the best time, which is during the dark of the night. I was standing waist-deep in the cold, clear waters of the Rio Grande at about 10 p.m. when the guide needed to take the other fisherman back to the lodge, over twenty miles away. I happily chose to carry on fishing alone in the dark. It was pitch black, the nearest building was the lodge, there were no towns or villages for over a hundred miles and hence no light pollution. The only light was generated from the stark, crisp moon and bright, glittering stars. I stopped fishing to look up and experience the night sky; I mean to really look, open up my eyes and my mind to visit a truly dark, star-filled night sky.

While I had lived, worked and hidden in a seething, dark underworld, doing some bad stuff, I never knew I had missed many astonishing realities. Why, at that moment in time, was I totally caught in the moment – experiencing the awe-inspiring vastness of the sky? Why did it grasp my attention so strongly? I can offer no answer. The wide powerfulness of the dark liquid of the river, in which I stood alone, with the occasional fluorescent flash, became almost incidental; the land, immense as it is, became reduced to nothing more than a black mass, all sheltering under the majestic sky in its silent and brooding splendour. It was humbling.

On our trek to Everest Base Camp in 2013 we stopped overnight at Khumjung. As a knackered bunch, we were all getting ready to turn in when Lucas Bateman called us all to witness a starry phenomenon. Tired, we reluctantly trudged out into the cold. What we witnessed expelled any lingering brain fog. The crystal-clear skies offered us a mind-boggling view of a celestial twinkling display that was also magically reflecting off the snow- and ice-covered peaks surrounding us. Life is not measured by the number of breaths we take, but by the moments that take our breath away; this was one of those moments.

I often told my daughter, Georgina, when she was little that if she ever feels alone, frightened or needs support to overcome a difficulty, look up in the night sky. I'll always be there for you!

CHAPTER 26

Confusion and Misconceptions

It was around the time when a spectre from my fairly recent past (2013/4) was rattling my cage, that I was approached by someone very close to me to commit a serious crime. To say I was thunderstruck was an understatement. I had gone straight years before the person asking was even born; they had a skeletonised gist of my past, but they appeared to have colourfully fleshed out the gaps in my past themselves, misreading me, both then and now.

It seems to me there's a confused and potentially blurry void between reality and fantasy. Sure, we all know murder happens, but as for professional hired assassins or hitmen, there are very few walking the streets. Far less than books, video games and films lead us to believe. Brief incidents opened my eyes to how reputations can be formed, twisted and easily destroyed.

I remember a time back in the mid-1990s, I had the privilege of assisting a bit of a lump called George H, who had been in plenty of trouble, usually connected with football hooliganism.

For a time we spoke almost daily on the phone; on one occasion, Georgina complained I was talking too much to him and I was her daddy not his. Point taken! However, a couple of weeks later he asked me to go with him to a magistrates' court as moral support; I agreed. I picked him up early, giving us a chance to chat and arrive less tense. While we drove to the court in Croydon, George asked if we could drop in for a coffee in a fancy coffee shop, because another friend of his wanted to meet up with us. George added that I would know his friend, so we pulled into the local Starbucks.

We sat, with me facing the door, expecting to reunite with an old friend, which would dilute the tension radiating off George. A guy sat down with us; either I was experiencing a senior moment or I didn't know him. George started chatting to the guy – from the relaxed banter they knew each other reasonably well. I gradually joined in and at the same time seeded the conversation, looking for mutual ground. Eventually I struck gold. Our paths appeared to have collided in recent times, we both went to the same meeting place in Kensington. We chatted about people we knew, mainly relative to the meeting place. He said I would know this other 'Roger' that went there. Big guy, with a dark and sordid past.

Then he proceeded to paint an unromantic description of said villain, including a colourful collection of ugly, aggressive incidents this 'Roger' was directly linked to. Oh yes, I did indeed recognise the other Roger and some of the incidents, which had been lumped together, coloured and dramatically jazzed up. Eyeballing him, I asked him directly if he personally knew this terrible 'other' Roger. Without hesitation, 'Oh yes,' he boldly replied. 'No you don't,' I said 'you're talking to him – that's me!'

In the mid to late 90s I shared an office in New Malden with two other small businesses. One was a quasi-civil engineer and the other a financial adviser. It was a tight-knit community, we could all hear each other's telephone conversations. The experience gave me a new angle on life. One telling example was that the engineer, Mr Birdy, spent 50% of his time playing political games. If someone did something he didn't like, he would promptly search for a weakness; for example, if he could find a fault with your car, he would immediately contact the police. Mr Birdy said putting it in writing forced the police to take action. I even witnessed him phone the boss of a person he didn't like and stir the shit by making up some bogus hearsay to create serious problems.

What it taught me was to be aware of what you say and whom you can really trust. Start off by smiling, it is easy to growl later.

Try and be open-minded, and accept that others have likes and dislikes.

Generally, people are territorial and sometimes they react in strange, totally unexpected ways, from a gentle shrug of the shoulders to outright vindictiveness. Once there was a violent incident in our office which happened through no direct fault of the financial consultant, who was a congenial and straightforward man.

I had come back from lunch to the office early, only to see a stranger attempting to nail up the front door from the inside. I shouted out what did he think he was doing? He waved back to me, though not displaying all four fingers. He thought he was safe behind the glass front door that he had secured from inside, but I could see how he had got in. He had created a hole in the wall by smashing a four-foot opening in the plasterboard stud wall. I quickly ran around the back of the building (the back door was open), ducked into a short passage that led to the back room where the hole was and climbed through.

He was incredibly surprised to see me. We locked eyes; we were the same age and height but not the same fitness. For some stupid reason he waved the hammer he had in his hand in a threatening manner, even attempted to hit me. This triggered me into the offensive. So I gave him a friendly dig on the chin and wrenched the heavy steel claw hammer out of his hand. I bent him over an office desk and spiritedly chastised him with it, in a manner he would remember for a very long time.

I marvelled at his dexterity as he scurried, hunched over, back through the hole in the wall, with both hands firmly clutching his damaged bottom, while squealing loudly like a little baby pig. I called the police and reported the incident; the perpetrator appeared, still nursing his wounds. We both gave versions of what happened. He shouted at the officer and was promptly reminded of the seriousness of trespassing, wilful damage and threatening me with an offensive weapon. In his defence he offered to show the policeman his injuries. The PC declined with a poor attempt at keeping a straight face.

It transpired he was the ex-business partner of the financial adviser, against whom he was holding some kind of grievance; I had given him a reason to cultivate a new one. I slowly learnt that to survive I had to become more giving and flexible. It's not about becoming tolerant, but I try hard to practice acceptance; I cannot change people, places or things, so I do my best to work co-operatively with others.

I strive to maintain mental flexibility rather than appear physically rigid, but strong and resilient like bamboo. Respect yourself enough to say 'I deserve better'.

I recall my dad didn't let me over the threshold of the family home until I was two and a half years clean and sober. It wasn't that my mum and dad didn't love me, they just had plenty of real reasons not to trust my behaviour. I deserved arm's length banishment – talk and empty promises meant nothing any more. Dad just wanted me to prove I had turned the corner and changed.

My younger brother Brian was also on the missing list but for different reasons. He didn't have a bad bone in his body; he had never harmed a soul and loved to entertain. He was a gifted musician, his genre was country and western. As a lad he played the piano, later the guitar and banjo.

In 1990 my parents asked me to go and find my brother and talk with him, bring him back into the family. He was living on the Isle of Wight. I drove down to his last known address, he wasn't hard to find.

Seeing Brian for the first time in some years was bittersweet, he was my little brother whose family nickname was 'Titch'. So it was a shock to see his poor physical shape, he was as tall as me but was carrying an awful lot of spare bulk.

He could see I was well dressed, looking fit and driving a fancy BMW. I attempted to tell him how I had changed. He was not impressed and promptly listed my faults, 'You are a thug, a criminal and totally untrustworthy. You maimed, robbed and have probably done even worse. No doubt you paid for your car with drug money or you've stolen it.' I tried to talk him down, after a long chat he did accept I may have changed but adamantly denied he was anything like me and said there was nothing wrong with him!

Eighteen months later I got a call from my dad. Brian had been found dead in a bedsit in Brighton. He died alone and was not discovered for at least a week. An autopsy report determined a heart attack as the probable cause of death. He was 42 years of age.

I stood with my dad and mum in the crematorium chapel; quietly my mum said, 'Here's Brian.' I turned to see a coffin ...

Mortality was brutally made real to me for the first time.

CHAPTER 27

Mt Toubkal and the High Atlas Mountains, 2013

We were a very mixed and friendly group of seven: three men – Benno, Adam and I, and four women – Lesley, Julie, Annabelle and Kay.

Our challenge was to summit Mt Toubkal and trek the High Atlas Mountains of Morocco. On arrival at Marrakech Airport my old friend and team leader Stephen Pinfold, with his local right-hand man, Ibrahim Ahmed Amzil, was there to meet us. We dropped our gear at our small, comfortable hotel in the heart of Marrakech old town, minutes from the world-famous souks. Marrakech's souks can be loud, colourful, aromatic, overwhelming, chaotic and fun.

The standard international way to avoid hassle is to offer a friendly smile and firm 'No thanks'. Usually, that's sufficient to ward off overeager stallholders, con artists and beggars. However, walking through the main square of Marrakech, we were plagued by a group of Arab children of around ten years of age, for whom the word 'no' didn't seem to have any immediate effect. One little rascal's response was unexpected. 'F*** you!' he said, in a pitch perfect South London accent! For a moment we were all speechless, until the pause was usurped by surprised grins, shrugs and quiet admiration for the cheeky, pint-sized little shit. When you walk around the labyrinth of souks, each one is laid out according to the commodities being sold. Little has changed, aside from some modern tastes, the basic goods are how they would have been in biblical times.

A people carrier picked us up from our hotel in Marrakech and transported us up to the start of our trek. It dropped us and our entire luggage off in what seemed the middle of nowhere. Steve and Ibrahim instructed us to repack what we needed for the six-day trek. The highlight of the day was the discovery, amongst the 'necessary kit' required for trekking over the Atlas Mountains, of a hairdryer and a set of straighteners!

Our gear was to be transferred to the local mode of transport. That's Sherpas in the Himalayas, porters in Africa – and mules in Morocco. The mule is a multifunctional donkey/horse hybrid. They are strong, sure-footed and enjoy a ruggedness that has made them indispensable and fundamental to life in the Atlas Mountains. The mule is an unsung hero, especially the one I rode, sitting astride it with the grace and poise of a bag of spuds. My mounting and dismounting were a source of great amusement for the Berber guides and muleteers. It also gave my fellow trekkers plenty of ammunition for days of amusing banter at my expense.

The High Atlas Mountains are home to the resilient Berbers. They are hospitable and tough, matching the unforgiving land in which they live, traits that have served them well over centuries. Berber villages consist of simple, square, earth buildings, with the animals sleeping on the ground floor and families above. The picturesque view of the villages is unchanged from early biblical days. Set strikingly amongst the valleys of the Atlas range, they offer a fascinating insight into a more traditional way of life in Morocco. While electricity was slowly penetrating some villages, the values and way of life in the mountains still offered a welcome contrast to the cosmopolitan city life of Marrakech. Villagers collect their water from the central well, keep livestock in their yards and hang rugs from their homes to dry.

As with most trekking destinations, most trekkers head straight to climb the big one, Mt Toubkal, ignoring the rest of the magnificent High Atlas range. The question intrigues me, why do so many people always head for the big name walks? One of the primary delights of trekking for me has always been the solitude. The first day of our trek, Steve and Ibrahim led us off the beaten track, far away from the usual tourist routes, allowing us to ramble freely on less frequented trails. The plan was to acclimatise while enjoying an off-piste four-hour trek which gradually turned into a nine-hour beasting. The weather was dazzling as was the mountain vista. We passed through lots of small villages, and found that we were the children's entertainment. They were fascinated by us and it was lovely to see the girls from our group giving them sweets. Watching their facial expressions when they tested the new, unfamiliar flavours, ranging from lip-smacking and mouth-watering to face-twistingly sour, it was priceless!

At night we stayed in gites, very simple guesthouses, each consisting of a long-room ringed with cushions which served as a multifunctional dining room, sitting room and bedroom. It would be hard to describe the accommodation as anything approaching comfortable, but there was a simplicity to it that was entirely in keeping with the mountain setting, and without exception all had incredible views.

The weather changed dramatically two hours before we were to reach our first gite; the wind picked up and the heavens just opened. If rain could be called fat it was fat rain! It came at us face on, in swarms of large wet lumps, thoroughly soaking us all in minutes. After an hour, cold and drenched, the feelings of elation were replaced by 'six days of this is going to be shitty'. It was dusk when we arrived at our first overnight lodgings; we were led up to the roof terrace, to a sight that was not quite what we were expecting. A cross between an open-sided circus tent and antiquated gazebo greeted us, bringing about the opportunity to enjoy the incredible view of the mountains even from our sleeping bags. Over the floor, there was a generous scattering of horse blankets, which were our beds.

All of us were absolutely soaking wet. Our first priority was to strip and put on warm dry clothing, which we began to do, when a local lady came in out of the rain, and walked over to a light socket that was attached to a hanging wire. She pulled a light bulb out of her damp pocket, reached up and started to screw in the bulb. I thought the power must be off, but if the bulb came on, I immediately anticipated there would be a loud, pain-filled yelp and smoke, or at the very least an electrocuted hairstyle. With mixed emotions of expectation and relief, we got light without the expected fireworks!

The villagers were proud that they had electricity; it had been put in just six months previously, and unfortunately nobody had given them any proper instruction as to its dangers. Wet skin has 100 times less resistance than dry – she was one very lucky lady.

In three days of trekking in the Atlas Mountains we came across just three other couples. Our trek started in Imlil Valley, at a modest altitude of around 2,000 m. The terrain at this altitude has a Mediterranean feel, with dusty red earth thick with fragrantly aromatic gnarled juniper bushes, wild mint and thyme. The neighbouring Azzaden Valley, however, was a photographer's dream, lush autumnal walnut trees densely crowding mountain streams on the valley floor and perfectly offsetting the rocky, dusty monochrome valley flanks.

During these initial days we ascended close to 3,500 m above sea level up to the head of the valley, where we witnessed yet another amazing photo opportunity, the photogenic landscape of snow-capped peaks, topped by Mt. Toubkal. While trekking, we passed goats and sheep well tended by shepherds accompanied by their very protective dogs. The most amusing time was when we stopped at a peaceful oasis, with a little stream running through shaded trees. Everything was going well until the mules decided to escape and off they went, cantering into the distance.

It was our turn to chill and be entertained. We watched as the leader of our porters sent the youngest muleteer off chasing frantically after the escapees. His boss stood on a rock bellowing instructions, waving his arms and openly mocking the young lad, who was chasing around the shrub-filled mountain slopes after the runaways.

It became more apparent the young muleteer was being told to focus on capturing and keeping a strict eye on the instigator, a light brown mule. Once caught, he was not trusted for the rest of our travels together. When we all stopped, especially at night, he was gently but firmly tethered and the young muleteer slept close by.

Climbing the Atlas range was harder than Kilimanjaro, or was it the route Ibrahim guided us along? Outside of the urban areas, Morocco is visually stunning. Every village we passed through the locals smiled and we said Bonjour! (French is their second language and Arabic their first.)

One evening we were unexpectedly entertained by all the men, singing and banging on anything including pots and pans. I joined in, bashing a table with a big metal spoon (I am, oh, so very cultured!). Good fun was had by all.

After a long day trekking uphill, we arrived at an alpine-style refuge. Steve decided for us that instead of a dorm inside the refuge with hot showers, we would camp. We set to work erecting our tents in the snow, laying out our sleeping bags and getting equipment sorted for morning. One tent was up but empty – two of the team had gone AWOL. Much to Steve's disgust and everyone else's envy, Lesley and Annabelle had snuck off and bagged the last available double room, with its own bathroom – pure luxury. Why hadn't I thought of that!

The refuge's restaurant was full of fellow trekkers, plenty of good friendly banter flying about. However, with an early start and a full belly of good food, most of us trudged off to the tents. On waking we lit the fire in the base of our trusty old Kelly kettle for our hot morning brew. Then we left the refuge just as the sun rose above the jagged mountain range. Our route zigzagged up the South Col, a long and fairly steep scree slope, to the Tizi-n Toubkal pass. After three and a half hours of strenuous climbing the snow thinned out and we reached the bare rocky ridge at last. It was slippery underfoot and the path edged alongside sheer cliff faces. As the path wound its way up we got our first proper sighting of the metal pyramid at the top of Mt Toubkal.

On reaching the summit we looked out over the surrounding High Atlas range to a panorama of craggy peaks. Rows of rocky ridges interspersed with snowbound valleys opened themselves to us. In contrast, a good way southwards, stretched the Sahara Desert, an unforgiving land; you could see the various hues of orange and yellow of its dunes. This remarkable backdrop sparked my attention; it was a vision for later consideration!

We spent a good half hour absorbing the experience and the view before we began to descend from the summit, retracing our steps over the slippery, icy, rubble-covered trail; it was a long and treacherous journey down. If my bionic knee struggled and ached a bit on the ascent, it seriously hated the descent.

Tired and leg sore, halfway down the mountain we stopped on a roomy ledge for a five-minute break, when spontaneously we all engaged in a crazy snowball fight. We were acting like a cross between naughty little school boys and rugby players on tour, just letting off steam and thoroughly enjoying the moment.

After four hours we got back to the refuge but decided to

continue on through. It took us about three hours to reach Sidi Chamharouch, running late; we were concerned we would lose daylight, so we walked as quickly and as safely as possible. Half an hour later and we were at the zigzags above the floodplain, continuing on down to a small village called Imlil where it was arranged that Ibrahim's brother would come to meet us in his ancient but serviceable mini bus. We arrived back in Imlil just before dark.

Hell hath no fury like a woman whose suitcase is missing – especially since in that particular suitcase are the infamous hairdryer and a set of straighteners! Grown men, including Steve Pinfold, chased around like chickens trying to locate it while being verbally castrated. I sat very quiet! Peace eventually was restored when the bright red suitcase was presented to its owner, Lesley.

We had a great night in Marrakech, savouring the delights of a hot shower and a real bed. We arrived at the airport the following evening with plenty of time to spare, only to be told there was no plane. That particular scheduled flight no longer even existed. Three of us had prepaid tickets that were redundant. The airline staff were not overly concerned and booked us on the next available flight, at 6.30 the next morning. Marrakech airport was closing, there were no facilities, not even coffee, only some hard benches on which we were expected to spend the night.

On returning to the UK I contacted the airline by email and phone. They accepted no responsibility for changing their schedule, and offered no recompense, not even an apology. We had been sleeping rough on the High Atlas Mountains but a hard airport bench is really tough on the butt. However, overall, this adventure with great friends was worth every little hassle.

CHAPTER 28

Everest Base Camp, Nepal, April 2014

Kathmandu was the real start of our journey. It is a remarkable city, full of vivid colours, sounds and smells. It's packed with guest houses, restaurants, shops and markets, mostly set out to fulfil travellers', climbers' and tourists' necessary or frivolous needs.

One morning we were wandering around and came upon Pashupatinath temple, which seemed to be home to umpteen eye-catching sadhu (holy men). Some were gaudily dressed, others more scantily covered. The sadhus depend on gifts to survive. They certainly knew how to entertain and play the crowd, happily posing for photos in exchange for a few coins.

Looking across a drying up Bagmati River, there were plumes of white smoke coming from what I first thought were bonfires. I was way off! They were actually funeral pyres evenly spread along the opposite riverbank.

A boy of about ten years old was standing a little downstream from where the family had scattered their relative's ashes into the river. He was tossing and retrieving something weighty tied to a length of twine, possibly some local primitive type of fishing. Well this is true in a way! The boy's bait was a magnet. He was fishing for any trinkets or coins that had been thrown or lost in the waters.

Our journey to Everest Base Camp

Our journey to Everest Base Camp, on the lower slopes of the world's highest and, arguably, most majestic mountain, was as spiritually uplifting as it was physically challenging. Trekking here is doubly difficult, the terrain is energy sapping and there is always the risk of altitude sickness.

After our second night in Kathmandu we rose early, setting off for STOL airport. We flew in a small plane, called a Twin Otter. Guides advised we get a seat on the left-hand side for the best views. The pilot waited until we were all seated and told us that Lukla, our destination, was temporarily closed due to bad weather. Off we got, and trudged back to the airport to refuel with coffee and chocolate bars. A couple of American pessimists, posing in brand-new kit at the airport, suggested that we could be waiting for days. However, our luck was in, half an hour later we heard that there was a weather window and we were good to go. We never saw those drama queens again! From Kathmandu to Lukla's tiny airport is a distance of 139 km (flying time 30 minutes); from here our classic Everest Base Camp trek through the Kumba valley could begin.

Lukla Airport, otherwise known as Tenzing-Hillary Airport, has the reputation of being the most dangerous airport in the world. In 1964, Sir Edmund Hillary bought the farm land from local Sherpas and built the airport. It has no modern comforts, like a control tower or even radar – a pilot lands and takes off by keeping an eagle eye on the short runway. Due to the terrain there is very little chance of a successful go-around on the final approach. The pilot aims at a point on the runway that starts just past the edge of a precipice. If he misses, you hit the rock face and drop 9,000 feet into an abyss. I never worried about the drop, only the landing!

From Lukla we trekked downhill towards the Dudh Koshi (the Milky River). It originates from snow and glacier melt from high-altitude areas of Mt Everest. The milky white water is coloured by rock flour from the glaciers. It is reputed to be the world's highest river in terms of elevation, relentlessly cascading its way down from the source, the Gokyo Lakes, located at an altitude of 4,700–5,000 m above sea level. The trail is fairly easy and well marked, meandering its way around fields in which potatoes and wheat are grown.

Walking on we saw many a 'Mani Wall'. These structures are stone tablets each carved with Buddhist chanting inscriptions, such as 'Om Mani Padme Hum', which loosely means 'Hail to the jewel in the lotus'. The guides asked us politely to respect these walls, which should be passed from the left side, in the clockwise direction in which Earth and the universe revolve, according to Buddhist doctrine.

We passed through many small traditional villages before arriving at Phakding for our first night's stay at a Nepalese teahouse, a small bed-and-breakfast-like hotel. A large sign outside read 'tea, coffee, hot showers here and we have electricity'. We all took the opportunity to shower in warm water, and charge up phones and cameras. Chicken curry seemed to be the food of choice, actually it was the only choice!

Lucas was my roomie on the trek. I had shared adventures with him before, to the North Pole and Kilimanjaro. We knew each other, and this time we had the opportunity to talk on a deeper level – what a good friend and companion to have.

Next day our destination was Namche Bazaar, five and a half hours at a steady pace. After an early breakfast, Annabel put Clive Hagley through his paces at yoga, much to the amusement of the guides. Once out on the path the vista was changing as we gained height; we passed through a pine forest and terraces, crossing and recrossing the Milky River. As a group we were all aware of the need to acclimatise to altitude slowly so we could fully enjoy our time amongst the breathtaking views. The spectacular peaks of Nupla, Kongde RI and Thamserku towered majestically above us.

Unfortunately, from day one, Jan struggled big time. It was what it was, a challenging trek. After a few days she developed a poorly tummy from the altitude or chicken curry, possibly a mix of both, which didn't help. Jan is a tough old bird and we all wanted her to fulfil the trek. We were especially mindful since similar afflictions had hit her previously on Kilimanjaro, forcing her to turn back.

Her progress was so alarmingly slow that the team could not hang back without risking health issues for others. Walking well below your natural pace leaves you open to the effects and risks of the extreme cold and this can also spoil the general morale of the group. Speed was unimportant to Jan, she had her own gentle tempo.

To assist Jan I had a word with our head guide. I slipped him a generous donation with an added promise of a completion bonus – a deal was struck. Jan was given her own porter, nicknamed DK, a big strong lad who gave her his arm and carried her day bag. He stayed by her side at all times.

We entered Sagarmatha National Park, a World Heritage Site, walking along the bank of the Dudh Koshi. On rounding a bend, I looked skywards to see two suspension bridges. The lower one was disused, and the higher one meant a steep climb up. Once at the mouth of the long suspension footbridge, you looked down at an impressive drop of about two hundred metres, although it seemed an awful lot higher when you stepped on. What was more impressive was when a Tibetan caravan of yaks and dzos started to cross.

These are big boys; a domesticated yak weighs in at 350–580 kg (male), and 220–260 kg (female). The dzo is a hybrid between the yak and domestic cattle in Tibet, and weighs in at up to 590 kg. They can carry loads up to 200 kg and walk for about 15 km a day. Both have large horns. On a path or bridge it's their right of way – who is going to argue?

We were busy watching these big, hairy beasts of burden slowly make their way across, when suddenly we all heard a commotion on the path we had just climbed.

Behind us was a string of heavily laden mules; they were heading for the footbridge at a steady plod. We clambered up on to rocks away from the impending confrontation. The leading yak was within feet of the end of the bridge and solid ground, just as the

Me with my fellow adventurers – Nepal

Yaks crossing a footbridge

leading mule attempted to start on his chosen path: the bridge! The Nepalese mule handlers arrived just in time to intervene; they had to physically manhandle the leading mule to stop him launching himself onto the narrow suspension bridge and confronting the yaks head on. The lead mule was not happy and kicked up a fuss. Rather them than me; neither the yaks nor mules cared who got in the way. Each believed the right of way was theirs. Even the biggest and toughest trekker better step aside or someone's going to light a candle for you!

We walked through many of the most incredible traditional villages, where time has stood still for centuries. Coming from the modern, high-tech world, you can't but be amazed at their lifestyle, handed down to them by their ancestors. Dressed in colourful traditional garb, the locals see scores of walkers pass through each season; they're always polite, and often smile, although for the most part, they pay little attention.

However, Lesley was extremely popular with the kids – or was it the sweets she distributed? It was both!

As we arrived in Namche I began to relax. It had been a long hard day's trekking and I was looking forward to a hot drink, dinner and a shower. I was somewhat peeved when our guide pointed up to our teahouse, perched at the top of a very formidable flight of steps. The teahouse was worth the extra effort. It was here I was introduced to a new drink – hot mango, my new favourite. Followed by a hot shower and good food!

Many of us intrepid trekkers staying at the teahouse were parents and grandparents, so we were a soft touch when the daughter of the proprietor, a four-year-old Nepalese girl called Tigi, introduced herself to us all. She sat amongst us, always smiling, constantly chatting, and drawing pictures, treating us all as if we were her personal house guests. Tigi certainly brought out the soft side of the roughest and toughest of us.

It was very important to acclimatise for the challenging ascent ahead of us. Next day in Namche Bazaar was a rest day; those of us who were acclimatising well and feeling fit just walked uphill above the village for a couple hours. Jan was unable to join us, but used the rest day to build her strength for the days ahead. As with the rest of the climb we were gifted with spectacular views of huge mountains, including our first sight of the biggest of them all, Mt Everest.

I recall a private moment standing at the Everest View Hotel, slowly absorbing what I was witnessing. Before me soared the highest mountain on earth, 29,035 feet (or 8848 m) high. I could see the raw beauty that only nature can create, it resonates with a feeling of power and arouses a sense of mystery. For a moment, I wished my dad could have shared the moment with me. I was blessed to have good friends with me, especially Lesley, to share the fantastic things happening. A couple of years later my relationship with Lesley organically grew from friend to soulmate and wife. We drank tea on the hotel's terrace, taking photos.

Stupidly I attempted to copy young Annabel's yoga moves while balancing on a wall; it was strongly suggested that I should get down before I fell down.

Next morning, after a breakfast of porridge made with water, as we were advised to avoid milk – bad experiences on my travels of explosive diarrhoea have taught me to take notice of local knowledge regarding food and drink – we set off. Our next destination was Khumjung, a three and a half hour trek at a steady pace along a trail that heads up over the ridges, allowing us spectacular views. Alternating between ascending, descending and ascending again we were all in a festive mood. Annabel got us to dance and sing 'Happy' by Pharrell Williams, high on a beautiful mountain slope, much to the delight and amusement of our guides – they just thought we were crazy. Rumour has it that there is a video of our impromptu performance somewhere. That would make a You've been framed TV moment, worthy of the £250. I hope it never sees the light of day!

We experienced a complete contrast when we got the opportunity to spin the prayer wheels on approaching Khumjung's 500-year-old Gompa monastery. On arrival the Buddhist monks made us welcome and began showing us around. A monk led us to an important-looking box draped with a red velvet cape; he said in a hushed voice that we would be allowed to see a fascinating sacred relic kept under lock and key, at a special price to each of us of only five US dollars. Wow! Cheap at the price! I paid to see the 300-year-old scalp of a yeti.

As we continued our day's journey to the 'City in the Clouds', Khumjung, Mt Everest could clearly be seen in the distance, until we found ourselves descending through a splendid blooming rhododendron forest, with their gnarled branches covered in moss.

Sir Edmund Hillary returned to Nepal in 1960, seven years after he had become the first man to summit Mt Everest, with Tenzing Norgay, and built the original 'school in the sky' in the village of Khunde, which we visited and met the lovely kids. He went on to create sixteen more schools, clinics and hospitals, all maintained by the Himalayan Trust, which he set up for the benefit of all the people of Nepal. It was a major ambition of his to establish a small hospital in the village of Khunde at an elevation of 12,600 ft (3,840 m), and this was achieved in 1996. In 2014, eighteen years later, we had the privilege to be shown around the hospital by the Nepalese duty doctor, who gave us a little talk about the day-to-day events. He was very keen on telling us how a lot of children locally were born 'cretin' because of iodine in the water. Sir Edmund Hillary assisted in funding mass immunisation and in 1963 he arranged for an airdrop of smallpox vaccine. What a good bloke. Not just a world-class climber, but a real humanitarian.

It was good to get to the local teahouse; the higher we climbed, the lower the temperature dropped. Lunch, hot drinks, warm showers and friendly banter always boost me. Annabel and Max, our in-house cabaret, entertained us and other guests and staff with their antics, either it was yoga or playing 'shitface', a bizarre card game, all done in fun and with plenty of cheek.

After a good night's sleep and breakfast of watery porridge and black coffee, we set off to a less-visited farming village called Phortse. The local main crop is potatoes – they fed us a lot of potatoes! This route allowed us to explore the Gokyo valley, through which flowed a river whose water was a milky blue, an exceptional colour that I'd never seen before.

The breathtaking views made it irresistible to constantly take photos. While walking we met the tiniest little old lady who just constantly beamed, it was infectious. It turned out she was the proprietor of the teahouse we were heading for where the food was the best we had enjoyed so far. Seeing her constantly smiling prompted me to ask one of our leading Sherpas, 'Why are you, and most Nepalese we meet, always happy and smiling?'

He said, 'We are Buddhist and we have learnt that being grateful helps to focus on the positives in our lives, which makes us happier.' What a strange coincidence. When I stopped drinking, long-term members of my fellowship often told me 'a grateful man is a happy man', who won't drink again.

My Buddhist Sherpa pal told me to greet each morning with a smile. He said you don't have to be a Buddhist to be happy, just greet each and every morning with a smile. Not a cheesy grin or a forced grimace, a real happy smile. That simple positive piece of advice would have cost thousands of pounds in therapy and counselling fees.

Next morning we set off on the gradual uphill trail towards our next destination, Dingboche. Our trail skirted the side of the valley with the river Imja Khola far below, passing beneath the spectacular Ama Dablam. We trekked on up through beautiful rhododendron forest. On reaching Thyanboche Monastery at Pangboche we took the opportunity to explore. We entered the monastery to the sounds of a monk chanting, accompanied by various musical instruments that included the dungchen (a Tibetan horn), the damru (a small two-headed drum), the gyaling (a traditional woodwind instrument), and a series of cymbals. Music is a reflection of Buddhism, giving the capacity to express the deepest feelings of the human soul. It also plays an integral role in common cultural practices. We were being treated by a dozen or so Buddhist monks to a wonderful musical performance. It felt spiritually uplifting.

The teahouse faced Mt Ama Dablam, 6856 m, one of the world's most exquisite peaks. It was a stunningly beautiful view to appreciate during our rest and acclimatisation day. Since it was our last rest day and we were only going out on a two-hour acclimatisation trek, I felt optimistic about organising a photoshoot.

Since I received my total knee replacement, I have had to wear a medical knee brace while trekking. It was not supplied by the NHS, I paid nearly £500 for it myself. In preparation for this trip I'd spoken to the supplier of my knee brace,[2] and they were very keen on sponsoring me. They supplied me with a small amount of kit – a pair of shorts, a T-shirt and a hoodie all with their logo of the carbon frame and titanium hinges that make up the brace. To support them I trekked up a snow-covered Himalayan mountain with stunning backdrops in -7 °C wearing shorts! My exposed legs went pink and my bits turned blue. Many photos in many poses were taken, I endured the cold and plenty of good-hearted piss-taking comments.

Later, back at the teahouse, a trekker with another group who had witnessed the shoot, introduced himself to me and asked why? As I was in the process of explaining, he pressed me for more info on my knee operation; he chuckled because he was an orthopaedic surgeon who had done that same operation many times. He shook my hand, said he was proud of me, that I was a great example to others with a similar condition and encouraged me to keep doing what I was doing.

The new day started with a grinding trek up the high valley on the barren slopes above the treeline to Lobuche, along the lateral moraine, covered in ankle-twisting rubble that had been carried and deposited by the huge Khumbu Glacier, the longest glacier in Nepal.

Once in a while there would be a need to scramble up these rocky pathways, on and over various moraines, skating occasionally on

2. Össur UK, https://www.ossur.com/en-gb

202

the icy glaciers and some of us (me) wheezed and coughed ourselves up. We were all now feeling the effects of the thinning air as the hike took us up to the Thukla Hills, a remote and solitary place where there are many stupas[3] and rock cairns erected in memory of Sherpas and climbers who have died on expeditions on these unforgiving mountains. It was a bleak and desolate place, but in spite of that, for me it was thought-provoking. You could see the area was visited and respected by the vast display of colourful prayer flags adorning the stupas. Buddhist prayer flags waving in the wind were a welcome sight; their purpose is to promote peace, strength, compassion and wisdom. On a personal level they stimulate and inspire me to see the brighter side of life.

The Buddhist prayer flags do not carry prayers to gods, which is a common misconception. Rather, the Tibetans believe the prayers and mantras will be blown by the wind to spread the goodwill and compassion into all-pervading space.

During the day the cough I had developed became much worse; it was my second day on penicillin but it had yet to take effect. I have no one to blame, it was my own fault for prancing around half naked the previous day.

The path wasn't all that steep and we were taking it at a relatively easy pace. I am embarrassed to admit I gasped for air between coughing bouts.

As we gained altitude I could feel the temperature biting; we were far more exposed and the camp at Lobuche is sited alongside the chilling glacier. It was a long, cold plod, with the constant chilly wind cutting through us, to get to the next welcome stop, the teahouse at Gorak Shep. On arrival hot drinks (hot mango for me) were quickly enjoyed followed by a second round and a lovely lunch. Then off to our rooms for a nap. DK and another guide had all but carried Jan for days, but the tough old girl made it.

---

3. A mound containing relics and usually the remains of Buddhist monks or nuns. It is a place of meditation.

The lodge was freezing, it was like living in a refrigerated cold store. I was definitely not the only person wearing a coat while eating breakfast inside the main building.

Using the toilet turned out to be an experience. In the accommodation block we were provided with plush European sit down and flush WCs. However, the toilet next to the communal area was of the infamous long drop style. To flush you bailed water from large butts after first smashing a hole in the frozen ice to reach the water. A large wooden mallet was thoughtfully provided.

On Monday 14th April we were due to reach Everest Base Camp. En route we stopped off for lunch at Gorak Shep, a small Himalayan village that is not inhabited year-round. The village is inside the Sagarmatha National Park, homeland of the Sherpa people.

One step at a time! It was treacherous underfoot in some sections and we were subjected to poor weather conditions. During my dark past I learnt that the best way to keep fear or anxiety at bay was to focus ruthlessly on the task in hand. I now had to make a constant effort to relax my head and just keep putting one foot in front of another.

Gorak Shep is actually a frozen lakebed, with pools of fragile ice-covered water that you certainly didn't want to dip your tootsies in. For safety, we followed our Sherpa guides closely along a narrow trail heading north over the top of a ridge that follows the spine of a mountain. We were very exposed, trekking the ridge; the wind was blasting us with sharp snow crystals and my chest infection reduced my physical ability to a slow plod.

Nothing, even the constant coughing, could have detracted from my appreciation of the sheer scale, the noble and stark beauty of the majestic Himalayas. They were awesome.

For me our trek to Everest Base Camp confirmed that it's far more about the journey than the spectacular destination. I believe we spent no more than twenty minutes soaking up the majestic views, posing for photos and congratulating each other. Lesley stripped off a couple of outer layers to be photographed wearing the Super Nana T-Shirt that one of her grandkids had given her. Her pride overcame her fear of frostbitten boobs.

I have a confession ...

After two or three days with a distended tummy due to the regular evening helpings of chicken curry, we were out on the trail and I wasn't really thinking when I asked our head Sherpa to 'pull my finger'. He obliged and I exploded! 'Pull my finger' is a joke regarding flatulence, in which a victim (in this case our head porter) is asked to pull the finger of the joker (me), who simultaneously farts so as to suggest cause and effect. It was his fault I farted!

He stared at me wide-eyed and open-mouthed. It was obviously the first time he had been presented with such childish humour. His expression made me laugh, he waggled his head and began to giggle, which grew to loud and unrestrained laughter. A couple of days later, out on the trail, I asked his fellow Sherpa to pull my finger. He must have overheard and raced over towards us, waving his arms and shouting in Nepalese. His shouting attracted all the other guides' attention. He wagged his finger at me with the biggest of grins; his explanation to the guides included some very expressive hand gestures of what I was about to do, and now they all joined in the amusement.

A tragedy occurred at base camp just forty-eight hours after we had left. Information about the avalanche that struck the Khumbu Icefall early in the morning on 18th April 2014 was given to us by our guides, bit by bit, as the news filtered through to them from different sources. It was very apparent that those who had died and those few who survived were known to many. Every local we met was connected in some way to one or more of the victims. The guys who died and were injured were Ice Doctors, the very best of the best. They were a highly experienced team of Sherpas who have the skills necessary to create new paths by placing ladders across potentially dangerous crevasses. They set up fixed lines which are anchored to the mountainside marking the route climbers should take, with ropes made out of thin nylon (about the thickness of your thumb). These fixed lines are secured by screws and anchors to make them safe to use, so climbers are able to walk safely across the huge gaps in the ice, using the ladders and ropes. Simply, they prepared the way for climbers by keeping the pathway open throughout the Everest climbing season.

The toughest part of the Everest Base Camp trek was when we arrived back at Lukla. As we walked through the village, I was aware of a lack of the usual hustle and bustle of daily life; instead, there was nothing but gloom and silence. Our lodge and Lukla airport stood at the far end of the village. As we reached it, we were greeted by a sight that humbled me. Nepalese people, men and women of all ages, were standing in hushed stillness at the chain link fence around the little airport.

We watched as a helicopter came down the valley towards us from the north and landed. Sixteen bodies were respectfully unloaded, carefully carried and laid without ceremony – but with much dignity – onto the grass bordering the airstrip. The injured were also taken off, ready to be airlifted to a hospital in Kathmandu.

On returning home I chewed over the extremes of our experience of the spectacular beauty of the mountains and the unexpected tragedy that occurred. For me it was all about meeting the world's friendliest people, who live and walk among the giants of Nepal. Occasionally, I have recognised and acknowledged my personal health issues and lack of sanity, to which, mostly, I turn a blind eye. In quiet reflection, weeks or months later, I fully absorb the enormity of my achievements.

CHAPTER 29

Kenya 2014

Living amongst extreme poverty opened my eyes

The first step of a journey usually starts with a thought, an idea or even a dream. In my case, it was a living nightmare of dangerous consequences, extreme and terminal, that triggered the dire need to walk away from my world. I couldn't think straight with so many crazy dark thoughts flying around. On one side I had serious concern for the long-term wellbeing of Gloria, Georgina and Mya, balanced against my deep cold anger for an ex of Georgina's, an absolute tosser.

That's how I came to go to rural Kenya, away from all distraction; I needed time and space to focus on what is really important.

Orphanage – Moving Mountains

A friend, Gavin Bates, gave me the opportunity of working in an orphanage in rural Kenya that would give me the time I needed for reflection. Over two decades Gavin has built a team of local staff to create life-changing experiences for adventure-driven travellers and nature lovers. They all have extensive knowledge of organising guided outdoor trips in East Africa. Through regular training and first aid courses, they ensure that all their trips are safe, fun and successful. He has also created a charity, Moving Mountains, and because of their close partnership with Adventure Alternatives, several of the staff are also involved in both. This gives a holistic experience for anyone looking to visit or volunteer to help in the community projects they support.

The orphanage was home to fourteen girls and sixteen boys from the age of five months up to eighteen years, many with truly horrendous life stories. Many were abandoned in the street; one boy was so ill it was thought he had only hours to live. All have mental scars, and some have physical ones. Younger ones smile and want contact. The adolescent boys and girls are somewhat less communicative, same as normal teenagers all over the world.

On a school day they all get up at 5.30 a.m., some wash and shower while others prepare breakfast, and then they swap around. All kids of school age leave before 6.30 a.m. for school. Primary school kids get back by 4.30 p.m. and secondary school kids at 5 p.m. Saturdays are half days.

At weekends they have real chores, washing their school uniforms and other clothes, cleaning their rooms and general areas. However, they enjoy plenty of playtime and some even make little trinkets. There is an amazing amount of genuine laughter and play, they all mix and support each other. Everything is out in the open, no secrets, and they all eat together as a very big family. For me this is a far cry from what I was used to, a fresh experience. I lived in a small room within the orphanage, with the permanent staff, all of whom were locals. I was the token Mgeni (white) visitor for many miles around. Actually, I didn't see another white face.

Kenya's national tongue is Swahili, and the official language is English, which they are taught from year 4. Conversations were interesting and punctuated with laughter, yet somehow lacked the informality and comfort of home.

Education in Kenya is free but oversubscribed, at the very least there are two children for every available place. In addition, there are shortages in all areas including teachers, classrooms, books and the fundamental necessity, money. Often parents are asked to chip in to pay for extra teachers, the princely sum (to them) of 25 Kenyan shillings per month (20p in sterling). Not all can pay.

Kenya school breakfast

Kenya school break

Classes are large; I was in one packed classroom of seventy 6 to 8-year-olds, with one teacher in sole charge. Education is a priority to all Kenyans, it is the only way forward. For assisting in schools and in the orphanage, I was paid £15 per 7-day week. This was to cover my food and any luxuries. I was given access to the children's records and while reading them I realised many are just too difficult to record here. I offer a couple of typical stories, to give you a sense of what some of these children have been through.

Donathan

Donathan's parents divorced shortly after he was born. At the tender age of 18 months his mother brought him to his father's home and then ran away, deserting him. Don's father worked and when he went to work he locked him in a room for the day. Having watched Don play with the other kids I have a problem imaging him as a toddler, how isolated and frightened he must have felt being locked up on his own every day. The nightmare only ended when Don got his head stuck between a bed and the wall. The neighbours heard him screaming and called the police. By the time they arrived he had lost his voice. The police released Don and took him to the children's office, then brought him straight to the orphanage. The orphanage staff took him to the hospital for treatment.

On the surface he is recovering well from the trauma, he is very active, loves football and socialises well. Don is enjoying school, wants to study at college and become a doctor.

Ruth

Ruth, seven years old, was found wandering the streets and in need of medical attention. She remembers staying with her mother, but reveals very little else, which is hardly surprising after she confided to Mama Rose that her mother tied her hands together and burnt them with a giko (charcoal oven/grill), then told her to leave. The parents were sought but have remained missing. She works hard at school, is well disciplined and organises others well.

Collins

Collins lost both parents; his father died before he was born, and his mother was found dead with him feeding on her milk. Initially he was cared for by his grandmother, who sacrificed a lot for him. Due to circumstances, it was thought best that he was admitted into the orphanage. On arrival he was very cold and sad, always shivering, but after about a month he started to be happy. Unfortunately, during this brief period his grandmother died. Collins is dedicated to looking after animals, helping with the cows and goats. He enjoys school and wants to study at university. He plans to be a farmer.

These kids have experienced more hardship in their tender years than most of us are lucky enough never to have endured in a lifetime. Yet as a group they laugh, play, and share together. These are happy little kids – the takeaway for me was that it's best if I avoid taking myself too seriously, for nothing of consequence is achieved without reflection, contemplation and a healthy dollop of fun.

My Kenyan friends told me that I, a white man, smelt musty, like a wet dog. Although, on another trip, a Congolese local said I smelt like a sheep. There is a myth that we white folk have flesh that looks like beef and tastes akin to pork and veal. Or, at least I hope it's a myth!

Equator Water Test

I witnessed with my own eyes the equator water test. Less than a stone's throw north of the equator, when you pull the plug, the water goes clockwise down the drain and just a short walk south of the equator, the water goes down anticlockwise. On the precise line of the equator, no swirling, no whirling, the water goes straight down the hole. Whoa, now that is real magic! For a few dollars, a local lad will demonstrate the equator water test for visiting tourists. It's a nice little earner for the smart local operators!

Living amongst extreme poverty opened my eyes to how easily I get bogged down with self-centred worries over my perceived position in modern society, size of my car/house and job title etc. Yet I do and will always enjoy a few material benefits including a hot shower and electricity 24/7. Am I soft and spoilt when I add a car, Wi-Fi, TV and a Starbucks to my little list? Speaking for myself, I have found that an extreme challenge, climbing a mountain or helping others, creates changes in me to varying degrees, some are little and some bigger. Certainly each small step alters my perspective of my place in this world.

I notice that I am like a recent non-smoker who doesn't want to smoke but checks his pocket, feeling something is missing. For me it's the umbilical attachment to my mobile phone.

Kids in Africa play the same way children throughout the world play, but without shop-bought toys and none of the hovering supervision of overprotective adults suffocating their harmless creativity and innovation. I watched them making their own toys from just about anything – sticks, pieces of string, empty plastic containers, water and mud. Add vivid imagination and enthusiasm and it equals happy kids. Many of the same children go to school without having had any food, arriving to enjoy a cup of water before the first class. The water will have come from a borehole, rainwater tank or a stream. The infants have a mid-morning cup of maize porridge, which is similar to the gruel that would have been fed to kids in an 18th-century UK workhouse (colloquially known as a 'spike'). These little Kenyan kids queued up and devoured every last drop.

My guide and friend, Francis Kioni, came from the shanty town slums of Nairobi; he was one of Gavin Bates' success stories. Francis has been with the sister charity Moving Mountains, since it was established in 1991. He is based in Naro Moru, where he works as a project planner and manager. Occasionally, Francis also leads mountain climbs for Adventure Alternatives and he has summited Mt Kenya more than 30 times by various routes.

Kioni and I were invited to meet with the local village Elder; Moving Mountains Charity, who we were representing, were supporting his school. Always on these occasions we would be invited to eat, and this was an honour. Kioni knew I disliked ugali; so before we left for the meeting, I asked Kioni to make an excuse and say I had an upset tummy. When we arrived at the Elder's home, he greeted us with handshakes and customary hospitality. He took me aside and said, 'Kioni informed me you don't enjoy ugali, but mine is different. We have killed and cooked a couple of chickens to go with it.' What could I say but thank you. The ugali, a starchy blob of thick semi-dough, sat in a perfect off-white mound on the centre of a large plate. Everybody attacked the mound, each breaking off a small piece and rolling it into a piece the size of a golf ball.

It has no obvious seasoning and is pretty flavourless, so you press a dent into the middle of the ball with your thumb and use it as an edible spoon to scoop up whatever it is served with, usually stew or sauce, or fried kale – on a good day beans or fish. On this special occasion it was boiled chicken. The texture of ugali is like chewy, coarsely mashed potatoes.

Rescue Centre and Feeding Station for Street Kids

In many towns, Moving Mountains' main priority is the high number of street children. To address this serious problem the charity has created rescue centres providing hot and substantial meals seven days a week for every kid that shows up. There is no discrimination between street kids and those attending school who suffer from extreme poverty. In a high number of cases children from poor families, but who are attending school, will have had no evening meal and no breakfast. Being constantly hungry seriously limits concentration and the ability to learn.

In addition, at the rescue centres, we provided free educational classes, toilets and washing facilities. Most importantly of all, they are a safe and welcoming environment where the kids get encouragement, support and medical help. The Embu Rescue Centre for Street Children, in Eastern Kenya, provides a safe and open contact point for the street children of Embu, where they can seek and receive help from caring adult staff and volunteers.

Kenya feeding station

Mama Lillian is the cook and mother to all at the centre. I had the privilege of assisting her, in a small way, with the daily feeding programme.

Mama caters for between 100 and 200 children from deprived backgrounds that come to the rescue centre every day to get a decent meal. Mama insists that all attending, including me, enjoy a plate of her maize and beans. I tended to leave a vapour trail in my wake on my 4 km walk back to camp.

Football, a universal language that unites all

Gavin Bates and his team of Kenyan local kids launched the hugely successful 'Black Cats' sports programme, which initially used football to attract street children, boys and girls from the rural and slum communities. When the kids are playing and training, they are distracted from the dangers and pitfalls that go with living on the street; this includes crime, glue-sniffing, drugs, prostitution and alcohol abuse. The charity provides kits including boots, and also football coaches to supervise, support and encourage. Once trust is established, they have been highly successful in introducing the street kids to the benefits of education. They are assisted in returning to local schools. In many cases, where need and commitment is shown, they are sponsored by the charity. Life for the street kids takes on a new meaning.

For me and all the many other volunteers, to see loneliness and isolation vanish, to be gradually replaced by friendships and team spirit, was a deep and meaningful experience. I confess to having been materially driven and more than a little macho, and when I was told in my past that it is through helping others that the greatest rewards are to be found, I would have suggested they should get out more. Now that I have been in a position to offer, in a small way, useful and effective assistance to others, I have had to swallow my pride and eat my words. In my limited experience, if you have been going through a rough patch or a serious case of the blues, helping others can help you to help yourself, to get back on track. I can never repay what those young Kenyan street kids taught me.

Surprises come in strange ways

I was totally unaware of the relatively high level of alcoholism and addiction in Kenya and in the developing world, especially as two-thirds of the population just don't drink. For the most part, it is people on lower incomes who succumb to the problem. In Kenya, as in most African countries, bootleg liquor is cheap and readily available. For example, over a couple of weeks during October 2014 while I was there, six people died and many went blind in one small township from a lethal, locally brewed cocktail.

It seems to me that modern Africa's cheap home-brewed booze is equivalent to what happened in Britain during the eighteenth century from drinking gin. Both brews, while keeping people warm at night and disguising hunger pangs, drove them to madness, suicide, death and even the gallows. I realised that there were children resident in the orphanage as a direct result of the parents' and grandparents' addiction to alcohol and glue-sniffing.

One morning I watched as two small boys came into the rescue centre; they were very grubby, in poor clothing and bare feet. They wanted to shake hands and bump fists, which I did. We played, alternately I tossed them in the air and swung them round. Both were laughing and having fun while waiting for the day's meal. Kioni asked where they had come from; the boys told him they had walked from a slum over a mile away. Where were their parents? It seems the mother was home but did nothing. Looking at these two playful four-year-olds and then seeing who they were mixing with – what real chance have they got without help and support?

Many of the street kids who came to the refuge each day for a hot meal were addicted to glue-sniffing. The problem is enormous. Glue takes away feelings of hunger, it gives a sense of wellbeing, and they can sleep in the open, anywhere. You could buy enough glue to get high on for pennies. Children from the age of seven were already treading on the slippery slope of addiction. The source of the thick, industrial glue is right there on the street: shoe repairers. Shoe repairers buy glue from the local hardware store, rarely in large quantities. Usually, they bring a half litre bottle that the hardware store then half fills from a larger container. The shoe repairer pours 100 ml (that has cost him only ten shillings) into a little child's bottle for 20 shillings, thus making 100% profit. Certainly not caring a damn about the real damage done.

My new vocation – teacher

I tried my hand at teaching, and was invited around the local schools to give motivational talks about the real benefits of education, and more generally to discuss modern life in the UK and the developed world, which stimulated lots of questions.

I saw first-hand the struggles and sacrifices parents make in a genuine attempt to better the lives of their children through education in rural Africa. Once, I was part of the same experience, disappointing my own parents in not taking the opportunity I was given. Later, however, my ex-wife and I did make sacrifices educating Georgina and Mya, giving them the very best we could provide, as do a great number of parents and grandparents. But, in the UK we have so much more ...

In Kenya they have far more challenges than any British children ever do, including sharing one book among three pupils. This is true even in class 8, when they have to take important exams in order to get into secondary school. Failure at this stage usually means the end of education. School starts at 8.30 a.m. and finishes at 4 p.m., but the pupils arrive much earlier and leave later, often experiencing twelve-hour days. The reason for this is homework, they need to share their books and they have no electricity in their homes. At one college I visited, there was the opportunity to take computer lessons, but with only one teacher and ten computers for 60 students. Today, I have a far better understanding of the value of education.

Mama Sarah Obama

Mama Sarah Obama is the 94-year-old grandmother of former US president Barack Obama. I was fortunate to spend a few thought-provoking hours visiting her at home shortly before she was due to visit her grandson in Washington DC in 2014. She was remarkably sharp and enthusiastic, with a great sense of humour. She talked passionately about her efforts to promote education. Mama Sarah confided to me that she had never attended school herself, nevertheless she was adamant in recognising that this was a terrible lost opportunity. Mama Sarah told me, 'I realised the value of education when somebody would bring me a letter and I could not read it!'

Mama Sarah made certain that all her children received an education, including Barack Obama Snr, whom she pedalled six miles to and from the nearest school every day. The Mama Sarah Foundation has already personally supported, through education, many Kenyans who have gone on to become doctors, university professors, engineers and senators. We also spoke of the huge number of children supported by her Foundation and by the orphanage in which I was assisting, of whom a great number were orphaned as a result of AIDS and poverty.

With a great big beaming smile on her face, Mama Sarah spoke proudly of her son and grandson, observing how remarkably alike they are in looks, mannerisms and tone of voice.

Mama Sarah Obama imparted a personal message to me: 'Without school the cycle of poverty continues. I believe our future and the future of the world lies in the hands of our children; their future lies in our hands – we hold the key – education.'

Dinner and Flying Termites

One night in Kenya there was an enormous hatch of what looked like mayfly or big flying ants. However, on closer inspection they were in fact large winged termites. Kioni explained that the termites come out of their holes, fly around for a short time and, on landing, their wings drop off. The males and females find each other, then go off to establish new colonies.

Children were enthusiastically running around chasing them. It was noticeable that the poorer ones were catching them and eating them with relish. I pointed this out to Kioni who told me how tasty and nutritious termites are. There is real poverty here and the poor seize any opportunity to eat whatever may present itself. Since I was living on a Kenyan diet, I joined in the spirit of the event but whether they have any nutritional value at all, I have no idea. Each time I caught a flyer I popped it straight into my mouth whole, chewed, choked and swallowed. I found them flavourless.

While chasing around catching and eating these flying termites, I collected quite a crowd of kids and locals, all of whom found my antics highly amusing. Were they laughing at me or with me? The Kenyan kids were plucking off the wings and only eating the body. For antisocial reasons I do not recommend the Kenyan diet while sharing a tent!

Revenge of the Termites

With my travelling companion Kioni, we travelled from Siaya District, crossing the Rift Valley, to a small town on the slopes of Mt Kenya, near Nanyuki, where the British Army has a large base. I booked into a hotel that caters for Wazungu (white people) who are planning to climb Mt Kenya.

That evening there was a tremendous storm. I was in bed reading under the canopy created by my mosquito net. Suddenly there was a build-up of crashing and a buzzing racket; my room was being invaded by hundreds of flying termites! This particular species is a similar size to UK dragonflies, but they looked far bigger.

Attracted by the light, they were marching into my room in droves via the gap between my door and the threshold. Once inside they then launched off into flight, careering around crashing into the walls, into the light and my mosquito net. I watched fascinated as they gradually began to land, shedding wings and walking off. In the morning my room was covered with thousands of gossamer wings and no sign of the termites. How did they know it was me that had eaten their friends?

CHAPTER 30

The Sahara: Trekking alongside Camels, March 2015

To me, the Sahara displays an awe-inspiring uniqueness, as did the North Pole. They share extremes of contrasts, yet are alike in so many ways: legend, mystery and raw beauty. Both can and will kill you if you don't respect them.

The Sahara is the largest non-polar desert on our planet at 3,320,000 sq. miles (8,600,000 sq. km). The desert is a great place to explore, but it can be one of the most dangerous. If you take the wrong dune and lose your way, you're in deep trouble. A desert is a barren area, defined by averaging less than 10 inches (25 cm) of precipitation each year. Clear skies, light winds and dry air help the air temperature cool off significantly at night – insufferable heat during the day can turn into unbearable chill at night.

During a business visit to Niger in 1996, I briefly saw the mind-boggling vastness of the Sahara. And later, from up on the northern heights of the Atlas Mountains, I observed sweeping before me an immense vista. What I witnessed blew me away, triggering a worm of curiosity deep in my skull.

Eighteen months after my trip to Morocco, I called Steve and Ibrahim to see what was possible. Six months later eight of us, Roger, Lesley, Maria, Clive and Max Hagley, Dave, Julie R and Michelle, flew to Marrakech to start a new adventure. Our local guide, Ahmed Amzil Ibrahim, teamed with Steve Pinfield.

We spent the first night in a colourful and comfortable Marrakech hotel before departing next morning in a crowded minibus that twisted its way through the ruggedly beautiful Atlas Mountains.

Once free of the mountains, we motored along a flat road until we reached Ouarzazate, known as the 'door of the desert'. Ouarzazate is perched on the edge of the Sahara Desert just south of the High Atlas Mountains. It's a film producer's dream location; the city has provided an exotic backdrop for such productions as Game of Thrones, Black Hawk Down, Gladiator and many more. At last we emptied out at the small desert hotel that was to be the starting point for our rare, off-the-beaten-track Saharan adventure.

We spent ten days in the Northern Sahara, riding on and walking with camels at a gentle pace along the ridges of sand dunes in early morning or late afternoon, surrounded by an open blue sky. We also passed through gorges, valleys and oases, crossed rocky plateaus and climbed numerous dunes, big and not so big. Wherever we trekked it was harsh and unforgiving terrain, and the main culprit was sand. Sand is soft and difficult to walk on, and it is incredibly tough on your leg muscles. Added to which, no matter how tightly you tie the laces, sand constantly fills your boots. This is very uncomfortable and can cause sores, so you regularly need to stop and empty your boots. We sometimes stayed at a traditional Berber camp, other times we set up camp on the warm dunes, taking time out to relax and enjoy a breathtaking desert sunset. It's surprising how quickly darkness descends, giving you a feeling of timeless tranquillity, then giving way to a rich red Saharan sunrise.

The Sahara interior is remote and pollution free, creating a dark sky that is ideal for stargazing. According to our guide we were roughly 80–100 km from the nearest large city, 30–40 km from the nearest large town and 10–20 km from the nearest village. The night sky creates a wonderful backdrop for the most spectacular views of the stars on earth. I slept in the open, lying back and looking up at the stars. I'd drift off to sleep with a smile on my face. In the mornings, the silence of the desert is rudely broken by moans, groans, bellows, bleats, farts and a disconcerting rumbling growl – the sound of our camels complaining about Clive Hadley's snoring!

After a week's trekking in the Sahara's boundless space, with only the company of camels, there was a momentary cultural shock when we suddenly, from high on a dune, caught glimpses of a car barrelling along a desert road that snaked through the remote valley below, leaving a heavy dust cloud in its wake. This turned out to be the Rally Morocco Classic – La Route du Coeur. The Sahara is not as empty as it seems.

Another time three runners came jogging gently over the arid sands towards us. As they got closer, Ibrahim puffed out his chest, and proudly informed us that one of the runners was one of the Moroccan ultramarathon brothers, Lahcen and Mohamad Ahansal, born to a nomadic family near Zagora in the Saharan desert; they were both prolific winners of the toughest foot race on earth, the Marathon des Sables.

Ibrahim suggested we should stick to the windward side of the dunes' ridges, avoiding steep bowls full of deep, soft sand, even when it appeared to be a good short cut, unless you are a masochist wanting a really good workout. OK, so the locals walk in sandals, the brave play barefoot on the sand for a while, the less adventurous keep their socks on.

Next to most of my adventures it initially seemed like a holiday, but I totally underestimated the challenges of ten days of trekking through soft sand in 40 °C heat.

Me and my trusty camel

Conquering the Sahara!

CHAPTER 31

My friend 'Pentonville Johnny'

Back in my early recovery days I was helped by Phil M; he had solid long-term sobriety and was a highly respected businessman, with a pal named Johnny C, AKA 'Pentonville Johnny'. An unlikely pair at first glance – little and large! They were staunch members of a recovery fellowship and both were keen golfers. Johnny grew up in the East End of London, and worked and knocked around with many colourful characters; he was closely associated with the well-known gangsters of the 1960s.

I came on the scene from a different direction, a decade later. At that time I was linked with the firm that filled the vacuum the East End gangs had left behind when they headed for Her Majesty's pleasure. I identified with Johnny's unconventional background. He was the only person I knew who had been involved in similar criminal activities to me, had stopped drinking and had gone straight. He had over fifteen years of sobriety when we first met; I was so lucky I had found someone that actually understood where I had come from and where I was at. We talked and shared experiences on the reality of what it was like, what happened and what it was like now we were sober. The difficulty for me was that I was still 'involved', while staying sober. It's like having one foot on the river bank and the other in an unmoored boat!

In 2002, while holidaying in The Gambia, Johnny and his wife, Chrissy, had been approached by an elderly couple to join them in a venture to build a nursery school. Subsequently they became heavily involved in supporting the building of a nursery school in the area known as Tallinding, which is a part of Serrekunda, the largest town in The Gambia, West Africa.

In 2004, they formed a charity they named the Tallinding Project, committing a great deal of personal time, energy and money. It started as a short-term fundraising project to help with the establishment of a four-roomed nursery school. The first four classrooms were completed in August 2004 and enrolment took place for opening in September. There were places for 160 children, but nearly twice that many turned up. October 2004 saw a big party and official opening with many local dignitaries, parents and visitors.

Johnny and Chrissy were ultimately responsible for the success of the nursery so the village elders asked them to continue with more building to accommodate the children as they got older, in order to prevent them having to walk many miles to a lower basic school – if indeed there was a place for them in the few schools available. Thus they embarked upon a further two blocks each of four classrooms with a headmaster's office and store. Enrolment in these new classrooms commenced in 2007, so taking the children on to the age of 11. The villagers and local school governors decreed that the school should be called the Carter Nursery and Lower Basic and registered it as such.

In July 2016, Johnny called me, inviting Lesley and me to join him and Chrissy for a holiday in The Gambia. Do we endure a cold and damp November in the UK, or the opportunity of enjoying the sun, sand and sea in the company of old friends? Such a difficult choice! A booking was arranged, and the deposit paid within an hour. A couple of months later, we flew into Banjul Airport where Johnny and the hot African sun greeted us. From the open back of a pickup truck we enjoyed a colourful, dusty and somewhat smelly ride to the Senegambia Beach Hotel, located on a picturesque stretch of beach in the popular resort of Kololi. It was situated within easy walking distance of several interesting local shops and restaurants, all displaying come-hither banners. Johnny wanted us to see the school he and Chrissy had built, of which they could be justly proud. What we witnessed on visiting the school was gobsmacking. From the original twenty kids, the school now had 1500-plus students. Before leaving the school on the first day, Lesley and I had signed up to sponsor two boys, Mustapha Bah (12 years old), Bakary Marong (7) and a little girl, Nyima Jammel (5) for the duration of their Tallinding school life.

On our third visit to The Gambia, while Chrissy, Lesley and I were sitting soaking up the sun by the hotel's swimming pool, Johnny thought it was an appropriate moment to drop a small bombshell in his raucous East London voice, which really carries, guaranteeing all the other sunbathers within half a mile would also be party to our conversation. His announcement, cleaned up for print, went something like:

'Rog, Phil M asked me to make a call for you.'

I nodded, unsure what was coming.

'He asked me to speak to the 'renowned London crime family' you were working for!'

'I spoke to the 'Man', told him you're out, and that I'm vouching for you.'

That was a big favour Johnny had done; even though belonging to a large and well-connected 'family' himself, he had put himself in the firing line with some extremely dangerous people. I was out, clean and free. What Johnny had done was not a total surprise; Phil had given me a nod about it almost 30 years ago when the call was made. To hear it from Johnny himself had a positive impact on me.

In January 2017, the newly elected president of The Gambia, H E Adam Barrow, invited Johnny to visit him. It was a privilege for Johnny, Chrissy, Lesley and me to be his personal guests in his private home. Some of the new president's top priorities were to revive the economy, to end human rights abuses and to introduce free primary education. It was Johnny's positive contribution and future plans for the Gambian schooling system that the president wanted to discuss and support.

The Tallinding School building and the happy pupils

CHAPTER 32

Rowing the North Atlantic

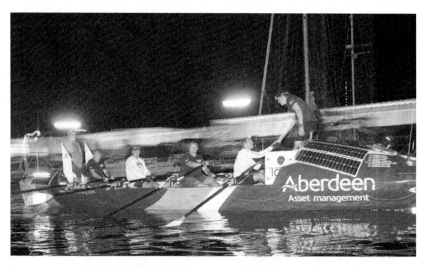

It was approaching midnight on the 28th January 2016. I was sitting in my rowing position on the 'Toby Wallace', a lightweight ocean rowing boat, primed and ready for an attempt on a world record. Our challenge was to row across the North Atlantic, setting off from Marina Puerto De Mogan, Gran Canaria, rowing 2,992 miles to Port St Charles, Barbados, faster than anyone before.

My daily training preparation consisted of a 3-hour, physically demanding session on a rowing machine in the gym. Therefore, achieving diddly squat in preparing me mentally for the Atlantic row I was about to begin. As a team we would row in excess of 1.5 million oar strokes. Ocean rowers row for twelve hours in every twenty-four, two hours on and sleep for two. However, Simon had worked out a new system; every day for the next thirty-four or more days on the Atlantic, we were to row twelve hours per day split into five watches. One hour at midday and a four-hour session during the wee hours, two hours and then three hours. On the upside, we did each have a three-minute break every hour to take a drink, eat sweets, poo and pee.

A couple of weeks before I was due to meet the team and spend a day training on the water, Lesley, Abi and Jacob, her kids, their best friends Charlotte and Luke, plus me, had a holiday on a canal barge. My first unfortunate mistake. I was bouncing along the towpath with the elegance of a young buffalo, rope in hand, when I tripped, landing on a heavy-duty mooring stake. I had a couple of injured ribs, and was banned from rowing for three or four weeks.

I was still injured when we went to meet the rest of the Atlantic team for an important training weekend, rowing the Toby Wallace. Lesley took my place on the oars!

The next experiment was to crew on a sailing boat from Hamble, Hampshire to Las Palmas and become acquainted with the sea. My second big mistake. We set off out of the Solent, down the English Channel and headed across the Bay of Biscay, which lived up to its fearsome reputation. I personally attempted to feed most of the fish all the way. Sea sickness is bad enough, but I fell awkwardly during a heavy squall and gave my knee a real walloping, causing a swollen lump to rise up to  the size of an orange, on the inner side of my metal knee. More crucial time away from training. I suppose those injuries were not as bad as the heart attack I had eight months before I pulled a pulk 350 miles to the North Pole.

Just before we actually set off, Lesley and I were in our apartment; all my clothes and kit for 35-plus days had been weighed and packed, totalling a maximum of two kilos. Yes, 4.4 lbs. Lesley created a braided wristband and tied it on as token of love and commitment between us. I was wearing it during the tragic incident on the Atlantic, which I will tell you about soon, and it has never left my wrist. It reminds me of the preciousness of life and helps keep me grounded.

Minutes before we would be departing I was lying on the bed collecting my thoughts in preparation. I can still see Lesley sitting quietly by the window; it is an image imprinted in me and I will never forget it.

During our time in port, skipper Simon Chalk decided who was on each of the two teams, and what our rowing positions were to be. Each oarsman is numbered by boat position (one to four) in ascending order from bow to stern. The person seated at the bow (sharp end) is number one and the closest to the stern (blunt end) is the stroke, number four.

Simon decided it was our watch (Team A), that was to set off in the dark from Puerto de Mogan in Gran Canaria. This was only the second time I had actually rowed in the Toby Wallace. It felt good to get going.

While resting in the cabin after finishing my second shift on the oars, the first violent attack of seasickness hit me. I knew I must not honk up inside our tiny living space so I made a dive for the hatch, and got my head and shoulders out. Uncontrollable retching started – I never made it to the side! I am ashamed to admit poor Dolores received what she didn't deserve – all over her back. I am still very sorry.

I suffered for a full three days from seasickness. Nothing stayed down for long, including my seasickness tablets! Sips of water were all my stomach would accept. When we came off our watch, we boiled water and reconstituted our freeze-dried meal. In the first week we did not eat very regularly but I did always try to keep myself hydrated. The Toby Wallace has two underdeck 'coffin berths' in the keel that run directly below the rowing stations, where two sleeping crew acted as human ballast. Since I was taller and generally bulkier than Richard, we decided after 72 hours, once my constant seasickness had abated, that it was best if I slept below in the coffin berth as the better counterweight. Each coffin berth is approximately two metres in length, shoulder-width wide and 40 cm deep; it is regularly awash with a couple of inches of lapping sea water for company. Reader, try and imagine me shuffling my 107 kilo frame feet first into my bed!

The moment I was horizontal I didn't just fall asleep, I lost consciousness. Next thing I would hear was the dreaded 'change over' shout, ten minutes, followed by five minutes. Sometimes I thought I was dreaming or it was a stupid prank; I couldn't even believe I had slept yet!

The skipper, Simon, had made it plain that the shift change was to be slick and speedy. While changing over the boat speed would drop, so six shift changes each day, over say 30 days, could make all the difference. I could not sit in the cabin. I was too big, the hatch was small; squeezing in and out then crawling to our rowing position, with a bottle of water and one's personal sheepskin seat cover in one hand was not easy. Whilst rowing the sheepskin reduces friction on your butt and dangly bits. After a week my knees were both open wounds. I tried to crouch instead of crawling. Another learning opportunity happened.

Poor Balance

My balance is shit – an unexpected swell tipped me into the South Atlantic!

At its deepest, the ocean is 8.5 km/5.28 miles deep. Half measures were not an option, I grabbed the gunnel and clung fast. I noted the water was warmer than I expected – or was I leaking?

A shout went up, 'Man overboard!' It was daylight so everyone could see me. I was gripping on and struggling to get back on board. Simon's expression told me he was unimpressed. It was Murray who came to my assistance and he put his hand out. We linked hands on each other's wrists. He pulled, I grunted and slowly flopped back on board. Incident over, I got on my seat and started rowing.

In turbulence, I too often lost my balance and fell off my seat, and it was a struggle to get quickly back onto my rowing position. This required me aligning my feet correctly, folding my uncooperative metal left knee and assuming a squatting position. The rowing seat is on tracks and slides, so timing before dropping my bum was crucial.

Balancing, when hovering, over the shit bucket was a nightmare for me. A mistake would be messy. All happening on a see-sawing boat. Not a pretty sight for the other crew members.

When the urge hit and you needed to empty your bowels, the shared black plastic builder's bucket was passed to you. You leant over the side to add 2–3 inches of seawater into the bucket, and when ready, you positioned it into your personal rowing space. Wet wipes in one hand, other hand steadying said bucket. Aim, squeeze and strain. Finish and wipe. Wash out bucket, remove any skid marks; hand it back all pristine, ready for the next user.

On the 2nd February 2016 I asked to use the sat phone, I wanted to make two important calls to Lesley and my close friend Michael Broderick. Why? Because I was celebrating my 35th anniversary of turning my life around and remaining sober every single day over all those years.

After six days I was beginning to become used to the conditions, when totally out of the blue, a very sharp electric pain shot through my left knee. I immediately feared the worst – my total knee replacement coming apart! Every time I tried to bend my bionic left knee I was hit with a further electric shock, forcing me to cease rowing. Gerry Kavanagh, on my return, suggested it was either nerve damage or neuropathic pain; it can go away on its own but is often chronic. I was lucky it was temporary, although I still get the occasional shooting twinges.

Simon Chalk was somewhat pissed off. Threats flew in the wind. He even asked me, in no uncertain terms, if I wanted off.

That's when I recognised and acknowledged his wholly blinkered obsession. At times you do need to be very focused and even obsessed, and I take my hat off to his achievements on the oceans. But with respect, fanaticism must be tempered. Ask any number of veteran adventurers (mountain, sea or polar) for their single, most important advice, and most will say, 'Say only positive things to each other.'

Chalky was totally starry-eyed on attaining a world record. He was blind to the physical pain I was in; however, more importantly, he was not equipped to ruffle my feathers. My troubled journey through life had made me brutal on myself. I knew deep down that if you want to reach the impossible, then you must continue where others stop. At 68 years of age, experience has proved to me many times that I can achieve real goals if I break it down into small pieces – one day at a time – one rowing watch/session at a time. Don't think; just keep going. Never stop.

I was always on my rowing seat on time, although unfortunately, I was unable to row for two shifts before the spasms ceased, never to trouble me again during the row. My metal knee sets off every security system throughout the world, especially at airports; the appearance of anybody in rubber gloves makes me nervous.

We had been at sea for eighteen days. Watches, either during the day or night, became a way of life. My body was coping well with physical endurance, the sea and living conditions.

As for what was going on inside my head … I recalled a conversation with my friend and mentor, Jock Wishart, a doughty wee Scot, and maritime and polar adventurer. 'Roger, why are you going to row the Atlantic? When I did it, it was the most tedious thing I have ever done in my life.'

I didn't understand when he said that – but I did eventually, 1,000 miles out in mid-Atlantic!

North Atlantic heading towards Barbados

Valentine's Day

In good spirits I called Lesley on the morning of Valentine's Day; the wind was strong and in our favour, and Toby Wallace was on course to break the world record. On my return to the UK, I saw a message sent and posted on our blog by Lesley at 2.58 p.m. on February 14th:

> Hi Rog & All,
> Valentine's Day is postponed this year until 29th Feb!
> Stay safe, praying for strength & good winds.
> Lots of Love xx

I believe the wind must have picked up significantly by the time Michael, Simon, Richard and myself took to our designate rowing positions that night and started rowing the scheduled 10 p.m. to 2 a.m. watch in difficult sea conditions and high winds. I learnt later that the watch before had been forced to cease rowing for a while due to high winds of 40+ knots pushing the Toby Wallace along at five knots. For our first hour we managed 3.5 to 4.6 knots; we were running before the sea, keeping the stern perpendicular to the oncoming swells. We were told to expect waves up to 20 feet high. Simon called out to me to take my three-minute break, thus confirming the time to be 11 p.m.

I had just restarted rowing when Simon gave a loud warning

shout, 'Big wave.' I looked up to see a monster swell coming at us fast out of the dark; it was the size of a two-storey building. This rogue wave was arriving from an unexpected direction, intent on broadsiding our row boat. It didn't break over but pummelled through us like a water tornado.

The immense power of the unstoppable maelstrom of angry sea water lifted me and ripped my rowing seat from its fixings, luckily dumping me in a tangle, hard into the small corner of the low gunnel and cabin bulkhead, not over the side. Moments later I heard Simon shout those most dreaded words, 'Man overboard.'

My hardwired primal instinct for survival kicked in. I looked around at the watch crew. The stroke seat was empty. Mike was gone.

With adrenaline as fuel I fought to free myself of my damaged seat, which was jammed tightly into my thigh and crotch. I dragged my bruised arse back to where I could reach both oars and immediately dropped both blades into the sea to hold water, in a desperate attempt to slow the boat.

It felt like only moments after the 'man overboard' shout that all four others came to assist us, while I was still struggling to get up and back to my station. My memory of events is vague but I do recall instructions called out by Simon, clear and concise. He asked who was at the bow. 'Roger,' I replied.

'Pass me back the EPIRB,' he shouted.

The EPIRB (Emergency Position Indicating Radio Beacon) was mounted on the forward bulkhead. I handed it back with great care. I didn't dare drop it, it was the only one we had on board. When activated, the EPIRB sent a distress signal via satellites, immediately alerting search and rescue authorities of our location.

It was probably at this time that Simon pressed the man overboard button, which immediately gave our position to MRCC Falmouth (Maritime Rescue Coordination Centre).

Some of the team dropped our last remaining bucket and anything else that might slow the boat down into the sea. Simon called out, 'Drop the daggerboard.' I had no idea what he was talking about, but thankfully Richard did. I learnt months later what a dagger-board is for. It is a retractable centreboard; during heavy seas it can help reduce the tendency of a rowing boat to tip over.

We lowered our oars into the sea and kept them in a static position to hold the boat, reducing the drift as much as possible. My position holding water was difficult because I was too low, sitting directly on the deck with both arms raised – not very practical, but it was the only thing I could do at that moment. This was shortly improved by me and Richard taking an oar each; bracing ourselves back-to-back we created a more efficient holding position. At all times we were shouting Mike's name as loud as possible; Murray led us by example. He constantly shouted Mike's name and words of encouragement while he stood on top of the aft cabin waving an oar on which a lamp was tied. I was instructed to stand at the bow and take my head torch in my hand and wave as high as possible in an attempt to give Mike sight of us and for me to try to locate him.

Staring back, suddenly I saw a small red light in the darkness – I blinked and wiped my eyes. It didn't belong out here. Bang, my brain switched on – it was Mike!

The sea swells cut off the light and he was gone. I stared fixedly into an inky black spot; again I did see a red flash of Mike's head torch at my two o'clock looking from bow towards stern – he was 300 metres away, possibly more; that is a long, long way under the circumstances.

No matter how hard we tried to slow the boat, a furious 35-knot wind was hitting us and sweeping us farther away from Mike. To my recall, my last sighting of Mike before he was lost to the sea was 60 or 70 minutes after going overboard.

I think it was Simon who deployed the sea anchors and the drogue. It took Graham some time to untangle the life raft before he could let it drift out with as much rope as was available – if it swung out it would act as a lifeline for Mike. Simon was on VHF sending out mayday calls and giving all necessary info.

Three or so hours after Mike was lost overboard, we heard that the nearest vessel, the Sea Pearl, a freighter, was a little over 100 miles from our position and was now heading our way. A search and rescue aircraft would also be with us at first light. We were all soaked through and some were suffering from mild hypothermia. Simon ordered us to leave the deck and get back into our cabins until morning.

We sighted the freighter just after daybreak. It passed us, to conduct a search pattern. French and Portuguese fixed-wing aircraft search and rescue planes also searched, but to no avail. The sea had taken my friend and colleague, Mike Johnson.

The Sea Pearl returned and picked us up that evening. The ship's captain and every member of his crew went out of their way to look after us. The captain's seamanship was amazing; he positioned his 600-ft-long cargo vessel, weighing 38,760 tonnes, in order to shelter the Toby Wallace from the huge ocean swell. Consequently, it gave us the opportunity to board far more safely when transferring from our little bobbing row boat to the safety of the Sea Pearl.

I was first to climb up a flexible Jacob's rope ladder hanging down the side of the freighter. A couple of the crew assisted me over the guardrail and led me to a safe seating position, a relieved man. The rest of our crew followed and the Toby Wallace was cut loose and abandoned.

I hadn't realised my physical condition; I walked like a drunk on wobbly legs. A crew member steadied me as he guided me to a single cabin that had a bed, chair, table and little bathroom – pure luxury. First for me was a cup of real Java, drunk while stripping off ready for a hot shower, with lots of soap, and a proper sit-down dump, followed by another hot shower. The crew supplied each of us with orange boiler suits and boots, then they fed us with lots of good food. Most of our crew spent their time in the lounge enjoying a beer and a smoke. I preferred to sit up in the quiet of the bridge, nursing a coffee or sleeping on a real bed. They dropped us off a week later in Brazil, and from there we flew home.

How did I feel during the incident and how do I feel with hindsight?

Rowing the Atlantic seemed such a good idea. However on reflection, the reality, as with much of life, it's not all it seems.

I first met Mike Johnson on our Toby Wallace training day; he was a nice young man and he was a pleasure to be with. A couple of months later I hired an old whaling boat used in the film Heart of the Sea, starring Chris Hemsworth and Tom Holland, a local lad from Kingston, for a group of my friends to row in London's Great River Race 2015. Mike was one of the team, he arrived a day early and stayed overnight at my home in Surbiton, along with an old friend from the Polar Race, Lucas Bateman. It gave us the opportunity to chat, joke and get to know each other.

At his age I was a pain in the arse to all and a big disappointment to my parents. I was involved in many criminal activities, some very serious. I was unreliable, untrustworthy, unpredictable and violent. I earned my money through violence, theft and selling drugs. Unlike TV and films, a criminal way of life is not glamorous. I was an active alcoholic – a polite way of saying I was a knob-head and a drunk.

My life changed at the age of thirty-three. The same age as the infamous twins, Reggie and Ronnie Kray's lives changed – they never saw freedom again! I was sixty-eight years old with an iffy past: Mike was twenty-one, a fine young man with a wonderful future ahead of him. Why him?

The moment I saw he had been swept overboard, a voice in my head said, 'We've lost him.' My heart desperately wanted me to be wrong. Mike had a very slim chance of survival; the odds were heavily stacked against him.

With Mike Johnson (wearing the cap) rowing the Thames

CHAPTER 33

Silence and Solitude

Silence is the absence of deliberate sound, a rare commodity in today's world.

Valued by some; feared by many. The deep silence of nature can be both calming and unnerving. When you stop walking and take a moment to tune in to the deep quietness, it can overwhelm you.

It has been said by some that silence is a medium for growing human consciousness, an invitation to be fully present, and a doorway to a sense of connection with the universe. These sacred moments provide an amazing energy and capacity for life.

As I understand it, the Buddha was an advocate of silence as an alternative to idle chatter. He also encouraged silence in the face of anger and provocation. It has taken me most of my life to learn to keep it simple and count to at least ten before I give my tuppence worth. I have noticed my silence in the face of bullshit can be most disconcerting to a loudmouthed braggart.

After a short time in intense silence one starts to hear internal sounds: the heart pumping blood, lungs and other organs working and the buzz of tinnitus in the ears. The feeling of enormous emptiness is brought closer, creating a form of intimacy with your immediate surroundings – obscure logic says in the vastness there must be sound but not right here. However, in the Arctic, or high up on a mountain, if you linger too long listening, the cold will start biting. So you start up again and once you are moving the quiet is taken over by the noise of your feet, the dragging of the pulk, your harness and ropes brushing; then there is the wind against your hooded head, not unlike holding a shell against the ear as we all did as children on a beach.

Replace that sea shell with a mobile phone; over the last decade noticeably more and more people's ears are glued to their mobile phones, listening to music, idle chatter or occasionally business. Craving distractions of any kind from TVs, iPods, all forms of social media available 24/7, rather than endure a terrible few quiet moments when you are faced with you, yourself, and the dreaded silence. Checking or sending texts or emails, stalking on Facebook or following on Instagram etc., we are addicted to the fear of missing out and the desperate need to be in the know.

The Arctic is one of the last great quiet places on the planet; in all that vastness, nobody ever mentioned the eerie silence to me. Out on the ocean, high on a mountain or in the desert, you can relax and bathe in the stillness of silence. Also, I can talk to myself and get the right answers!

The famous line 'Listen to the wind' is out of place up on the very top of the world. In this desolate and unforgiving landscape, there flows, sweeps and often rages, a silent wind. You can only feel it. Wind chill makes temperatures even worse and creates one of the planet's most inhospitable environments. The savage Arctic wind, if not respected, is more akin to a silent assassin as it carries a chill factor that can literally maim you in moments or freeze you to death in minutes.

Silence gave me a chance to listen to that inner voice, making me come to understand that listening is far more powerful than speaking.

Solitude restores me, loneliness drains me.

There is a lot of confusion between being on your own and being alone; to some, solitude and loneliness look a lot alike.

If I allow myself, I can feel desperately lonely in the midst of a crowd, cut off and completely isolated from those around me.

At times like that my inside is filled with the powerful feeling of emptiness and a desolate sense of loss. But today, and for many years past, I don't allow myself that feeling; it's dangerous and pointless. Instead, I embrace feeling alive and full of life. Whether on the very top of the world, where I am just a speck in the immense remoteness of the frozen Arctic Ice Cap, high up in the vast Himalayas, on the giant Erg Chebbi sand dunes of Morocco; indeed, just sitting quietly fishing on a chalk stream in Hampshire, I find and enjoy solitude without loneliness.

I jog/run, row, workout, and fly fish alone, in total comfort with myself; as a matter of fact it's often in the wilderness I have found both stillness and vitality. While far from excluding companionship, I do relish occasional spells of solitude.

Silence and solitude is where creativity grows.

CHAPTER 34

Sea Kayaking

I had my first experiences of kayaking off Hastings beach in the summer of 2017.

It is tricky getting a kayak launched with me on board. I would drag the kayak down the beach to the sea. It needs to be in just enough depth of water so it floats, roughly knee-high. The plan is to be in control of the kayak at all times. However, at this point the kayak always seemed to try and float off without me. It is difficult to look cool when you're a large unit with your legs akimbo in a semi-squat pose, hovering over a bobbing kayak. It's all down to timing and luck, somehow dumping my bum, accurately, onto the piddling excuse for a seat.

Landing on the seat, I would try to keep my weight evenly balanced, then quickly swing both legs on. I even used the paddle as a third leg to keep me steady during this process, but the surf has a different agenda, and at this moment there was usually a 50/50 chance of an early bath. On hitting the seat, with legs in place, and if still upright, I paddled hard; once through the surf and into deeper water, kayaking is fun and good exercise.

I enjoy riding the waves and probably breaking the rules when dodging under the famous, award-winning Hasting's Pleasure Pier. However, I get the same experience in reverse when disembarking, more often than not, taking a second dip into the English Channel.

Undoubtedly, I have poor balance but clearly it's the waves that magnify the problem.

Living in St Leonards-on-Sea and looking out over the English Channel every day sparked a wacky idea, now deeply implanted in my head, 'Why don't I merely kayak over to France for a coffee and croissant?' I know they are my own thoughts but it's just like dangling a carrot in front of a donkey. There was no question of whether, no ifs, buts or maybes, only when.

I had survived a harsh lesson on the Atlantic; it was my intention not to repeat the basic mistake, but always respect the sea.

I needed to start learning to sea kayak and buy a beret. So, I booked myself and Lesley a morning's training on the quiet upper reaches of the River Rother with a highly respected kayak instructor, Cliff Meadon of Epic Life[4]. On arriving we had a few minutes of general instruction and tips from Cliff, then carried our kayaks to the placid stream. We placed them parallel to the bank in 2 foot of water where you could step off the bank straight into your kayak. There was even a solid timber post you use to support yourself. Paddle in hand, I stepped into the kayak's cockpit and as I lowered myself gingerly into the seat, the kayak gently tipped me into the stream: Ha! Ha! Ha!

To heighten the amusement for my audience, the same performance happened whenever I tried to get out of the kayak, thus confirming what I already know: it's not the sea, nor the kayak that's responsible. I accepted my need for a good wetsuit!

I spent many happy hours training and finding that comfortable rhythm on the quiet River Rother. Feeling free from modern techie distractions, just enjoying a relaxed paddle on the water – the difference was highlighted as I glided past the fourteenth-century Bodium Castle, surrounded by nature and close to wildlife.

In the spring of 2018, I commenced training on the sea. I joined the friendly Hastings Motor Boat and Yacht Club, where I keep my own sit-on-top kayak. Attired in a rash vest, life jacket, Sealskinz socks and a pair of very fetching Neoskin shorts (everyone's arse

4. www.epiclife.co.uk/

looks big in these) I paddle to Bexhill and back, a three-hour nonstop round trip of approximately 10 miles. This became a routine three or four times each week for me.

Kayaking on the sea is always subject to water conditions, if I see 'white horse' sea waves on the open water, created by either high winds and/or proper breaking waves, I forget about launching. On those few occasions, I swap the freedom of the open sea for the pedestrian confines of the gym and spend an hour or two of healthy, bumaching cardiovascular exercise on the rowing machine.

All was going well, and the date for the crossing was set. The safety boat was booked for the week of 3rd September 2018. The actual day for the crossing during that week would depend on weather and tides. But then an unexpected, alluring call from Jock Wishart put kayaking on temporary hold. I had a better offer. So I swallowed and lost the deposit. An often forgotten and ignored fact: extreme challenges don't come cheap!

CHAPTER 35

Everest Rugby Challenge, 2019

Plans of mice and men

I got unexpectedly hit from out of left field. This was the unexpected, alluring call from Jock Wishart that put kayaking on temporary hold. 'Do you fancy playing Rugby with Altitude?' asked Jock. 'In April 2019, we're going to trek in the footsteps of Mallory and Irvine, up Mt Everest's Magic Highway to base camp in the Rongbuk Valley, Tibet, which is just below the North Col, to play two games of rugby on a glacier! You will make history and become double world-record holders!'

He made it sound fun. A mere two weeks after the tempting phone call from Jock, I was introducing myself and Lesley to the Wooden Spoon Everest Challenge, and we were invited to attend a training weekend.

Our first group day training was on the Fairfield Horseshoe, a circular hillwalking ridge route, reputedly the most famous of the classic Lake District walks. Contrary to the previous day's weather forecast, we enjoyed a dry, warm and clear day, granting us the opportunity to bask in the glory of this stunning part of the Lakes.

The route, as distance goes, is not excessive, a modest 16.4 km (10.2 miles). However, it's the interesting ups (the ascent is over 900 metres) and downs of the ridges that took their toll on my knees. The following morning, with stiff legs and knees in torment from the Horseshoe, off we went to the cutely named Stickle Ghyll car park. That name conveys a totally false impression of the Stickle Tarn trail we were about to ascend; as we very quickly discovered. Stickle Ghyll gained height fairly rapidly as the path became steep, rougher and still steeper. I remembered my own advice to lift my head up to take in amazing views across the valley. Close to hand we observed rock pools and a dramatic waterfall. The beautiful surroundings did nothing to camouflage my using every opportunity to pause and catch my breath.

The group had a good feel, lots of support and plenty of amusing banter; overall a tiring, friendly and thought-provoking weekend, but my muscle memory had not been working! I recognised I had become soft and lazy. My trekking fitness had lapsed. It highlighted my need for spending more time on my feet, outdoors.

On returning, our Labradoodle, Dolly, could not conceal her delight at the new regime; two-hour, early morning walks over the Fire Hills in the south-east of Hastings Country Park Nature Reserve. I supplemented this regime with a gym training schedule that included the rowing machine (Ergo), pumping a little iron and the stair climber (Stairmaster). The evils of the tedious, mind-numbing Stairmaster amount to a regime of pain, boredom and more pain. The benefits are it provides a great cardio workout, making the lungs burn and the heart pound, while toning your body, strengthening the legs and glutes. Shame was my initial driving force, promptly followed by pride as the drive to succeed. After three weeks I had built up to 90-minute sessions, 4/5 times per week. This continued for four months until ...

Health issues

Our first encounter with HCA (HCA UK is a private healthcare provider) was via an email from Laurie Dennard, on behalf of Wooden Spoon, dated 5th February 2019, to arrange pre-trip health checks.

The earliest appointment we could get was 8th March 2019 at RL Chiswick with Carin Bernard. One of the health checks was called, the Bruce protocol, which is a standard test in cardiology and is comprised of multiple exercise stages of three minutes each on the treadmill. There were guarded conversations regarding my test results!

A conversation with HCA's doctor confirmed I had a serious heart problem.

They can't clear me for any altitude events

They said I had blocked arteries and there was a possibility of a heart attack at any time. This was extremely worrying for me and Lesley. With this knowledge I would be unable to go to Tibet. I found myself in the same position as Paul Watkins and Graham Allen, both of whom had to pull out, after being integral to the squad's build-up, due to accident and injury just weeks before departure. I could not allow my selfishness to impact on the rest of the team. Furthermore, to continue to request monies from sponsors after being told verbally, and in writing, that I had been medically diagnosed as unfit, and thus was unable to be a part of Wooden Spoon's Rugby on Everest Charity Event, would constitute misrepresentation – fraud. Plus, my insurance would be automatically invalid.

So, important questions needed to be addressed:

- How ill was I?
- Was my life in danger?
- What could be done to improve my health?

I needed to see a cardiologist urgently and have further tests. Arrangements were made for a CT coronary angiogram on 25th March 2019. However, on the morning of 25th March, I recall entering the gym in a pissed off, angry mood and vented my frustration by attacking the rowing machine. Bizarrely, I rowed 15,481 m in 60 minutes and smashed the British indoor rowing record for my age group by a hefty margin!

I knew I had rowed much faster than normal, but I had no idea that it was especially quick. My efforts were witnessed by Karolina

Kasprzak, an in-house personal trainer, and others present at Bannatyne Health Club, Hastings. I snapped some pictures, on my phone, of the rowing machine's monitor display for confirmation, creating photographic evidence showing the displayed distance and time. Although it was witnessed, it's totally meaningless as a record because of the lack of one continuous video shot and insufficient official paperwork.

For me personally, the record meant nothing – it's just a piece of paper. Far more importantly, I did it while apparently suffering with a life-threatening heart problem.

Back to see the pointy heads, then. On 26th March a CTCA cardiac scan showed signs of moderate coronary disease. On 29th March a dobutamine stress echo test showed no abnormalities at peak stress. A few days later I received the all clear from the cardiologists; it was safe for me to climb Mt Everest.

This medical misdiagnosis created all sorts of psychological and financial difficulties for both of us. For days, I woke restless with a sense of impending doom. It's a giant psychological leap from being told by experts, and therefore automatically believing, that I was a very, very ill man and out of action, to making history by playing rugby on the highest mountain on earth.

Now we had a new problem. Lesley and I had only five working days to get ourselves together and shrug off the mental heebie-jeebies. I drew token confidence from a quote I recalled:

Any expedition to the North Pole is ten times more difficult than climbing Mt Everest

Eric Larsen, an American polar adventurer known for his expeditions to the North Pole, South Pole, and Mt Everest

Between us we had already raised about £10,000 for the Wooden Spoon Children's charity. Lesley talked to schools and raised money (averaging £200 to £300 per school). She spoke to 1800 pupils in five schools, spreading the word. I reactivated my major sponsors, but with little immediate success. I had serious conversations with our local Wooden Spoon regarding my circumstances. Going forward they still asked me to act as an ambassador for them at local events; it was a privilege to be asked and a pleasure to do. We were invited and attended a Brighton and Hove Cricket social funding event.

In regard to the incorrect diagnosis, I visited HCA and followed up on the previous tests. At a meeting at HCA, it was strongly suggested that the 'naive timing' of the medical health check, as arranged by Wooden Spoon, most definitely did not help. Mr Schalk Blom, head of cardiovascular services for HCA, suggested he would speak to the financial director to waive the additional costs for the tests. Which they did, and I am appreciative.

Additional health issues

In February 2019 I visited my GP with a cough. I had a blood test and was later sent for a chest X-ray. I received positive results for a chest infection and was given penicillin. After the original diagnosis I had another chest X-ray and, at 1 p.m, on 5th April 2019 a doctor from my local surgery phoned my mobile. At that moment I was in my favourite jewellers buying a beautiful ruby and diamond ring for Lesley's birthday present. The doctor began by telling me that the X-ray had revealed a serious lung problem and suggested strongly that it may be lung cancer. She told me I urgently needed to get a scan.

All my energy drained out of me. I turned my back on Rolf the jeweller; I felt I had been punched in the guts and sat down so I could take it in. The time and place were all wrong. But it could have been worse, I could have been driving!

In April 2019 I went to Conquest Hospital for a CT scan. Then I visited my surgery as an emergency to see my GP and have a discussion with him. We were acutely aware that, after the confusion, depression and then elation regarding my heart misdiagnosis, I would not receive the results until 7th May, the day after my planned return from Mt Everest. We mutually decided that going or not going in three days wouldn't make much difference. Grumpily, I accepted I was powerless over the results; worrying was not going to fix anything. But the pendulum hadn't stopped swinging.

Departure Day

The plan was for the team and families to meet at the Hilton Garden Inn at London Heathrow Airport for a send-off celebration. We arrived early to find chaos – a bad omen. Wooden Spoon had explicitly suggested a dress code, requiring the squad to wear WS's favourite sponsors' branded hoodies and polos. The event turned out to be just a thinly disguised set up for a PR photo call. When the session finished, no transport had been arranged to get us and our kit to the airport. We were rather dismissively told that we could either ask our loved ones to drop us off or take a local bus. As everything seemed so chaotic and disorganised it was easier to say goodbye to our families, who were already bored with the circus, and get the bus.

A senior staff member of Wooden Spoon confidently led a large group of the Everest team off to a distant bus stop, each of us dragging our loaded bags filled with a month's worth of hefty kit. She wished us good luck and, with a smile, turned back to the hotel. Oh bless, we watched her go weighed down by her cute little handbag. It was the wrong bus stop! The 423 bus was heading towards Hounslow; we needed to go in the opposite direction. A friendly bus driver took pity on us and gave us all a lift back to the central bus station where we eventually got the correct bus to our airline terminal, so we could actually start our journey.

This minor incident unfortunately became a fairly typical example of much of the next few weeks and our experience of Wooden Spoon's practical organisational skills. WS had obviously not heard of the sacred mantra of business and expeditions, the six Ps: Prior Planning Prevents Piss Poor Performance. It was from this point on that the wheels started to slowly fall off.

Wooden Spoon's in-house office staff pulled all the strings on the adventure. They were lovely people – kind, enthusiastic and well-meaning, ideal at creating publicity and raising money, but totally lacking actual experience in practical know-how and on-the-ground organisational skills for an extreme challenge; their decisions sadly proved time after time to be naive and incompetent.

Once airside I felt more relaxed. We were going; it was too late for the dreaded tap on the shoulder to tell me I'm not fit enough or I'd been found out and it's all a mistake. I had long since learnt that worrying about things you cannot change is utterly pointless, but it was no wonder that Lesley and I felt somewhat rattled.

The adventure had begun and it was a brand-new page in my life. For the next 25 days Lesley and I were part of a group of new friends who were all excited and ready to go. We were members of a pack of rugby players off on a jolly.

After an uncomfortable 10-hour flight we arrived in Chengdu, China, and were met by our Chinese driver, Billy, who took us to our hotel, which was of a higher standard than I had expected. The next day we travelled on to Lhasa, where our formidable jaunt and acclimatisation process began. Tibet was full of surprises for me, what I was witnessing was not as dull or uniform as I had been led to believe. Everywhere you looked there were bright new buildings and many more were under construction.

In 2012, along with friends, I tackled the UK's Three Peak Challenge; climbing the highest mountains in Scotland, England and Wales (Ben Nevis at 1345 m, Scafell Pike at 978 m and Snowdon at 1085 m, in under 24 hours). The total height we summited was 3408 m (11,181 ft). That evening, while relaxing in my modesty bath, reflecting the lofty altitude of our Tibetan hotel at 3656 m (11,995 ft) above sea level, I had an 'Aha' moment – we were already 248 m (814 ft) higher!

For the first week we were not treated as adventurous, rough, tough rugby players, but as a group of tourists on a tour bus. In fact it turned out to be the best way, for us as a group, of avoiding the serious effects of altitude sickness; the tourist route enabled us to increase altitude gradually and systematically, sightseeing and visiting various tourist attractions. The group was a bunch of interesting, fun loving, strong individuals, a law unto itself;

sightseeing was all part of a deviously sneaky plan to keep us entertained and out of mischief while aiding our acclimatisation. Rugby high jinks are synonymous with players on tour and they were not going to break that tradition. The locals were friendly, they took pictures of us – we were their entertainment.

Eating yak had never crossed my mind up until our first dinner in a Lhasa restaurant where yak was on the menu. Up until that moment, to me, yak were big, shaggy, impressive beasts of burden – Tibet's monarchs of the mountains. Yak meat is as lean as venison or bison, tasting juicier, sweeter, and more delicate than beef. I was spoilt for choice, yak curry, yak stew, yak chilli, yak stir fry or yak burger. I chose a very tasty and tender yak steak. In the evenings some of the lads and lasses explored. Occasionally high jinks and a little horseplay happened, it was all harmless fun. Owners of some of the bars we visited may not have been in total agreement, but they weren't shy in taking our money.

We visited the impressive Potala Palace and later the Jokhang Monastery, with their colourful paintings and detailed carvings. Walking on those well-worn steps I became acutely aware of the tens of thousands of feet that must have trodden them over the centuries.

Off again, on a long drive, crossing some high passes. From the highest pass so far, Kampala La (4,990 m), we marvelled at the turquoise lake, Yamdrok Tso. We gained more height and topped a pass at 5010 m. Stopping at one of the high points, the views were incredible. Later we began dropping back down to stay the night at Gyantse.

I understand the locals need an income and tourists are possibly the only source, but as with all tourist spots, you have to tolerate the sad attractions – miniature goats dressed up and imposing Tibetan Mastiffs wearing sunglasses and silly hats.

The boys were getting frustrated and needed to let off steam. To the entertainment of the locals and Chinese tourists we started racing each other, then practised scrummaging drills and finally played a short, crazy game of rugby in a mini car park. That came to an end when the ball went over the touchline and bobbed off down the mountain.

Next morning the buses drove on to Xigatse, the second most important city of Tibet, where we visit the Thashilumpo temple and, for me, more interesting, the fortress Samzhuze, dating way back to 1363, the residence of Panchen Lama.[5]

The buses took us up a long winding road that swept higher. The scenery dramatically changed from brown plains with rolling hills to spectacular and majestic. On topping a pass, a wholly awesome sight greeted us – we were confronted with the North Face of Mt Everest.

On Saturday 20th April, after travelling in minibuses for 800 km over seven days, we arrived at Everest Base Camp. The weather was fantastic, bright, sunny and clear, allowing us to experience an unrestricted, breathtaking view. How different it felt arriving by a minibus rather than on foot; I felt I had cheated. I vividly recalled the difference when, five years previously, Lesley and I trekked 65 km from Lukla to arrive at Everest Base Camp in Nepal, in the midst of an icy blizzard delivering blasts that cut through us. Unfortunately, our view of Mt Everest's Southern Face varied from patchy to obscure.

It had been a long drive and my ageing bladder suffered. The moment the bus stopped, out I jumped and asked, 'Where can I have a leak?'

Our head tour guide, Tashi, said, 'Follow me.' Obviously his need was as urgent as mine. We trotted briskly over to a snowy bank bordering a flat white expanse, which I guessed was a frozen lake. Standing a few feet apart we started, and just as I began to make decorative patterns in the snow, Huw shouted, 'You're pissing in the wrong place!' Apparently we were christening the pitch. Kari 'Charlie' Kobler, the base camp boss, turning a blind eye to my indiscretion, greeted us all with a big friendly smile.

---

5. Spiritual authority second only to Dalai Lama

During our time in camp I had the opportunity to enjoy conversing with him. He told me he had had the Everest bug since the 1970s, quietly speaking about summiting Mt Everest a number of times over the years, until semi-retiring to become the Tibetan Everest Base Camp boss.

Our new temporary homes were bright orange two-man tents. Camping at altitude is deceptive; when the sun is out, it is very warm, but when a cloud masks it, the temperature drops suddenly, and wow, does it feel cold! We sorted out our kit, and went off to the dome mess tent for dinner and the first of many befuddling daily meetings. A running joke throughout the trip was that Dr Georgious always aimed to be first in the food queue. On one occasion Jon Ingarfield beat him to the first scoop of food amid cheering from all the team.

The Tibetan camping food is not too bad under the circumstances, but with hindsight, perhaps I should not have eaten the hard-boiled green eggs. For most of the team, it was their first experience of sleeping under canvas in fiercely freezing temperatures plus altitude, then there were the unofficial WS snoring contests, which broke out as soon as darkness fell. All things considered, an uncivil wake-up call for the majority!

Lesley and I didn't sleep well; the cold, poor sleeping mats and the eggs turning to hydrogen sulphide all played a role.

The next morning was Easter Sunday, and the top of the world revealed herself in all her golden glory.

Contrastingly, over breakfast, I heard lots of moaning from the team; everyone seemed to be suffering from lack of sleep. A good night's sleep is not a luxury but a necessity, vital in these conditions. The team were issued with the barest minimum sleeping mats by Adventure Peaks. For a small sum we all should have had, at the very least, the basic benefits of a Therm-a-Rest air mattress. They are self-inflating, durable, and give a tired trekker a smooth, stable sleeping surface, with additional insulation, all for the princely sum of around £40.

This may seem a small, even petty observation but we were on a mountain and all members of the team were cold, suffering from fatigue and altitude. Chronic fatigue makes it hard to carry out everyday activities, let alone the challenges encountered in an extreme environment. It affects your mental and physical health, also your ability to make good decisions. And I am not unique, when over-tired I have been known to get a little grumpy.

Our first full day at base camp was scheduled as a rest day to acclimatise us to the altitude. It was decided to use the opportunity to hold a photo shoot on the frozen lake, with Mt Everest in the background. The team was instructed to wear the main sponsors' gear while holding up all our own individual sponsors' banners. It was assumed that the ice would take our combined weight. Fortunately, it did!

On 22nd April (Earth Day in the United States and Easter Monday in the UK) we set off on our first acclimatisation walk; not aiming to go higher, but to get meaningful time on our feet. Our 9 a.m. start was delayed by Chinese police being a bureaucratic pain – we got going an hour late.

We eventually set off at a sensibly steady pace, but we soon got our first casualty, Lee Mears. Next casualty was Tamara, with a bad headache and feeling sick. Both returned to camp and were temporarily transferred to Dr Georgious's tent, so they could be closely monitored. Lee was on oxygen, possibly suffering from pulmonary oedema – not good at all.

The most common cause of pulmonary oedema is congestive heart failure. Heart failure happens when the heart can no longer pump blood properly throughout the body. This creates a backup of pressure in the small blood vessels of the lungs, which causes the vessels to leak fluid.

It wasn't too long before the group spread out into three: yompers, trekkers and plodders. On our return to camp Matt Franklin collapsed and passed out on the floor of the mess tent with an oxygen saturation level of 55 – dangerously low. Lesley began to suffer from classic altitude sickness, nausea and headaches; I thought a good night's sleep and Diamox may help her. Next morning she didn't look good so I suggested speaking to the doctor before we embarked on our second day of acclimatisation involving a steep climb.

Sadly, the chest infections began to take their toll. The man who brought the infection with him and infected others was the first to fall. I had absolutely no sympathy for him. He had openly bragged to me and Lesley that he chose to ignore his own doctor's advice not to come on the trip. If you take a handful of laxatives why are you surprised when you shit yourself?

We were barely out of camp when it became clear that today was not going to be Lesley's day; forcing herself would only make the symptoms worse, she needed to rest and recover. Doc said the same – probably the only time I ever fully agreed with him. Towards the end of the walk we hit a stiff climb, I dug in and reached the top. On the way back down to base camp I could feel my legs becoming a little achy. Could it be because my pace was quickening? I wanted to reach camp to make sure Lesley was OK; I'm really glad I made the effort.

Much to my relief she had made a full recovery, aided by her first 'luxury' tent shower. Before I had a chance to feed my face, I too was dispatched to the shower tent; women's priorities are odd.

Hot water showers are very refreshing after a hard day's trekking but they are not very healthy for the skin; water strips the skin of its oils and nutrients, causing early wrinkling and ageing. I shower once a week even if I don't need one (joke!).

Acclimatisation generally takes 2–3 days; Lesley had sensibly opted out, giving herself time to recover from altitude sickness, in readiness for the major section of our journey.

While all of the team were still able to stand, including Lee, Matt and Fenton, it was decided to take the opportunity to create a world record for the highest ever game of mixed seven-a-side touch rugby, at 5,119 metres above sea level. On the pitch, pre-kick-off, as replacement for the national anthem, the whole team sung an impromptu 'Happy Birthday' to Lesley.

Our birthday girl kicked off, starting the second highest 14 minute rugby game in history!

Our group was composed of a diverse range of people mainly from the rugby community including international rugby legends from the men's and women's games.

The local Sherpas, cooks and yak herdsmen, all watching from the touch line, were clearly a touch bemused by this strange game of running, staggering, throwing and chasing an oddly shaped ball.

Team Taylor-Phillips took on Team Mears-Williams and the game was played in good spirit. In sight of Mt Everest, on a frozen lake, a huge cheer resounded when Lesley scored the first try.

Within minutes of the start, with oxygen levels at around 50%, players began to reduce the pace of the game to a jog; actually, a more apt description might be a stagger. As the game progressed there was an occasional slip and fall. Amazingly, no real injuries other than a few bruises.

A further exchange of tries left the score level at half time. Phillips was first to score in the second half, touching down in the corner, but Mears took advantage of a gap in the Taylor-Phillips defence to run in a sixth try in the dying seconds. Each team scored three tries and the match ended in a deserved draw.

On the final whistle, our local fan club was still laughing at us – a bunch of crazy men and women collectively making strange vocalisations while gasping for breath. Birthday girl, Lesley Davies, was unanimously voted as MVP (most valuable player) by all four captains, despite making her rugby-playing debut.

The highest trek in the world

On the 27th April we advanced higher up into the mountains. The journey started from Everest Base Camp and continued upwards along undulating moraine hills, taking in the towering ice pinnacles beside the Rongphu Glacier, to reach the Intermediate Camp.

Our plan was to continue next morning, passing the East Rongphu Glacier, until we reached Advanced Base Camp; all the time we were meant to slowly acclimatise.

The long trek was broken by enjoying a picnic lunch amongst jaw-dropping glaciers, sculptured in infinite shades of blue.

Unfortunately, as we ascended towards 6000 m our team began to lose people. Jordie and Ben were bothbattling a chest infection compounded by the increased altitude.

The team strung out into roughly three parties: medium, slow, and slower; Lesley and I trudged along steadily in the middle. Although Lesley struggled on the training treks, she was getting to grips with altitude now. Deano, Tamara and Jess brought up the rear. It wasn't a race, we all just kept going, one step at a time, at our own pace.

Intermediate Camp was very different from Base Camp. There were no frills, but on the other hand, we were welcomed with much appreciated warm food and hot drinks. Unfortunately, Viv Worral chose to return to Base Camp with mountain sickness. The tents were pitched on very rocky ground, which was bad enough, but worse, our sleep was disrupted by the constant movement of 500 kg yaks loosely tethered just metres from our tent. Lesley was fearful of being trampled on.

For me it was the constant dull clanging of the Tibetan yak bells. Yak bells are made of iron and bronze; they come with a hand-woven, strong woollen or dyed yak hair neck strap. The bells are spectacularly functional in the remoteness, so that yak herders can hear them from afar. We were all trying to sleep just a few metres away with only a sheet of canvas between us. For me, yak bells are like bagpipes – best heard from a considerable distance.

I have slept in far worse places than in a tent, but one place I haven't tried is where 'real' climbers sleep, in a Portaledge. A Portaledge is a lightweight device consisting of stretched nylon over a metal frame, which can be hung from a vertical rock face to provide a place to sleep on big wall climbs. That's one of the reasons I take my hat off to serious mountaineers, they are a gutsy breed of raving nutters! They're a different type to those who queue to walk up Everest; anyone who fronts up to the physical and mental challenges with the knowledge that they will be entering the 'death zone', where dead bodies lie as testimony to small margins of error, deserves our high regard. But it is the icefall doctors, a team of elite local guides who string the ropes and set the ladders in place for those that follow, I truly admire.

Sleep in a Portaledge? Yeah, b*****ks!

As we neared the Advanced Base Camp, Lesley and I found Matt Mitchell alone, freezing cold and exhausted. It was very obvious he had lost his bearings and focus. These mountains are absolutely unforgiving of any mistakes. Lesley mothered him and told me to lead the way for the final hour or so to ABC3.

On reaching Advanced Base Camp, the oxygen levels were about 40% of sea level. We had reached the harsh tract of rock and ice where we would spend a couple of nights, and play a game of rugby. This is the limit of where the yak caravans can reach. That says something!

Tuesday 30th April was game day and more. First there was a matter of a long, tough glacier hike, wearing crampons, from Advanced Base Camp 3 to the East Rongbuk Glacier. We trekked through the brutal, unmatched beauty of stunning ice formations where you occasionally hear the eerie sounds of the ice shifting. The trek included a short section of abseiling, making the glacier hike a unique experience. Then, under the supervision of Rob 'head groundsman' Callaway and in accordance with Guinness World Record specifications, we constructed a full-size rugby pitch with posts, lines, flags etc. on the ice.

The start was delayed. Matt Mitchell had mislaid the necessary paperwork needed for bureaucratic authentication of the world-record attempt. He had to phone home! The UK is seven hours behind Tibet, so who received the 4 a.m. call? Who knows, but, big-hearted, blushing Matt Mitchell got it all sorted.

Tamara Taylor, the referee, blew the whistle to signal kick-off for the world's highest ever game of full contact rugby sevens. Our team started strongly, but within a minute, charging towards me as fast as it is possible over the glacier, came Simon Wright with the ball tucked under his arm. I ignored the instructions Lesley gave me to be careful and take it steady. I bone-headedly launched a full-on rugby tackle, hitting him low with my shoulder. At the age of 71 years I forgot that I no longer bounce, especially on solid ice! Unsurprisingly, the impact of landing hurt. At first, I was uncertain what damage I had done to myself and I was having problems getting up. Testing, I gently moved different bits of my body – nothing broken, merely a rather painful dead leg.

Luckily, it wasn't serious. Also just as well nobody else picked up an injury during the game, because we lost our doctor; just before kick-off, he was urgently needed to attend to Jay. Doc's priorities were spot on. I just had bruising, but Jay had a very serious condition.

One of the lads made a break covering some ground then passed to Arthur Prestidge, a former Northampton Saints hooker, who a month later summited Mt Everest with my friend, from the North Pole race, Julian Evans. Arthur passed the ball back as he was being tackled, leaving Ollie Phillips an amble in for the game's first try.

Next attack from the Whites was stopped by the Blue teams' captain, Shane Williams. He showed his incredible turn of pace, despite oxygen levels down to around 40%.

If that wasn't enough, he was running on a frozen river of ice, but he still completed a try-saving tackle.

In the second half, Team Phillips worked hard to maintain their lead but failed to clear their line in the final moments. A loose ball was fielded by Rob Callaway, who scored an equaliser for Team Williams. Tamara blew the full-time whistle to mark a fiercely contested and breathless 5-5 draw.

Every team member on the pitch and those in supporting roles contributed to a great seven-a-side game of rugby. It was a privilege to play with and against such a great bunch, including four Sherpas. Together we had battled against exhaustion and altitude to compete in a tough, record-breaking match.

Throughout all the ups and downs of travel, trekking and the two games, Sam Tongue, our intrepid cameraman, was there with us every step of the way. He even played briefly in the full-contact game; hats off to him.

As team captain Shane Williams put it, 'In arguably the world's most spectacular setting for a rugby match but also the most inhospitable conditions, the game was incredibly tough. If you ran during the match it took ten minutes to recover. That said, everyone put in 100%, I can't praise the team enough.'

Match referee, Tamara Taylor, said, 'The time spent at this altitude has taken its toll on all of us but the group summoned a second wind to play the game. The energy has been tremendous, with everyone rallying together to spur each other on and, even though we're exhausted, we're buzzing at the achievement. After days of having to deal with one of the world's harshest environments, we're looking forward to coming down off the mountain and enjoying the feeling of having broken two world records and raising a lot of money for very worthwhile causes.'

She was right, we had raised over £250,000 for children with disabilities and facing disadvantage across the UK and Ireland.

For all our efforts and achievements, there was one near tragedy and four medical emergencies. My previous experiences, especially the tragedy on the North Atlantic, make me more aware of the great risks and dangers that are part and parcel of these sometimes heroic endeavours.

Jay became seriously unwell after walking from ABC3 to Pitch Rongbuk and was supported back to camp by Sherpas and Dr Georgious. That's where the real medical troubles hit him big time; a lesser man would have been brought down in a body-bag. Doc and two Sherpas balanced Jay on the back of a yak and during the trip down to Base Camp, we were told that he toppled off a couple of times. Accompanied by Doc, Jay was transported from Base Camp by minibus to Nepal, along with Matt Franklin, Paul Jordan and Ben Harvey, all of whom had chest infections, albeit less serious, also Lee Mears, with a heart condition aggravated by altitude. Four of the team were flown home. But due to the gravity of Jay's condition he was hospitalised for eighteen days in Kathmandu before returning. I met Jay at Heathrow along with Becky, his wife, and Nick and Matt. To say my friend looked poorly is a total understatement. He looked like a very sick man. He was to be admitted to Exeter Hospital for further treatment.

I do believe in charity work

My modest contribution towards various charities started with the 1984 London Marathon. Over the last thirty years or so I have competed in an excess of 100 running events, climbed mountains, rowed rivers and an ocean and taken an active role in many adventures. Given my past, I made a personal decision to give back something to society. I choose not to list monies donated, for me it is vulgar to do so.

In my experience, charities are businesses that do society and humanity a remarkable service. But I am sorry there is a need for them. Many charities and travel companies are a little blind to the realities of adventurous expeditions, and on occasions underestimate the value of the practical and local knowledge necessary to carry out a valid risk assessment.

After seeing avoidable tragedies; I ponder occasionally – do sponsors, charities, families and well-wishers think about the real challenges and risks they are expecting and encouraging amateur participants to face? Is it possible that enthusiasm blurred realistic assessments? Charity begins at home.

Return of the team

It took us two tough days to cover approximately 22 km (12 miles) of trekking up from Everest Base Camp to Advanced Base Camp 3. We were scheduled to get back down in one day's trekking!

Straight after breakfast we hit the trail; it was notably tougher going back over those ridges that caused so many difficulties on the way up. Already the team was spreading out. Jay, Doc and two Sherpas had gone the day before. Carrie, our leading guide, was struggling with sickness and on oxygen. As for the promised eight Sherpas, we never had the full complement at any time, probably just half. Adventure Peaks' other guide, Di Gilbert, plus a Sherpa, strode off with the front group; Carrie and a Sherpa followed at the back with Tamara, Jess and Deano.

I understand from Jude that she was alone on the trail down

for over two hours, as was Nick. Based on my personal experience over 30 years, I found this situation unacceptable.

If a solo trekker becomes disoriented in these mountains, it is extremely dangerous. Picking up a relatively minor injury, such as a sprained ankle, is bad, but a more serious incident such as a fall, causing a break or worse, alone with no shelter in sub-zero temperatures, can prove fatal. Lesley and I had Nick's company for part of the day.

I was leading the way, over ankle-twisting scree, when I spotted what looked like a dark brown branch or stake sticking up out of a pile of rocks. It was entirely out of place up here, way above the treeline. My inquisitiveness made me take a closer look. On mountains the air you breathe is clean, cold and fresh. So it was a complete shock to my senses when suddenly I was hit by a deeply rotten stench. The wooden stake turned out to be the foreleg of a dead yak. Herdsmen must have manoeuvred the body into the shallow ravine and covered it with rocks. Had they left the leg rigidly pointing to the sky as a macabre marker, so they could find it later? Did they plan to come back later to strip the carcass?

Yak bone is often made into exquisite handicrafts. Yak hooves are rich in protein, especially colloid protein. Yak hair is used to make rope; the yarn spun from long hair is also used for weaving tents, bags, rugs and slings. Yak hide is made into leather. Yak heads and tails, with or without hair and hide on them, are made into ornaments by herdsmen or given to guests as gifts. Yak recycling is not a job for the faint-hearted or those with a queasy stomach!

Passing the gruesome find we continued heading downwards, bypassing the East Rongphu Glacier, until we reached the Intermediate Camp, where we stopped and enjoyed a hot, but bland noodle soup for our lunch and on finishing immediately continued on down long, undulating moraine hills beside the Rongphu Glacier.

You can't afford to relax when trekking over rough, stony and rock-strewn paths made by yak caravans. Fatigue from the physical exertion of walking all day makes the descent a far more treacherous journey. Lack of concentration can lead you to momentarily dropping your guard, resulting in a loss of balance or a simple stumble, and that can result in a fall or a far more serious incident. Occasionally, on our route through the boulders, ice and scree from ABC we came across sections of dangerously narrow paths passing above the steep screes. A fall and you would tumble down a fair distance – in the dark and off the path you would be hard to find.

As we walked my mind turned to my balance, never a strong trait of mine. For me there are two types of balance – mental and physical; I am rubbish at both.

I used to believe that if a pill or a beer is good for you, obviously two must be twice as good and three even better. I looked up balance in my thesaurus and of all the synonym words, harmony leapt out at me.

Balance = harmony = peace of mind = a happier Roger!

But then there is physical balance. Our balance system is inside the inner ear, and I often wonder if the teacher's blow to my head, in the early 1960s, did far more damage than just rupturing my left eardrum.

While rowing on the Atlantic I got frustrated and pissed off at myself for getting constantly knocked off my rowing seat when caught off guard by an unscripted wave. Getting back on my seat was a performance, not helped by the rolling of the boat and the fact that the seat was on runners – it moved! In addition, my metal knee has restricted movement for squatting and timing a drop onto my seat, all done while attempting to control two great big oars. Which explains how I managed to take a dip in the Atlantic.

On reflection, I am one very lucky man. How many people have fallen overboard, into the North Atlantic, a thousand miles from land, and survived?

The afternoon began to fade, I sensed we needed to pick up the pace a tad, otherwise we would be trekking in the dark. My legs were feeling the effort so I could only guess how difficult it must have been for Lesley. I walked beside or behind her, encouraging and distracting in equal doses.

When I'm knackered, my endurance trick is to simply not let the negative worm burrow into my head. If I hear a little voice saying 'you can't go on' then I promptly grin and pick up my pace– that silences the monkey on my shoulder.

So I smiled, watched my footing and just kept plodding, one step at a time. I told Lesley (actually I told both of us) we are getting closer and closer to the mess tent, to friends and a hot drink. Dusk caught us on the lower slopes, but I was pretty certain we were close. Darkness came very quickly, bringing about still more hazards. We needed to get back so we couldn't drop the pace, but we couldn't hurry either; tiredness and darkness create uncertainty under foot. I didn't want either of us to go 'A over T' at any time, least of all at this stage of our journey.

Just as darkness laid a blanket over the mountains, downing a slope and turning a corner, we saw, 400 yards away, the shining lights of Base Camp. Uplifted and relieved, we trudged across the open expanse to see, coming towards us, a group wearing head torches.

Ackers, Jeff, Ollie and Simon, these guys having had hot drinks, were going back out into the cold night to help round up us and other stragglers. I find that a kind and unselfish gesture.

Jess, Tamara, Deano and Carrie were about an hour or so behind us, absolute troupers all of them. We went straight to the mess tent, where I took the weight off my feet and enjoyed a hot drink and plate of hot food that tasted wonderful; hunger really is the best sauce.

It was a bittersweet last night on Mt Everest. We had achieved what we had set out to do – played rugby at altitude. On the way we had seen friends sent home early. Twenty-seven of us arrived at base camp on 20th April and only 19 made it to ABC3 to play.

The following morning, we packed our rucksacks and headed off to the mess tent for our last base camp breakfast. Only two, not three, minibuses were waiting for us. It was a poignant reflection, illness and altitude during the challenge had taken a toll. We thanked Charlie and the Sherpas, gave them a few token Wooden

Spoon items and some of us gave them pieces of kit, such as a set of poles. It's very unlikely they will ever use the gear; more likely they will sell it. Wages, gratuities and gifts traditionally bolstered their family's kitties. On our previous trip to the Nepal base camp, we got closer to the Sherpas, witnessing first-hand that they are very family-orientated.

Lots of pictures of us with the Sherpas and AP staff were taken as we were getting ready; eventually we squeezed ourselves and our luggage onto the minibuses, and headed off on the long road trip back to Lhasa, followed by a ten-hour flight home.

The Teams: Oh boy. What a mixed bunch!

Top: Left to right: Lesley Davies, Jess Cheesman, Sam Tongue, Huw Lougher, Nick Stevenson, Jeff Broderick, Miles Hayward, Ollie Phillips, Jon Ingarfield, Roger Davies, Jude McKelvey
Bottom: From left to right: Matt Mitchell, Tamara Taylor, Arthur Prestidge, John Curtis, Rob Callaway, Mark Ackred, Phurwa Wangchhu Sherpa, Phu Rinjee Sherpa, Pemba Gelzen Sherpa, Shane Williams (MBE), photographer and player, Mark 'Deano' Dean

Shane Williams MBE, Roger and Mt Everest

THE TIMES | News
Tuesday May 7 2019

We made the papers!

Scrum up! Rugby game on Everest is a record

world record for playing the highest game of rugby, at 6,331m (20,771ft) above sea level. Lee Mears, 40, Shane Williams, 42, Ollie Phillips, 35, and Tamara Taylor, 37, played on the East Rongbuk Glacier, near Mount Everest's Advanced Base Camp, a week ago. The players faced severe shortness of breath, with oxygen levels at 40 per cent. They played full contact rugby sevens, with Taylor acting as referee. The match, which was a 5-5 draw, took place on a full-sized pitch, including flags and posts, in line with the Guinness World Records rules. Williams, a team captain, said: "The game was incredibly tough. If you ran during the match it took ten minutes to recover."

The game was organised by Wooden Spoon, a British children's charity. The previous week the group played the highest ever game of touch rugby, at 5,118m (16,794ft) at Everest Base Camp.

Below: Everest rugby full time

It's hard work playing at high altitude!

After the match – knackered but happy!

CHAPTER 36

Cancer and Chemo

On 7th May, two days after my return from playing rugby on Mt Everest, I visited the Conquest Hospital. The consultant told me I couldn't possibly have cancer; I would simply not have been able to climb to 6,500 metres on Mt Everest if I did. Then he surprised me with the information that, when I was poorly in February 2019, I had actually had pneumonia. He suggested that it must have scarred my right lung. That, he suggested, was what was spotted on the scan, and that had raised the alarm bells.

I was, needless to say, immensely relieved and without further ado (or pause for thought, now I think about it) I focused on the next potential challenge. You might say I was simply following a guiding principle that has changed my life and, possibly, saved it: we should never let go of our dreams and always strive to gain new experiences and enjoy life for everything it has to offer; there are so many great adventures out there to choose from!

As I looked back on all the challenges that I have had the privilege to be a part of, for me, one adventure stood out. I suppose I saw it as the one great environment I had not yet tried to come to terms with, the unfinished business of my adventures to date: Antarctica.

I decided that I should assemble a small team, to humbly walk in the footsteps of iconic – and heroic – Antarctic explorers. I have read and studied much of what has been written about those early pioneers, and as I did so, I looked at the scale of the challenge and what it would entail.

I narrowed my focus, and looked for the best 'on the ground' contact to further the plan. I had serious discussions with Steve Jones, expeditions manager of Antarctic Logistics and Expeditions (ALE). Now, things were beginning to take shape in my mind.

I wasn't planning to attempt the trek solo (I am probably crazy but I'm definitely not stupid). In fairly short order, a dream team formed: Ben Harvey, Rob Callaway, Mark 'Ackers' Ackred, Lesley and me. We were a group of capable friends, who I know would enjoy the adventure. Later, James Trotman, my North Pole buddy, was to join us.

We set up a meeting at Ackers's home, on the 25th of February 2020, to discuss the project in more detail. Everything was looking positive; my initial dream, and our initial planning, was turning into action.

On the 11th of March 2020, Covid-19 was declared a pandemic by the WHO, and the hammer came down.

Antarctica became all but closed, except to scientific researchers and military personnel. Talks with Steve Jones, and with major sponsors, inevitably stalled.

Disheartened, but not defeated, it became my long-term aim that, once the world had the pandemic in check, we would proceed with our plan. I realised we might need to look at 2023 rather than 2022.

In the meantime, I suggested that for a bit of fun we should kayak across the English Channel. Plan B received a resounding 'Yes' from the hastily renamed 'Kayaking Dream Team'.

I linked up with Will Chetwood, a safety boat skipper based in Rye, who explained to me that, in 2012, the French had made it illegal to cross their shipping lanes in anything human powered. We would have to kayak across at a wider point (from Dungeness to Boulogne), which meant a trip of 24 nautical miles, or 27.5 miles in old money. The safety boat would carry us for the five miles in the middle – the prohibited shipping lane – and then drop us back in the water again so that we would still paddle the full accepted distance for a Channel crossing attempt (18.5 nm/21.3 miles/34.3 km). There was no way round this arrangement and, since the change in the law, everybody is forced to do it this way.

I booked Will's safety boat to escort us on the crossing from Dungeness during the week of 24th May 2021. Now firmly committed, we purchased two tandem sit-on-top kayaks and the training sessions began in earnest.

My training included yomping over the Firehills with a 35-kg-loaded backpack. Unfortunately I took a little tumble and picked up an inconvenient but minor injury. Or so I thought. Nothing is simple in my life; I have discovered that, at seventy-two years of age, when I trip over my own feet I no longer bounce. Can a bad fall cause a hernia? Oh yes it can. On the 27th of August 2020 I attended an appointment at Benenden Hospital's private outpatients' department for a groin hernia repair with Mr Deya Marzouk. Mr Marzouk, on examining me, was not happy with what he found, so he sent me for a CT scan.

On Monday 21st September 2020 I underwent a CT scan on my thorax; and on the 29th, Dr T Nakos told me that I did indeed have cancer. A few days later Dr J R Jones, a consultant haematologist confirmed the diagnosis; I had B-cell lymphoma cancer. My first thought was 'game over'; but then my second was 'you bloody drama queen!'

After the initial shock of being told I had cancer, I felt numb, then slowly emotions of anger, anxiety and sadness jumbled around inside my head. I felt I had to ask the big question: 'OK, doc, give it to me straight. How long have I got?' The answer I got from the cancer nurse was, 'We never discuss that.' There went my John Wayne moment.

Luckily my third thought was, 'Me, disabled? Nah!' And my fourth, 'Don't they know I have plans? I'm kayaking to France with my friends,' brought me back to the real world. Self-preservation kicked in and, without further hesitation, I began to process the fact there is hope; through treatment and a positive mental attitude or, in my case, sheer stubbornness.

I needed to tell Ben, Ackers and Rob I had cancer. I phoned each of them in turn and their responses were uplifting.

Rob: 'Just sit in the front of the tandem; we'll get you across.'

Ackers: 'Bring a coat so you don't get cold.'

They might seem to be a pair of unsympathetic jokers but there was never even a suggestion that I should pull out. They are friends who inspired me and didn't even know it.

Timing is the secret of good comedy. The confirmation of our Guinness World Record for playing rugby at ridiculous altitude came on 19th October 2020, and my first cycle of chemotherapy was scheduled for the next day. Who says the universe doesn't have a sense of humour?

My first experience of receiving chemo was spending seven hours sitting in a plastic covered armchair with a needle stuck in my arm, while a cocktail of powerful drugs, designed to kill 'naughty' cells, was pumped into me. I had another five cycles of R-CHOP treatment to look forward to.

To add to my physical and emotional ups and downs, a week after each chemo day, I had an unwelcome five-day ordeal of self-injecting bortezomib into my own belly. Lesley decided this was her role; to say she chased me around the bedroom with a syringe in her hand is a slight exaggeration, however, once in the required position, she darted me. I suppose I shouldn't have been so surprised to feel unusually tired and generally weak; the nurses told me that chemo affects every cell in your body.

I had lymphoma cancer; the lymph node glands play an essential role in the body's immune defences plus the treatment of it, and chemo can weaken the immune system, so being particularly vulnerable is not ideal in the middle of a pandemic! I needed to take extra care.

- Wash hands
- Bump elbows

- Wear a mask
- Get vaccinated
- No tongues

However, breathing fresh air into my lungs and getting my heart pumping always helps. Doing some exercise every day keeps my spirits and energy levels up. Dolly the Doodle and I never missed our daily morning walk over the Firehills, in Hastings Country Park. During the first week after the chemo it may have been more of a gentle hour's amble, but then it was back to bracing ninety-minute walks until the next chemo session. I kept up this routine for the full fifteen weeks of treatment.

Between the second and third cycle my mouth was as dry as Gandhi's flip-flops, I lost my sense of taste, had no appetite and my digestive system swung from constipation to the trots, when farting was not an option. On top of everything else, I was quickly losing all my hair. Pride and vanity were a problem but Lesley came to my rescue by shaving off the tufty bits. By the third/fourth cycle I'd lost all my hair. In the privacy of my shower, I looked like a misshapen, oversized boy! Sometimes I wondered 'what the hell' but then I'd go back to my lifelong mantra: just put one foot in front of the other.

The cycle routine became the norm; I would go to the hospital for a blood test and, a week later, spend a day sitting in the plastic chair attached to a drip, then a rest week, followed by five days of belly jabs, another rest week and then it was time to start the next cycle.

As for food and drink, I found it easier to eat little and often. With my arid mouth, homemade smoothies helped to get healthy fuel into me. When needs must, you find out the strangest things; I discovered you can buy artificial spit (saliva)! It temporarily moistened and lubricated my mouth; however, I later discovered that chunks of pineapple worked better and they are decidedly tastier.

Throughout this time I visited Epic Life at the Hub near Bodiam Castle, on a regular basis, hiring their kayaks for a paddle on the River Rother. Often I went with Lesley, sometimes alone and occasionally I shared a tandem with my seven-year-old grandson, Kal-El, who sat in the bow enthusiastically giving me directions.

On 3rd February 2021, I had my last chemo in the Judy Beard day unit, Conquest Hospital. On my way out I rang the 'End of Treatment Bell'.

Our new tandem kayaks were delivered in May of 2021, giving the Kayak Dream Team the opportunity to test them – and ourselves – on the sea.

Rob came down from Coventry and Ackers from Oxfordshire. Ben was working in Dubai and his place was taken by James Trotman, my polar buddy from Brighton. It was great to meet up and to spend a few hours kayaking the English coastline with friends.

We met and parked up at the Hastings Motor Boat and Yacht Club, situated at Rock-a-Nore, where I am a member and store my kayak. The team got dressed for action, topped off by our buoyancy jackets and carrying with us only the essentials: drink, a few munchies and mobile phones in waterproof cases, and in Ackers case, his car keys in his pocket.

The next important decision was who sits where in a tandem? The fat boy is always best in the stern, unless we're in crosswinds, when the heavier rower ought to be seated up front. If the conditions change, tough luck, it's difficult to swap seats out on the sea. Though it is possible to do this, the chances are that one or both of you will end up in the water.

Rob and Ackers, and James T and I, launched our sit-on tandem kayaks into the surf and paddled hard to get out into deeper water, roughly three hundred metres out from the shoreline, where the sea surface was smooth(ish), and headed west towards Bexhill. James, in the bow, set an economical pace, suitable for endurance training. In the stern, my role was to match the cadence and steer.

The sea was best described as a little bouncy, which was OK. The bigger problem was the wavelets hitting us diagonally; they pack a lot of punch and push the bow off course. If you aren't ready to compensate, the next wave can hit you broadside, causing you to lose control and possibly capsize.

We had been out on the water for about 90 minutes when behind us we heard raised voices. We looked around to see Rob and Ackers messing about in the sea – that is to say, in the sea instead of on it. There was no panic, both men are tough and level-headed but we turned back to give assistance if necessary. The two lads got back onto their kayak – I've seen pregnant walruses heave themselves out of the water more elegantly. Good-natured banter continued on the way back with Rob and Ackers blaming the wind, a rogue wave and their weight distribution for their unscheduled, early bath.

On hitting the beach we dragged our kayaks back up to the club, where Rob and Ackers's vehicles were parked. Oh, how we all chuckled when Ackers produced his 'drowned' electronic car keys for his very nice car, but unfortunately it was a real pain for Ackers as his remote key was now dead. Help came in the guise of the RAC and their magic spray. Apart from the dunking it was a good day's training on the water with a great bunch of lads – three middle-aged plus one OAP.

Standing on a cliff path, looking south, out across the often dangerous English Channel, was enough to motivate me into action and upping my training programme: a daily ninety-odd minutes on the Firehills with Dolly, a ninety-minute to two-hour session on my indoor rowing machine three or four times per week, alternate days on the River Rother, where I gradually increased the paddling distance up to twenty kilometres, or on the sea which I'm lucky enough to have unlimited access to, along with the opportunity to enjoy a stunning coastline.

Piers Hopkirk, from BBC South East, interviewed and filmed me and James kayaking off Hastings beach for the evening news, aired on 25th of June 2021. Why? Because it's a remarkable true story, about a harmless nutcase, who's in remission from cancer, and has chosen to kayak across the English Channel to raise money for a cancer charity.

Yes, I'm on the telly!

www.rogerdavies.me.uk/kayak-the-english-channel/

Kayaking with my 'chemo curl'

CHAPTER 37

Action in Remission ... Kayak from Dungeness to Boulogne

The ideal conditions for kayaking across the Channel are little or no wind and a neap tide. However, Mother Nature makes setting a firm date at more than twenty-four hours' notice in advance a lottery. The 24th of May was cancelled, so we reset for 12th July, and again cancelled. Eventually, Tuesday 3rd August 2021 became our D-Day.

All the changing of dates had an impact. Ben Harvey, my original kayaking partner, was Covid red carded and marooned in Dubai. What a bummer! James Trotman, the dream team's first reserve, had already shuffled his work schedule twice, but just couldn't make the final date work. Rob introduced his friend Jamie Soden, an ex-Royal Marine, as a replacement; the team was back to full strength.

Plans were made, the hotel booked, all seemed ready. I phoned Will on Sunday, two days before kick-off, for any final instructions. During our conversation I asked about our kit, safety equipment and kayaks etc. Then I realised that Will wasn't saying very much. When the silence ended he dropped a bombshell; the French had banned the use of sit-on-top kayaks. We were forbidden by law to use them. They now defined them as 'beach toys', and anyone found using them would be stopped, the kayaks confiscated, and all involved would get heavily fined.

I felt like I had been kicked in the stomach. The kayaks we had bought and trained in for months were out of the question, and our preparation was all of a sudden turned on its head.

Before I had the chance to give a rather colourful response, Will offered us the use of his tandem sea kayaks; he also suggested I contact Cliff (who had advised us in the first place) to see if he could lend us a couple of suitable kayaks.

I immediately phoned Cliff, and told him the situation. He didn't believe me at first, but after realising my position he bailed us out. That evening, I went round to his home and loaded two single sit-in sea kayaks, with spray decks, on to my roof rack, and there they stayed until Lesley and I drove them to Rye harbour, where we were to launch from in thirty-six hours' time for Boulogne.

At 8.30 a.m., outside Rye harbour sailing club, I introduced the dream team to Will and his powerful RIB (rigid inflatable boat) for the first time. The three kayaks were loaded onto the RIB, plus each man's personal kit and food bag. Lesley had prepared ham rolls and homemade date flapjacks for all.

Off we went, on the six-mile journey to our starting point, Dungeness Power Station. On arrival one of the single kayaks was lowered over the side. Will and his mate held it steady for me, enabling me to get into it for the very first time, and without getting a dunking.

Sitting 'in' the sea surface, I looked ahead; there was no sign of France, only an indistinct horizon where the sea and sky blended. Too late to change my mind, time to accept I was a novice in a narrow sea kayak that felt very wobbly next to the far wider-beamed sit-on-top I had spent months training in. To stay upright it was necessary to focus hard on my technique. I told myself to relax, drop my shoulders down from my ears and just accept that the water was lumpy and bumpy. I didn't have time to waste on worrying; worry fixes nothing.

I did make one very silly mistake. Having a hernia meant I needed to wear medical support; when using the sit-on-top kayak it seemed unnecessary; I thought sitting for this long-distance endurance challenge, it would chafe and make me sore, so I decided not to wear it – what a bonehead! After a couple of hours paddling I started to experience a sharp burning pain that was only relieved when I took my left foot off the foot brace peg, and laid my leg down the centre, unbalancing the kayak. I carried out a brief reality check: I am kayaking on the busiest sea route in the world. This was not the time to get precious, it was time to get on with it.

The plan was for Rob and Ackers in the tandem to take the lead, Jamie and me in our singles to follow, all keeping within shouting distance of Will in the safety RIB.

We caught sight of France well before the halfway mark and got excited. Will had pointed out to us that the toughest thing about crossing the Channel is that France will seem so deceptively close. He was right, and the novelty quickly subsided; we had another three or so hours paddling.

The best entertainment for me and Jamie was watching the cabaret unfold in front of us. Ackers, the helmsman, seemed to have his imaginary satnav set on the scenic route. Their tandem never stayed in a straight line, zigzagging widely, criss-crossing the safety boat's wake. The lads' amusing, frustrated rantings made me forget any fatigue.

It wasn't until we hit the shipping lanes and linked up with the RIB that we found out what the problem was – the tandem's rudder was broken. From then on Ackers became a proper helmsman; he is still convinced his tandem covered forty miles (enough for there and back), not just the planned twenty-one.

We didn't get too close to any ships but near enough to appreciate their size. Those vessels are so enormous next to my kayak; comparing an elephant to a mouse doesn't come close.

Our kayaks were averaging about four knots and the big ships travelled at 20 knots. A loaded tanker could take as much as 3 km and 15 minutes to come to a full stop, so you don't 'play chicken' with those big boys.

As we approached the shipping lane, each kayak was lifted

aboard our support boat. We refuelled – drank water, shovelled ham sandwiches and flapjacks down our necks as quickly as possible – while speeding over the shipping lane. Once through we got back into our kayaks and started paddling.

After paddling 21.3 miles from Dungeness, a high-speed motorboat with its blue light flashing, crewed by armed Maritime Gendarmerie, intercepted us; we were a mere 250 metres from Boulogne harbour's entrance.

Gendarmerie: 'You don't look like migrants going the wrong way, so what are you doing?'

Us: 'It seemed a shame to waste such good sea conditions so we decided to go for a paddle, also it's a fun way to raise money for the Velindre Cancer Charity.'

Stern-faced gendarmerie response: 'Did you paddle across the French shipping lane?'

Us: 'No, we loaded three kayaks onto the safety boat for a quick blast over that short section.'

Amid the questioning, and speaking for all of us, Rob asked innocuously if we could take a group photo with them.– Anglo-French relations became confused. It is said that the French have a reputation for being a nightmare for red tape and bureaucracy. Tactfulness over petty issues has never been my strongest point, especially when I am hungry and tired. I accept that a little diplomacy is probably the best solution for this type of occasion.

The gendarmes spent a suitably lengthy period in waffling and debate over the radio with their HQ. Once they were satisfied, we mutually decided we had achieved what we came for, so we headed back home to England.

The return paddle

On 13th October 2021, to celebrate eight months since my last chemotherapy treatment, I arranged to kayak back from Boulogne to Dungeness.

For various bona fide reasons none of the lads could make that date, so I called James Trotman, our first reserve, and asked if he would like to join me for a days' paddling. He jumped at the opportunity to enjoy another great adventure and an unforgettable experience with me.

James knows me well enough; he realises that being mildly insane helps me thrive in challenging situations and bounce back in adversity.

Due to the pandemic, interest in water sports had exploded; sensibly priced tandem sea kayaks were as rare as hens' teeth. Luckily James managed to source two singles and I had two quality paddles – job done.

The first time I set eyes on the boats was forty-five minutes before we left Rye harbour for France, on the RIB skippered by Will Chetwood.

We sped over the Channel from Rye to Boulogne in 50 minutes, giving us a chance to see the water conditions and distance we would be covering at least 30 knots slower!

At 9.30 a.m. we started kayaking from Boulogne harbour in

our recently acquired, pre-loved yellow sea kayaks, about ten metres behind the safety boat on a sea that was somewhat rough and lumpy; riding the waves was exciting, but it can be dangerous. Quickly settling into an economical pace, strong, slow and steady, we headed out into the English Channel.

Our sea kayaks, which are longer and more slender than the sit-on tandems we had trained on, moved over the water with less resistance, and were consequently faster when propelled by capable paddlers, and even by us.

James and I paddled for much of the time loosely abreast. The advantage of being in close contact was that we could communicate easily with each other and with Will on the escort boat. Not just for safety issues, but also to exchange encouragement or vent how we were feeling – good, bad or just plain crazy.

In the couple of months since my last crossing I'd spent time training in a sit-in kayak and I certainly benefited, physically and mentally. Wearing my surgical belt this time relieved discomfort. Which reminds me, as a man of a certain age, my bladder is not what it was; it seems to have shrunk, and holding out for a couple of hours can be a problem. Hydration is way more important than any inconvenience. There are solutions: for boys, it's a pee in a bottle, or for girls a She-wee and a bottle; peeing into a sponge and squeezing it out works for some. My preferred choice is 'the golden arc'. On long trips slap on plenty of anti-rash cream, as even minor spills can cause chafing and ruin the day.

It's easy to get lost in the rhythmical flow of paddling; it's so peaceful, nothing but the sounds of the wind and water. However, after a while I started to miss the constant lively banter we had enjoyed during the last crossing. Without entertaining distractions I became more aware of my niggling aches and increasing tiredness. Distractions can be a positive tool that provides a much-needed mental break and helps to mask one's feelings. I remembered the Foreign Legion used singing as a distraction to help their long marches pass more quickly. So I started singing, loudly!

A long-distance sea paddle is formidable, and not necessarily just physically, it also demands mental strength and big balls. Or, as in my case, a stubborn septuagenarian, and a very grateful cancer survivor who wants to carry the message of hope to others.

The sudden dousing of cold sea spray when paddling hard through a choppy sea interrupted my routine stroke technique. The momentary shock was mentally refreshing, it awakened and stirred feelings of my achievements against the odds and reminded me why I was there.

Funnily enough, on long-distance kayaking trips, the only for-real memorable moments are the start and finish, unless you bump into something big and frightening like a shark or you flip the kayak.

Dungeness Power Station is enormous, poking high on the horizon, and on a clear day it can be seen from Boulogne. But I have to say, it doesn't matter how long and hard you paddle, frustratingly it doesn't appear to get any closer. Oh bollocks, just keep paddling – a rough day on the sea is better than any day in a pandemic lockdown; this too shall pass.

At 2.30 p.m., after 21.3 miles of paddling, the stark, flat shingle beach in front of the hulking Dungeness Power Station and old lighthouse was a beautiful sight.

Approaching Dungeness Power Station

Kayaking from Boulogne to Dungeness

CHAPTER 38

The forgotten Heroes of the Adventures

The porters in Africa and the Sherpas in the Himalayan region are the forgotten heroes; without their support it would be nearly impossible to reach our goals. They carry equipment and supplies to keep us hydrated, fed and sheltered, they guide us and keep us safe. I would also include our filmmaker, Sam Tongue. Daily he shared the demanding physical and mental challenges with 26 teammates. Sam captured footage that certified two world records. He created a legacy, giving each of us personal lasting memories.

When I get the opportunity to talk about my experiences, I am reminded that when I see and talk with ex-offenders, recovering alcoholics and addicts, they have the choice to restructure themselves, use their rebirth, to live a healthy and productive life, or scuttle back to their old ways. We all have our own personal mountains to climb, why not ask or listen to someone who has already conquered a similar mountain to share their experience with you?

Adventure is intrinsic to humanity. We can choose to explore and test our limits in different ways and each of us has our own personal Everest. The happiness of life depends on the quality of what's going on between your ears, not the externals. Externals can be the icing on the cake and I do enjoy the icing. So when a gym monkey or a middle-class bore asks me why I do what I do, my head leads me to wonder whether they are questioning my motives. Am I harbouring hidden agendas or are they making sad attempts at mockery, or could it be a smokescreen for envy or lack of self-esteem?

Wally Herbert, the first man to walk across the Arctic Ocean, when asked 'why?' is quoted as saying, 'Those who need to ask will never understand the answer, while others who feel the answer will never need to ask.'

If you asked me what Wally Herbert was saying before, during and soon after my time on the frozen sea I had no real idea, but now I've had a little time for the enormity of the multitude of facets of the real adventure to settle within me, I understand and completely agree with him.

It's in the isolation and lonely arena of adversity where a man gets to know himself. In a boxing ring, during a street brawl, on the sea, crossing a barren desert, high up a mountain or in the wilderness – real or imagined. It's not the challenge I conquer, but me. I just take a moment to chill, keeping my feet firmly grounded, that's when I find my calm centre and plug into a positive mental attitude. If I can – you can! It's your mountain!

My personal history has taught me to look at failures as a chance to learn and grow in this wonderful game of life. An injection of adrenaline has the power to turbocharge my psyche so I can focus the discipline needed during extreme adventures and sports.

Sitting in a tent in one of the remotest places on our amazing planet with just one other person is so very far from boring. The conversations can be remarkably raw. There is nowhere to hide, masks drop off; I am totally exposed. To become isolated in remote circumstances could be very negative, unproductive and dangerous. I don't take myself too seriously, I am the best source of my own amusement – I laugh at myself. I have learnt not to criticise or judge but try to accept and support.

Here's to friends who inspired me and didn't even know it ...

CHAPTER 39

But – Why?

I read a humbling, yet bittersweet story of two young lads, Rob Gauntlett and James Hooper, who in 2006, at the age of nineteen, became the youngest Britons to climb Mt Everest. In 2008 they won the coveted National Geographic's Adventurers of the Year for a 26,000 mile journey from North Pole to South Pole using only natural power – ski, dog sled, sailing boat, bicycle and foot. Right up to the very sudden end, doing what he loved, Rob Gauntlett's life was truly exciting, inspirational and packed with fun. He was killed after falling while ice climbing in the Alps on 10th January 2009. These young men had the courage to look life straight in the eye. They had discussed the possibility of dying and they both agreed, 'The worst thing of all would be to get to seventy, having done nothing with your life, and be lying in bed, waiting for the inevitable.'

I need to remind myself that each of us has our own personal mountains to conquer; for a few it's physical, others it's mental and to some it may be spiritual.

For me, it's a hotchpotch of all three. I accept that not every event is a positive mind-blowing experience, some are total flops. Flops and failures are not all about me, they are just events experienced. My first introduction to bruising failure was at four years old when I took a tumble while learning to ride my bike. It was my own fault; I had taken the training wheels off!

Failing to try, in case you make a mistake, leads to avoiding mistakes, which may be the biggest mistake of all. Avoiding or putting things off is the same as delaying a dump until ten minutes before the plane is due to land; it gets you nowhere and pisses everyone off.

I try to remember what is most important. It's not having everything go right, it's facing whatever goes wrong!

Today I have a soulmate and wife, Lesley, who brings an expanding family to the party, my daughter, granddaughter, grandson and many good friends. I am now feeling my age and my immortality is starting to creak, but I go on.

Believe in yourself: your mountain is waiting …
Tomorrow is promised to nobody

Lesley and me with golden Mt Everest

WHAT'S NEXT?

As this book goes to press, I am already planning another trip to trek up Mt Kilimanjaro. On descending we will play a friendly game of rugby against a local team called the 'Arusha Rhinos'.

We will be departing from the UK on 17th January and returning home on 29th January 2023.

We welcome all who join us to use the event as a platform to assist in their fundraising for their preferred charity.

To find out more about this trip go to:

www.adventurealternative.com/kilimanjaro-machame-route

www.rogerdavies.me.uk
Visit for tips on how to plan and survive your own adventures!

APPENDIX

The Highest Seven-a-Side Rugby Union match, played on 30th April 2019

Near Mt Everest Advance Base Camp 3, Tibet, China.
At 6,331 m (20,770 ft), (28° 06' 4.32" N 86° 51' 32.91" E).
The teams consisted of the following members: Shane Williams (MBE), Mark Ackred, Jeff Broderick, Rob Callaway, Jess Cheesman, John Curtis, Mark Dean, Roger Davies, Lesley Davies, Miles Hayward, Jon Ingarfield, Huw Lougher, Jude McKelvey, Ollie Phillips, Matt Mitchell, Nick Stevenson, Tamara Taylor, Simon Wright, Sam Tongue, Arthur Prestidge, Phurwa Wangchhu (Sherpa), Phu Rinjee (Sherpa), Pemba Gelzen (Sherpa).
Confirmation of Guinness World Record 19th October 2020

The Highest Touch Rugby Union Match on 25th April 2019

North Base Camp, Tibet, China.
At 5,119 m (16,794 ft). (28° 8' 29" N 86° 51' 5" E)
The teams consisted of the following members:
Shane Williams MBE, Mark Ackred, Jeff Broderick, Rob Callaway, Jess Cheesman, John Curtis, Mark Dean, David Fenton, Roger Davies, Lesley Davies, Matt Franklin, Ben Harvey, Miles Hayward, Jon Ingarfield, Paul Jordan, Huw Lougher, Jude McKelvey, James O'Malley, Lee Mears, Ollie Phillips, Matt Mitchell, Nick Stevenson, Tamara Taylor, Viv Worrall, Simon Wright, Carries Gibson and Sam Tongue.

Everest Rugby Challenge Team 2019

The team was comprised of a diverse range of people mainly from the rugby community, including international rugby legends Lee Mears (England) and Shane Williams (Wales), who boast almost 140 international caps between them, Ollie Phillips, an international rugby sevens star, and a legend of the women's game, Tamara Taylor, who represented England 115 times.

Ackers, the 'entrepreneur', with fingers in lots of pies – you can trust him.

Ben Harvey, doyen of Digital Ads, good man to have on your side when the shit starts flying.

Huw Lougher, a rugby-playing art dealer – a real one, unlike the dodgy ones from my old life in the 1970s.

Mark 'Deano' Dean, is not a bricklayer but an historical health and safety stoneworker, and an emcee in the making.

Miles Hayward, a 'finance man', yet far from boring.

Jeff Broderick, if you want to have fun and a good laugh, stick close to this man.

Paul 'Jordie' Jordan, boss of a global techie co., who has the gift of an infectious smile.

Jon Ingarfield, if only I could bottle his enthusiasm, I would be a very rich man.

Matt Franklin, a CEO at work, but a newly married man!

Jude McKelvey, a super-energetic entrepreneur, there's no stopping this girl.

Jess Cheesman, a Welsh-English self-confessed tidsoptimist, and an accomplished rugby player.

John and Viv, a cuddly little couple.

Simon Wright, an amateur rugby ref with a turn of speed (but I caught him).

Matt 'big hearted' Mitchell and his friend Nick, a football supporter – that says it all!

Jay O'Malley, ex-Special Forces, sent by Sarah Webb as her, I quote, 'Silver Back'.

Rob Callaway, it's important to have the courage to have fun, follow your heart and intuition, my pal Rob, does that 100%.

Lesley 'Super Nanna' Davies with seven grandkids.

Me – Roger, a septuagenarian adventurer.

The Polar Race 2009 – Five Teams and their members

1. Team Pole In One: John MacPherson, Iain Whiteley, David Stanton
2. Team Northern Lights: Ed Crowe, Julian Evans, Adrian Wells
3. Team Oman: Nabil Al-Busaidi, Claire Shouksmith, JP Downes
4. Team Magnetic Attraction: Lucas Bateman, Julie Jones, Arabella Slinger
5. Team Standard Life: James Trotman, Roger Davies

Jock Wishart is a maritime and polar adventurer, sportsman and explorer. Until his successful 2011 Old Pulteney Row to the Pole, he was best known for his circumnavigation of the globe in a powered vessel, setting a new world record in the Cable & Wireless Adventurer[6] and for organising and leading the Polar Race.

Serpentine Running Club

John Hadley, Hilary Walker, Johnny Walker, Uncle Bob, Peter Forster, Tom Blacker, Russell Stevens, Richard Smith, Ros Young, Cathy Crilley, James Godber, Wendy Wood and many more.

---

6. www.jockwishart.co.uk/about/

I competed in excess of a hundred running events between 1983 and until my knee replacement in 2011, including 10 km, 10 miles, half marathons, X-Countries and marathons including two London Marathons in 1984 and 1987.

Plus a few examples of the wacky-named races I have competed in

Tough Guy (5 times)	www.toughguy.co.uk
Man vs Horse	www.man-v-horse.org.uk/
Ballbuster	www.humanrace.co.uk/event/ballbuster
Welsh Castles Relay	www.lescroupiersrunningclub.org.uk
Nos Galan	www.rctcbc.gov.uk/EN/Events/NosGalan/
Race the Train	www.racethetrain.com
The Grizzly	www.axevalleyrunners.org.uk/grizzly
Benidorm Half	www.benidormhalf.com

London 2 Paris Rowing Challenge 2010

The Outloars, team members: Guy Fisher, Mike Roberts, Simon Pelly, Carlton Barnard, Virginie Vendiesse, Anne Maurissen, Christopher Nugee, Roger Davies, Steve Aquilina, James Datnow, Adrian Sharrott.

A scratch, mixed crew assembled from the UK and Belgium who tested ourselves against the elements and two other experienced crews in the nonstop six-day rowing race.

Mt Kilimanjaro 2010 and 2012

Machame Route 2010

We were a mixed bunch:
Clay Smith, Julie Jones, Claire Shouksmith, Lucas Bateman – all highly experienced and had been with me to the North Pole. And enthusiastic novice adventurers David Radley, Dr Eileen Feeney, Dave Bush, Robin Elwes, Mickey Pearce and brothers Mark and Sam.

Rongai Route in 2012

Lesley (now Mrs Davies), Sue Richards, Peter Wickenden, Jeremy, Tony, Adam Cole, David, Jeff and Andy Nunn.

Mt Toubkal and High Atlas Mountains 2013

Benno Rawlinson, Adam Cole, Lesley, Julie Rawbone, Annabelle Hancock and Kay Naldrett.

My old friend and team leader Stephen Pinfold with his local right-hand man Ibrahim Ahmed Amzil.

Kenya 2014

My guide and friend, Francis Kioni, who came from the shanty town slums of Nairobi. He was one of the success stories of Gavin Bates's, founder of Moving Mountains (charity).

Mama Sarah Obama, 94-year-old grandmother of former USA President Barack Obama (2009–17).

The Sahara 2015

Lesley, Maria Higgins, Clive and Max Hagley, Dave Radley, Julie Rawbone and Michelle Godbeer.

Our local guide, Ibrahim Ahmed Amzil teamed with Steve Pinfield.

Everest Base Camp, Nepal April 2014

Lesley Pender, Lucas Bateman, Annie (Annabelle) Hancock, Julie Jones, Jan Meek, Clive Hagley and his youngest son Max.

Nepalese Guides – https://www.mountainmonarch.com/

Rowing Crew of the Toby Wallace on the North Atlantic 2016

Mike Johnson	(stroke)	British/Zimbabwean (age 21)
Simon Chalk	(3)	**Skipper of the "Toby Wallace"**
Richard Wattam	(2)	Berkshire, UK (age 50)
Roger Davies	(bow)	South coast, UK. British (age 68)